Study Guide

Cram for the Exam!

Your Guide to Passing the New York Real Estate Salesperson and Broker Exams

FIFTH EDITION

Marcia Darvin Spada

OnCourse Learning

OnCourse
Learning

For product information and technology assistance, contact us at **OnCourse Learning & Sales Support, 1-855-733-7239.**

For permission to use material from this text or product.

ISBN-13: 978-1-133-49605-2
ISBN-10: 1-133-49605-9

OnCourse Learning
3100 Cumberland Blvd Suite 1450
Atlanta, GA 30339
USA

For your course and learning solutions, visit

Purchase any of our products at your local college store or at our preferred online store

Printed in the United States of America
1 2 3 4 5 6 7 16 15 14 13 12

Contents

(Continued)

Preface

Congratulations on your decision to invest extra effort to prepare for your qualifying courses and state exams. This guide will help you face the exams with greater confidence, which should enhance your test performance.

Cram for the Exam is exactly what it says—a quick way to prepare. Why spend more time than needed? Here you have a directed review in an easy-to-study format. *With Cram for the Exam*, depending on individual needs, you can spend about ten hours for a comprehensive review.

Before you begin your review, take a few minutes to read the first section, *Your Questions Answered*. It gives you details concerning test preparation, time, place, types of questions, and so forth. Also, review the *Quick Tips to Help You Pass*. Then read the instructions on *How to Cram for the Exam* to attain optimum results.

About the Author

Marcia Darvin Spada is owner of the Albany Center for Real Estate Education, a New York-licensed proprietary school. She also is owner of Cram for the Exam, a website that provides practice real estate exams for New York and New Jersey.

A professional educator and nationally known real estate author, Marcia teaches real estate and has developed content for numerous real estate courses. Her textbooks and courses are widely used by colleges, real estate-related organizations, and proprietary schools throughout the country. In addition to *Cram for the Exam: Your Guide to Passing the New York Real Estate Salesperson and Broker Exams*, she is the author of:

- *New York Real Estate for Salespersons*
- *New York Real Estate for Brokers*
- *New Jersey Real Estate for Salespersons and Brokers*
- *Real Estate National Licensing Exam Prep The Smart Guide to Passing*
- *Cram for Exam: Your Guide to Passing the New Jersey Salesperson and Broker Real Estate Exams*
- *The Home Inspection Book: A Guide for Professionals*
- *Environmental Issues and the Real Estate Professional*

Marcia holds a BA and an MA in English from the University at Albany and a BS in Real Estate Studies from Empire State College. She welcomes all comments and questions about the content in this exam guide. Her website http://www.cramforexam.net contains downloadable practice real estate NYS licensing exams and licensure information. Her e-mail address is cramforexam@hotmail.com.

Acknowledgements

Sincere appreciation goes to my husband, Eugene R. Spada, Esq., for his ongoing help and support in the writing of this exam guide. I am also very grateful to my editorial assistant, Jonathan Keats, who worked very hard to help me prepare the manuscript.

A very sincere note of gratitude to Senior Acquisitions Editor Sara Glassmeyer of Cengage Learning whose encouragement and assistance has been invaluable in completing all of the New York textbooks. I also appreciate the assistance of Senior Marketing Director Mark Linton, and Real Estate National Account Manager Shawna Hershey, all of Cengage Learning. I also want to thank Arlin Kauffman of LEAP Publishing Services for his superior expertise and assistance. I owe the clarity, readability, and beautifully formatted pages of this *Cram* to Joseph Malcolm and his production team at PreMedia Global.

The Cram that will Help you Pass!

Everything you need to succeed on your NYS real estate exam for salesperson or broker is in this *Cram* review

- ✓ Your Questions Answered- Important information you need to know about licensing requirements and taking your exam.
- ✓ Quick Tips to help you succeed on exam day.
- ✓ Comprehensive review of all NYS-mandated key terms and important points for each subject in the NYS syllabus.
- ✓ Links to websites that contain more information or forms for study or use.
- ✓ Quick View tables that summarize important information for each topic in the NYS syllabus.
- ✓ Marcia's List that summarizes the most important key terms or concepts that you must know.
- ✓ A total of 710 questions including 360 review questions and two salesperson and two broker practice exams with explanations and references to both *New York Real Estate for Salespersons 5th e* and *New York Real Estate for Brokers 5th e.*

Your Questions Answered

1. How do I obtain a salesperson license in New York?

Essentially, you need to complete three steps:

- ✓ Complete a New York State (NYS)-approved 75-hour qualifying course including the course exam
- ✓ Pass the NYS licensure exam
- ✓ Obtain broker sponsorship
- ✓ Be at least 18 years old

2. How can I obtain a real estate broker license in New York?

- ✓ Complete 120 hours of NYS-approved qualifying course education or its equivalent
- ✓ Be at least 20 years of age
- ✓ Meet NYS mandated experience requirements

Experience requirements for a broker real estate license can be either:

- ✓ Two years of active experience as a NYS-licensed salesperson under the supervision of a NYS-licensed broker

or

Three or more years of equivalent experience in the general real estate business

or

- ✓ Proof that an equivalent license was issued by a state with which New York has a reciprocal agreement

3. What exams must I pass to obtain salesperson or broker licensure in New York?

All applicants for New York licensure must pass a final online or classroom course exam at the completion of the qualifying course. Applicants must also pass an exam given by the NYS Department of State (NYSDOS), the New York regulatory agency that oversees the licensure process.

4. When and where are these exams given?

The qualifying courses may be completed either in a classroom setting or online. For the classroom format, the final qualifying course classroom exams are scheduled at course completion by the entity offering the course. The NYS exams are given at DOS test centers throughout New York. See **Intro Figure 1** for a list of exam locations. To verify these locations, check this list on the DOS website.

Note that if you take your course online for either salesperson or broker licensure, you must still take your final course exam in person at the entity where you signed up for the course. Sometimes arrangements may be made by your course provider to allow you to take your exam at another state approved school entity. However, the final course exam must always be completed in person.

Intro Figure 1

NYSDOS Salesperson and Broker Real Estate Licensing Exam Sites

Exams may be canceled due to weather conditions or other emergencies. If hazardous weather conditions exist in your area, you may call 518-474-4429 to see if an exam has been canceled. Please do not call the exam site.

If you need assistance or exam information, you may contact a Division of Licensing Services office in your area or call the Albany phone center at 518-474-4429. TDD users may contact the New York State relay operator at 1-800-662-1220.

No one will be admitted to an examination after the specified starting time.

ALBANY Exam Site
Alfred E. Smith State Office Building
80 South Swan Street
Albany, New York 12239
Located at the corner of Washington Avenue and South Swan Street

BINGHAMTON Exam Site (State Office Bldg.)
44 Hawley Street, 15th Floor
Binghamton, NY 13901

BUFFALO Exam Site (State Office Building)
65 Court Street
Main Floor Hearing Room, Part 5
Buffalo, NY 14202

FRANKLIN SQUARE Exam Site (VFW Hall)
68 Lincoln Road, Basement
Franklin Square, NY 11010
N6 Bus Route on Hempstead Turnpike
From the East, take the Southern State Parkway to Exit 16N, Franklin Ave.
From NYC/West, take the Cross Island Parkway SOUTH to the Southern State Parkway EAST. Take exit 15, Franklin Ave., turn left at the 2nd light onto Franklin Ave.
On Franklin Ave., turn RIGHT onto Hempstead Turnpike and go 5 blocks. Turn LEFT onto Lincoln Rd. (7-Eleven on corner). The VFW Hall and parking lot are on the RIGHT.

HAUPPAUGE Exam Site (Perry Duryea State Office Building)
250 Veterans Memorial Highway
Basement Conference Room
Hauppauge, NY 11788
Note: Building sits back off highway. Look for the green sign near the road.

NEW YORK CITY Exam Site
123 William Street, 19th Floor
New York, NY 10038

NEWBURGH Exam Site (Orange Ulster BOCES Adult Educational Center)
Federal Building, 471 Broadway, 2nd Floor
Newburgh, NY 12550
NYS Thruway Exit 17, take ramp toward Stewart Airport. Turn LEFT onto NY-17K, continue approximately 2 miles. Exam Site is on RIGHT.

PLEASE NOTE LOCATION CHANGE
PLATTSBURGH Exam Site (PARC Dining Hall - Part of Clinton Community College)

14 Dormitory Drive, Conference Room 1
From Clinton Community College, 136 Clinton Point Dr., Plattsburgh, NY 12901 US:
Start out going west on Clifton Point Dr. (go 0.06 miles),
turn left to stay on Clifton Point Dr. (go 0.08 miles),
turn right to stay on Clifton Point Dr. (go 0.58 miles).
Turn right onto US-9 (go 1.17 miles).
Turn left onto Connecticut Rd (go 0.79 miles).
Turn right onto Idaho Ave (go 0.29 miles).
Take the 1st right onto Dormitory Dr.,

14 DORMITORY DR, PLATTSBURGH, NY 12903 is on the right.

ROCHESTER Exam Site (Finger Lakes DDSO)
620 Westfall Road
Rochester, NY 14620
Take NYS Thruway to Exit 46, take 390 North to exit 16, turn RIGHT on East Henrietta Road, turn right at 2nd traffic light onto Westfall Road, Finger Lakes DDSO is on LEFT. Park in lot on right. Do Not enter through main lobby. Look for Sign, "New York State Testing."

SYRACUSE Exam Site ***Broker Exam Only***
333 E. Washington Street, Main Floor, Hearing Room A
Syracuse, NY 13202

SYRACUSE Exam Site ***Salesperson Exam Only***
407 East Taft Road, (park in the rear of the building, enter through back door)
North Syracuse
Syracuse, NY 13212

UTICA Exam Site (State Office Bldg.)
207 Genesee Street 1st Floor, Room 107
Utica, NY 13501

Source: NYS Department of State

5. Must I take the state exam at the test site closest to where I live?
You may take your state exam at any test center in New York State. Be sure to arrive at least 15 minutes before the starting time.

6. Do I need to schedule an appointment to take the NYS licensure exam?
Applicants are required to schedule their real estate salesperson exam on the DOS Occupational Licensing Management System, *eAccessNY.* In addition to being able to apply for the exam on *eAccessNY*, applicants can view their scheduled exam details or exam results and *apply for their salesperson license online.*

The initial broker license, however, must be applied for by sending the application and other application documents and payment to the NYSDOS. The mailing address for the NYSDOS is:

NYS Department of State
Division of Licensing Services
P.O. Box 22001
Albany, NY 12201-2001

If you use mailing services such as UPS or FedEx, you must use the DOS physical address:

NYS Department of State
Division of Licensing Services
1 Commerce Plaza
99 Washington Avenue, 6th Floor
Albany, NY 12231

The *eAccessNY* system requires that applicants create a personal ID and password when they register online. Persons with disabilities who require accessibility information should call 518-473-2731. Applicants who require testing modifications should not schedule an exam and should instead call 518-473-2731.

Useful Links

NYS Salesperson Real Estate Exam Procedures
http://www.dos.ny.gov/licensing/realestate/re_salesexams.html

NYS Salesperson and Broker Real Estate Licensing Exam Sites
http://www.dos.ny.gov/licensing/realestate/re_examsites.html

NYS Broker Real Estate Exam Procedures
http://www.dos.ny.gov/licensing/re_broker/re_broker_exams.html

eAccessNY
http://www.dos.ny.gov/licensing/eaccessny.html

7. When do I receive my exam results?

Exam results are reported as passed or failed; applicants will not receive a numerical score. Results are not given over the phone. Exam results are available online through your account in *eAccessNY.* The exam results are available as soon as possible after the NYSDOS Exam Unit receives the exams and scores them.

8. Should I first complete my salesperson or broker qualifying course before taking the NYS exam?

You can take the NYS exam at any time during the licensure process. Since the qualifying courses prepare you for the questions on the NYS exam, it is recommended that you first complete the course.

9. For the salesperson license, do I require broker sponsorship to take the NYS exam?

No. You may take the NYS exam and the 75-hour qualifying course without having a broker sponsor. Before taking the course or during the course, you should seek a broker to work for who will be your sponsor. This broker will sign and attest to sponsorship on your online licensure application.

10. For the broker license, if I have equivalent real estate experience and plan on obtaining a broker license, do I need to take the salesperson exam?

No. If you have prior real estate experience, you may choose to obtain broker licensure without first becoming a salesperson. You are still required to complete 120 hours of qualifying education; that is, the 75-hour salesperson course and the 45-hour broker qualifying course. If you have taken the old 45-hour salesperson-qualifying course (before July, 2008) and not the current 75-hour salesperson-qualifying course, you will need to make up 30 hours. In this case, to obtain a broker license, you will need to complete a 30-hour remedial course given both online and in the classroom in addition to the 45-hour broker-qualifying course. This rule applies to all applicants for the broker license.

Although you must pass the final exam given with your qualifying (and/or remedial) courses, you need only take and pass the broker NYS licensing broker exam if you do not plan to obtain a salesperson license. There is no "remedial course" state exam. The same rules apply, however, for taking the final classroom remedial course exam in person as for the other qualifying courses. (See Question 4). In addition to the required courses and passage of the exams, you must also demonstrate three years equivalent real estate experience.

11. How often can I take either the salesperson or broker exams?

Depending on the policy of the entity conducting the qualifying courses, you can generally take one make-up exam if you do not pass the first time. Inquire about this policy when you begin the course. You may take the NYS exam as often as you want until you pass. If you pass the exam, salesperson applicants, in most cases, should apply for licensure online utilizing their accounts in *eAccessNY*. Broker applicants cannot apply for their initial license online but must send it in to the DOS. Those who do not pass the exam can schedule another exam by utilizing their accounts in *eAccessNY*.

12. If I do not wish to be licensed immediately, how long is my passing grade valid for either the salesperson or broker exams?

Passed exam results for both exams are valid for two years.

13. Is there a fee for the NYS exam?

The fee is $15 for each time you take the exam. You must schedule a new online appointment to retake the exam.

14. What should I bring to the state exam?

1. Bring two #2 pencils. Calculators are permitted if they are battery or solar powered, silent, nonprinting and do not contain an alphabetic keyboard. PDAs are not allowed. You should bring a government-issued, signed, photo ID. Identification must be current and from the following list:

- ✓ Driver's license
- ✓ State-issued identification (ex, non-driver ID)
- ✓ Military ID
- ✓ U.S. Passport
- ✓ U.S. INS issued ID
- ✓ Certificate of US citizenship

2. You should also bring the page you were requested to print when you scheduled your exam on *eAccessNY*. This page is referred to as the "Summary of Your Submission" and includes your examination information, including your candidate number.

15. What question types are on the NYS exam?
All questions on the NYS exam are multiple-choice.

16. How many questions are there for each subject on the exams and what is the passing grade?
The numbers of questions on the classroom and NYS exams are weighted according to the number of hours allotted for each subject in the course. For example, for the salesperson exam, the subject *Law of Agency* requires 11 classroom hours, so that topic will contain more exam questions than the subject *Mortgage Brokerage* that requires only one classroom hour. For the broker exam, the subject *The Broker's Office-Operation, Management, and Supervision*, which consists of ten classroom hours, will have many more questions than that of *Taxes and Assessments*, which consists of two classroom hours.

The final salesperson classroom or online qualifying course exam consists of 75 or 100 questions. The NYS salesperson state exam has 75 questions. Each question on the NYS exam is worth 1.33 points. The passing grade is 70 percent. The DOS "rounds downs" the grade, which means that you need a minimum of 52 correct questions to pass (which would also mean that 23 wrong would give you a passing grade. You are given 1.5 hours to complete the classroom or state exam.

The final broker classroom or online qualifying course exam and the NYS exam consists of 100 questions, each worth one point. Note that the broker classroom exam has about five questions on local concerns, a topic chosen by the entity that offers your course. These local concerns questions are not on the NYS exam. The passing grade for the broker exam is 70 percent, so you can miss up to 30 questions and still pass. You are given 2.5 hours to complete the broker classroom or state exam.

17. Are all NYS exams the same?
Several different exams are developed from a large question bank. If you repeat the NYS exam, you probably will have a different set of questions.

18. Can I review my NYS licensure exam?
Yes, if you fail an exam, you may request an exam review. An exam review will help to evaluate your performance and the areas that require further study. You must request a review within 60 days of the examination date. You can ask for an *Examination Review Request* form at the exam and give the completed form to the Proctor. You can also call DOS to obtain one and then mail it back. You will have up to one hour for the review using your examination booklet and your answer sheet.

19. How should I prepare for the exam?

Completing the 75-hour qualifying course, and studying all of the topics covered on your class and state exams, is your primary preparation for the exam. After completing the course, review your textbook and notes. You should be familiar with the key terms, the important points, laws, and general theory for each subject. These items are summarized for you in *Cram for the Exam.*

Your completion of *Cram for the Exam* is an excellent final step in exam prep.

Other Preparation Sources

Here are some other sources for exam preparation:

- ***New York Real Estate for Salespersons, 5th e.*** This textbook completely covers the required New York syllabus for the 75-hour course. If you have not used this textbook in your course, have missed some classroom hours, or want to spend more time studying, you may want to review this textbook. The book provides additional information on the licensure process in the Introductory Chapter and Chapter 1, "License Law and Regulations".
- ***New York Real Estate for Brokers, 5th e.*** This is the textbook for those who are preparing for New York broker licensure and completely covers the syllabus for the required 45-hour broker course. More information regarding licensure and the duties of a real estate broker are included in the Introduction and Chapter 1 of this textbook.

The review and practice exam questions in *Cram for the Exam* are referenced to these two textbooks so that you can easily find further clarification of your answer.

- ***30 Hour Remedial Course Supplement.*** This companion text for the salesperson or broker course is for students who have completed the old salesperson 45-hour course (completed before July 1, 2008) and need to complete the entire 75 hours for the salesperson course or the 120 hours for the broker course.
- **Author website:** www.cramforexam.net. Marcia's website contains downloadable practice NYS licensing exams, other textbooks for sale, license requirements, and important information and updates for students and instructors.
- ***Live Exam Review Chat with the Author, Marcia Darvin Spada***

For personal help from the author, you may sign up through her website for a *Live Exam Chat* with Marcia which is an hour long real time review for the exam and includes downloadable practice exams.

To order a desk copy of this *Cram* or any Cengage real estate textbook, contact:

Shawna Hershey, National Account Manager, Real Estate & Appraisal
New Media Group & Consumer Markets
Cengage Learning
5191 Natorp Blvd. |Mason, OH 45040
Office: 513.229.1796; Fax: 513.229.1031
Email: shawna.hershey@cengage.com

To order Cengage textbooks online, go to the Cengage bookstore at cengagebrain.com.
To view the Cengage online real estate catalogue go to
http://www.cengage.com/realestate;
and to order textbooks by
Marcia Darvin Spada, go to
http://cengage.com/realestate/spada.
To order any textbooks directly, contact Cengage customer service at (800) 842-3636.

Quick Tips to Help You Pass

Before the Exam

- ✓ Try to get a good night's sleep.
- ✓ Know the exact location of the test, and arrive there about one-half hour before the test begins.
- ✓ Take the necessary ID, Record of Your Submission, pencils, and calculator
- ✓ Fear can be contagious; avoid pre-exam socializing and stay calm.
- ✓ If possible, sit toward the front of the examination room, where there are fewer distractions.
- ✓ Listen to all instructions.
- ✓ If you are physically challenged, you may call the NYSDOS and make arrangements for assistance.

During the Exam

Selecting an answer

- ✓ Answer every question as you go along. If you do not know an answer, take a guess or mark down the question number on scratch paper to return to it later. (DOS exam proctors collect all scratch paper after the exam).
- ✓ Read the questions *slowly* and *cautiously*. The question may ask for a negative answer rather than a positive one. Do not read into the question; read it as it actually reads. Do not look for deeper hidden meanings. If you have studied, the first answer that occurs to you is generally the correct one.
- ✓ Read every answer before deciding on your choice.
- ✓ Note that questions usually contain two distracters (incorrect choices) that are obviously wrong. Spot them and you have a 50% chance of selecting the correct answer. There may be a third distracter that is not as obviously wrong as the others are, so if you eliminate all three, all that is left is the correct answer! Often you can find the correct answer through this process of elimination without actually knowing the correct answer.
- ✓ Do not always apply the maxim-"I cannot change my first answer." You may have initially misread the question. One word you may not have noticed previously can change the meaning of the question upon rereading it.
- ✓ Watch out for "must" and "always". If an answer has any exceptions, these words generally indicate a wrong answer.

Timing Yourself

- ✓ Because every question counts the same, do not spend a lot of time on one complex question if it means running out of time. Finish the exam; go back to the questions you either guessed or could not answer.
- ✓ Use your allotted time. You have 1.5 hours to answer 75 multiple-choice questions for the salesperson exam. You have 2.5 hours to answer 100 questions for the broker exam. You might want to leave when you have finished, but use this time to go back to the answers you are unsure of. By rereading a question, you might see it in a different light.
- ✓ Before handing in your exam, review all of your answers. If you spot just one wrong answer, it could make the difference between passing and failing.
- ✓ If you are unsure of an answer, go with your first impression.

Marking Your Answer Sheet

- ✓ Be sure that your answer sheet is lined up correctly with each of the questions.
- ✓ If you erase, erase completely. The computerized test reader could pick up a faint mark.
- ✓ When marking answers you are certain of (and will not return to later), press down with the pencil on the answer sheet so that the test reader picks up the answer.

How To Cram For The Exam

1. First, review your textbook and any notes you have from your qualifying courses. Focus on areas where you had some difficulty. Then begin this *Cram.*

2. Next, use the "Subject Review" section in this book to review the key terms and key points for the qualifying course subjects. Note that the title of the topic is indicated in the heading for the salesperson course and the broker course. Although the topic headings are different for the salesperson and broker courses, the subject matter is essentially the same. *Remember that broker candidates are expected to know all content from the salesperson course for the broker exam. Also, salesperson and broker candidates who completed the old 45-hour salesperson course (before the new 75-hour course was instituted in July, 2008), are required to take the remedial course which contains 30 hours of the current salesperson course.* The only topic that salesperson applicants do not need to know from this review is *General Business Law* which appears in the broker course and exam only. Broker applicants must study the entire review.

The key terms, as well, included in this section, are identical to the key terms required by the NYS syllabus for the salesperson and broker qualifying courses. The key terms' section also includes other items that you should know. Knowing the meaning of these key terms is essential, as you will see them repeatedly in exam questions.

3. If you have questions regarding key terms or key points, refer back to your textbook.

This *Cram* is best suited for use with *New York Real Estate for Salespersons, 5th e* or *New York Real Estate for Brokers 5th e* by Marcia Darvin Spada. The textbook covers all content required for the NYS exams in an easy-to-understand format. See "Other Preparation Sources" earlier in this book for information on how to obtain a copy of either textbook.

4. Now, you are ready to begin your self-test review. "Questions for Your Review" contains questions for each subject in the qualifying courses. When answering the review questions, pay attention to all choices. Even the wrong choices may be terms that will be on the NYS exam. If you do not know their meaning, look them up in the "Subject Review" or your textbook. Do not time yourself for this review but complete it under exam conditions.

5. Use the Answer Key in the back of the book to grade your work. Then review the subject areas that are problematic. The Answer Key provides a rationale for each question. In addition, the Answer Key for the "Questions for Your Review" provides the page numbers from the Salesperson and Broker textbooks where the content in each question is found. Remember that sporadic wrong answers do not reflect weakness. You are doing quite well if you miss no more than 35 of the 360 questions in the review.

6. After you complete the review, complete the Sample Practice Exams. There are two for the salesperson and two for the broker. Broker applicants should complete the salesperson practice exams as well. These practice tests are similar in content and weightage of questions to the NYS exams. The exams are based on information that you should know according to the NYS syllabus. Take the Practice Exams under exam conditions with no interruptions. Allot yourself a maximum of 1.5 hours for the salesperson practice

exams and 2.5 hours for the broker practice exams as for the NYS exam. The Answer Key provides the correct answers, rationales, and page references in *New York Real Estate for Salespersons 5th e* or *New York Real Estate for Brokers 5th e*. If you do not pass these practice exams, further study is needed. The exams are divided into topics so that you can easily see problem areas. These sample exams are very good predictors of your performance on the NYS exams, so you should not attempt the NYS exam until you are comfortable with the content in this review.

A Word Of Encouragement

The best guarantee for success on any exam is preparation. Your willingness to spend time working with this *Cram for the Exam* will help you realize your goal. However, some people, no matter how well prepared, may not succeed on the first try. Many factors may come into play; how well you feel on that particular day, your level of anxiety, and sometimes just plain luck. Take care of the details that you can control, and try to relax. Most importantly, do not give up! If you do not pass on the first attempt, you have many resources available to help you succeed.

Disclaimer

The situations in the questions are fictional and the names of people and businesses are not related to real people or businesses. To simplify the text, the pronoun "he" is often used to refer to both male and female. Although the *Cram* offers comprehensive exam prep, use of the *Cram* does not guarantee success on your exams.

Subject Review

Review the key terms and key points for each subject before completing the review questions and sample exams. Instead of memorizing, strive for understanding. Additional content is fully explained in the textbook *New York Real Estate for Salespersons 5th e* or *New York Real Estate for Brokers 5th e*. The topic name in the salesperson syllabus appears first in the heading. The topic name for the broker syllabus, if different, appears after the slash in the heading.

License Law and Regulations/The Broker's Office: Operation, Management, and Supervision

Key Terms

Apartment information vendor An individual who, for a fee, furnishes information about the location of residential real property, including apartments, that are available to be rented, shared, or sublet

Apartment sharing agent An individual who, for a fee, arranges and coordinates meetings between the current owners or occupants of real property, including apartments, who wish to share their housing with others

Article 12-A of the Real Property Law Contains most of the law pertaining to salespersons and brokers

Article 78 proceeding The method for judicial review of determinations by regulatory agencies such as DOS

Associate real estate broker A licensed real estate broker who may perform the acts performed by a broker, but by choice wants to work under the name and supervision of a licensed broker

Blind ads Ads placed by a broker that do not indicate that the advertiser is a broker and do not give the broker's name and telephone number

Commingling The mixing of others' funds, such as deposit money, with a broker's business or personal funds; brokers are prohibited from commingling funds

eAccessNY The NYSDOS Occupational Licensing Management System that processes salesperson and broker licensure and other real estate licensure functions.

Escrow Account A fund deposited in an insured bank for the purpose of keeping deposit money

Felony Any serious crime above a misdemeanor and generally punishable by imprisonment

Kickback An improper payment by a broker or salesperson to someone who is not licensed or is not exempt from the license law; additionally, salespersons may not share a commission with other licensees

Misdemeanor A crime punishable by a fine of not more than $1,000 and/or imprisonment for not more than one year

Multiple Listing Service A system that pools the listings of all member companies

New York State Department of State (NYSDOS), Division of Licensing Services Governs the real estate licensure process and approves all real estate licenses

Pocket card A state-issued identification card that salespersons and brokers must carry in the course of business

Real estate broker Any person, partnership, association, or corporation that, for another and for compensation of any kind, negotiates any form of real estate transaction; also supervises and accepts responsibility for the activities of sponsored associate brokers and salespersons

Real estate salesperson One who performs any of the acts allowable under law by a real estate broker for compensation of any kind, but does so in association with and under the supervision of a licensed broker

Reciprocity An arrangement in which nonresident salespersons and brokers licensed in another state must take the New York exam and maintain an office in New York, unless their home state does not require New York licensees to have an office in their state or pass their exam to practice real estate there

Revocation Permanent removal of a license by NYS

Sponsor A broker that holds the license for the salesperson

Suspension Temporary lifting of a license by NYS for a designated time

Uniform Irrevocable Consent and Designation Form Gives the New York courts jurisdiction over unlawful actions of the applicant while doing business in New York and allows summonses and other legal documents to be served on the New York Secretary of State in place of personal service on the applicant

Key Points

1. License laws are an exercise of the police power of New York. Much of the license law pertaining to salespersons and brokers is contained in Article 12-A of the New York Real Property Law.
2. The purpose of license laws is to protect the public and elevate the standards of the real estate industry.
3. A real estate broker is a person or an organization that, for compensation of any kind, performs or offers to perform aspects of real estate transactions for others.
4. Real estate salespersons perform acts that a broker is authorized to perform, but they do so on behalf of a broker with whom they are associated.
5. Associate real estate brokers must fulfill the same requirements as a broker, but their status in the firm is the same as that of salespersons.
6. Attorneys do not need a license to practice real estate brokerage unless they employ licensees to work under their supervision.
7. The New York Department of State (DOS), Division of Licensing Services, oversees the licensure process. Most applicants can apply for the salesperson license online through the NYS DOS license management system *eAccessNY.*
8. The DOS has the power to deny, revoke, fine, or suspend a license.
9. The term of licensure for real estate salespersons and brokers is two years.

10 New York has reciprocal arrangements with other states for the licensure of nonresident licensees.
11. Real estate salespersons and associate brokers may not be officers of real estate brokerage corporations, hold voting stock in such a corporation, or be a partner in a licensed real estate brokerage partnership.
12. Brokers have a responsibility to comply with sign requirements, change in status and address notices, and termination notices, which must be completed online with a fee to DOS.
13. Other licenses and registrations related to real estate include mortgage bankers, mortgage brokers, and mortgage loan originators, apartment information vendors and apartment sharing agents, licensed or certified appraisers, and home inspectors.
14. Net listings, kickbacks, and commingling of funds are illegal. There are many other violations of license law.
15. The DOS has specific guidelines for real estate advertising by licensees and for the employment and duties of unlicensed real estate assistants.
16. Violation of the license law is a misdemeanor and is punishable by a $1,000 fine and/or a maximum sentence of one year in jail.
17. The revocation or suspension of a broker's real estate license suspends the license of the salespersons and associate brokers in the broker's employ.
18. Licensees must inform sellers that a Property Condition Disclosure Statement is to be provided to the buyer or the buyer's agent before the sellers accept the purchase offer.
19. A seller must disclose to the buyer the existence of any known uncapped natural gas wells on the property. The seller must disclose this information before he and the buyer enter into a contract of sale.

Useful Links

NYS Department of State
http://www.dos.state.ny.us

DOS Occupational Licensing Management System, *eAccessNY*
http://www.dos.state.ny.us/licensing/eaccessny.html.

Frequently Asked Questions, *eAccessNY*
http://www.dos. ny.gov/licensing/eaccessny_faq.html

Law of Agency/Real Estate Agency Disclosure (includes Independent Contractor and Antitrust)

Key Terms

Advance informed consent to dual agency Buyers or sellers can consent to dual agency on the NYS agency disclosure form in advance of it occurring by indicating consent on the NYS Agency Disclosure Form.

Advance informed consent to dual agency with designated agents Buyers or sellers can consent to dual agency in advance of it by indicating the name of the agent or agents who will represent them on the NYS Agency Disclosure form.

Agency disclosure form Mandatory written disclosure of representation form used for the sales or rental of residential one -to four unit properties and residential condominiums and cooperatives in any size building.

Agent When one person, the agent, agrees and is authorized to act on behalf of another person, the principal, an agency relationship is created

Brokerage The business of bringing buyers and sellers together and assisting in negotiations for the terms of sale of real estate

Broker's agent One who is engaged by a broker to work for that broker; in this relationship, the principal is not vicariously liable for the acts of any of the broker's agents; the broker who engaged these agents accepts this liability

Buyer agent One who represents the buyer of real property by entering into an agreement to work in the best interest of the buyer

Clayton Antitrust Act (1914) Supplements the Sherman Act and has the same general purpose; covers restraints on interstate trade or commerce not covered by the Sherman Act

Client The principal is also known as the agent's client

Cooperating agents Licensees from the same or other offices who participate as agents of buyers or sellers in a real estate transaction

Customer The party whom the agent brings to the principal as a seller, buyer, or tenant of a property

Designated agent A salesperson or an associate broker, supervised by a broker, who is assigned to represent a client when a different client is also represented by such real estate broker in the same transaction.

Disclosure and informed consent Explanation by a real estate agent of his position in the agency relationship and the verbal and written consent of the relationship for which the agency is created

Dual agent /dual agency An agent who attempts to represent both the buyer and the seller in the same transaction; must have the written approval of both parties after the agent's informed disclosure that the buyer and seller each will relinquish the agent's duty of undivided loyalty in the fiduciary relationship

Employee Employment status in which the employer must withhold federal, state, and social security (FICA) taxes and use special reporting forms; employee is supervised by employer

Estoppel An agency relationship created when an individual claims incorrectly that someone is his agent and a third party relies on the incorrect representation

Exclusive agency listing A listing with one broker as the only or exclusive agent; the broker is legally entitled to the commission agreed upon if the exclusive broker or another broker effects sale of the property, but not if the owner sells the property without the assistance of any broker

Exclusive right to sell A listing with one exclusive broker under which the broker is entitled to the commission no matter who effects the sale, including the owner

Express agency An agency relationship created by an oral or written agreement between the principal and agent

Fiduciary A position of trust; under a fiduciary relationship, the principal is owed faith, trust, and confidentiality by his agent

Fiduciary duties Reasonable care, skill and diligence obedience, accountability, loyalty and disclosure of information

First substantive meeting The first contact or meeting when some detail and information about the property is shared with parties who express some interest in the real estate transaction

General agent Someone authorized to handle all affairs of the principal concerning a specified matter or property, usually with some limited power to enter contracts

Group boycott A conspiracy in which a person or group is persuaded or coerced into not doing business with another person or group

Implied agency Creating an agency by words or actions of the principal and agent that indicate that they have an agency agreement

Independent contractor A work situation in which the employer does not have the right to control the details of a worker's performance; form 1099 misc. is filed with the IRS indicating the worker's yearly income

Market allocation agreement An agreement between competitors dividing or assigning a certain area or territory for sales

Net listing A listing contract that allows the broker to keep as a commission any money obtained from the sale above a sale price specified by the seller

Open listing agreement A listing with one or more brokers; any broker effecting the sale is entitled to the commission unless the owner sells the property

Price fixing A conspiracy by competitors in a group or industry to charge the same or similar price for services rendered

Principal The person who selects the agent to act on his behalf

Ratification The creation of an agency when a person claims to be an agent but has no express agreement, and the principal ratifies or accepts the agent's actions

Section 443 of the Real Property Law Requires that licensees present a written disclosure form that details consumer choices as to representation at the first substantive contact with a prospective seller or buyer; applies to the sales and rental of one- to four-unit residential properties and condominiums and cooperatives in any size building

Self Dealing Occurs when a broker has an undisclosed interest in a property

Seller agent A listing agent, an agent who cooperates with a listing agent as a seller's subagent, or a broker's agent who represents the owner of real property establishing a principal/client relationship to work in the seller's best interests

Sherman Antitrust Act (1890) Enacted to preserve a system of free economic enterprise and to protect the public against the activities of monopolies, contracts, or other combinations that unreasonably restrain trade

Single agent An agent who works only for the buyer or the seller and who may elect to reject subagency

Special agent An individual with narrow authorization to act on behalf of the principal; an example is a real estate broker who has a real estate listing

Subagents The principal's authorization of an agent to use other people to assist in accomplishing the purpose of the agency; these people are agents of the seller/principal and the broker with whom the property is listed

Tie-in arrangements Agreements between a party selling a product or service with a buyer that, as a condition of the sale, the buyer will buy something from the seller or the buyer will not buy the other's product or service

Undivided loyalty As part of their fiduciary duties, agents must remain loyal to the principal and work in the best interest the principal; the agent may not work for personal or for the interest of others adverse to the principal's interest without the principal's informed consent

Undisclosed dual agency A situation in which an agent represents the seller and the buyer in the same transaction but does not disclose his position

Vicarious liability One person is responsible or liable for the actions of the other. According to Section 442-c of the New York Real Property Law, a broker's license may be revoked or suspended for a salesperson's actions if the broker had actual knowledge of such violation or if the broker retains the benefits from the transaction after he knows that the salesperson has engaged in some wrongdoing.

Key Points

1. When one person is hired to act on behalf of another, an agency relationship is created. Agency is usually created with an agreement (express agency) but also can be implied by the parties' conduct. A position of trust, which is a fiduciary relationship, exists between every principal and agent in an agency relationship.
2. Real estate agents are special agents with specific authority.
3. The agent's fiduciary duties and responsibilities include obedience; loyalty; disclosure of information; confidentiality; accountability; and reasonable care, skill, and diligence.
4. A brokerage contract is created when the principal, usually a real estate owner, hires a broker (agent) to perform services relating to the real estate. Every agency relationship is consensual.
5. The principal can authorize the agent to use other people to assist in accomplishing the purpose of the agency. These people are subagents.
6. The nature of the compensation (commission or flat fee) (or the person who pays it) does not determine the agency relationship.
7. An agent may decide to represent the seller or the buyer in a real estate transaction.
8. A single agent works only for the buyer or seller directly and may elect to reject subagency.

9. A seller agent represents the owner of real property. The seller agent accepts the employment contract of a listing agreement, establishing a client relationship in the seller's best interest.
10 A buyer agent represents the buyer/purchaser of real property. The buyer agent accepts the employment contract of a listing agreement, establishing a client relationship in the buyer's best interests.
11 A dual agent is an agent who attempts to represent the buyer and the seller in the same transaction. Dual agency occurs in real estate companies when the firm attempts to represent the buyer and the seller in the same transaction.
12. According to New York law, an alternative for handling a dual agency in a brokerage firm is the designated sales associate or agent. With disclosure and informed consent, one sales agent in the firm is designated to represent the buyer. Another agent is designated to represent the seller.
13. Sellers and buyers may provide advance informed consent to dual agency with designated sales agents by indicating consent on the agency disclosure form. Advance consent to dual agency is allowed under an amendment to Section 443 of the NYS Real Property law effective January 1, 2011.
14. A multiple listing service (MLS) offers cooperation and compensation to participating members. It does not create an automatic subagency.
15. Although there is a fee for services and the possibility of less commission, multiple listing services generally offer a greater exposure for listed property, perhaps rendering a faster sale and a better price.
16. Cooperating agents are seller agents from another real estate firm acting as subagents of the listing broker and seller. Cooperative agents are also buyer agents from another real estate firm. These agents work through the usual system of offerings published within an MLS.
17. In the sale or rental of one- to four-unit residential properties and residential condominiums and cooperatives in any size building in New York, a dual agent must have the written approval of both parties after the agent's informed disclosure. The buyer and the seller each agree to relinquish the individual, undivided loyalty in the fiduciary relationship.
18. An undisclosed dual agency can result in a violation of New York Real Property Law.
19. New York real estate firms can provide consensual dual agency for in-house sales.
20. All agents must disclose what party they represent in a real estate transaction
21. In the sale or rental of one- to four-unit residential properties in New York and condominiums and cooperatives in any size building, the agent must present a mandatory disclosure form to all parties signing listing agreements. The form is also presented at other meetings and discussions between prospective buyers and sellers at the first substantive contact or meeting.
22. There are two separate agency disclosure forms: NYS Disclosure Form for Buyer and Seller and NYS Disclosure Form for Landlord and Tenant.
23. The IRS code classifies real estate salespersons and brokers as independent contractors. To qualify, the real estate agent must be licensed and the broker and the sales associate enter into a written contract.
24. As independent contractors, licensees do not receive sick pay or medical benefits and must file a Form 1099-MISC with the IRS. They pay self-employment taxes.
25. Antitrust violations are business activities in which a monopoly, contract, or conspiracy negatively impacts an individual's or a company's ability to do business. The negative compact is called "restraint of trade."
26. Antitrust laws are important to the real estate profession because it is unlawful for brokerage firms, real estate boards, franchises, and MLS services to conspire to fix commission rates. MLS cannot unreasonably prohibit a licensee from becoming a member and using its services.
27. The Sherman (1890) and Clayton (1914) Antitrust Acts and the creation of the Federal Trade Commission (1914) established legislation to control and regulate antitrust activity.

28. The Antitrust Division of the Department of Justice enforces the Sherman and Clayton Acts. Violators are subject to criminal liability and monetary damages.
29. Antitrust laws prohibit price fixing, group boycotts, market allocation agreements, and tie-in arrangements.
30. A series of lawsuits heard in federal district courts in New York and out of state sets forth activities prohibited under antitrust law and defines those activities allowable under the law.

Useful Links

National Association of REALTORS®
http://www.realtor.org

NYS Association REALTORS®
http://www.nysar.com

Legal Issues
Part I Estates and Interests

Key Terms

Act of waste When a life tenant abuses or misuses a property

Air rights Rights to the area above the earth

Beneficiary One who receives benefits or gifts from the acts of others given, for example, by a will or trust

Bundle of rights A visual concept that illustrates interests in and title to real property, including air rights, water rights, mineral rights, easements, leases, and mortgages

Chattel Another name for personal property

Defeasible fee A title subject to being lost if certain conditions occur

Dower and curtesy An automatic life estate owned by a surviving spouse in inheritable property owned by the deceased spouse alone during the marriage; for practical purposes, not valid in New York

Estate in real property An interest in the property sufficient to give the holder of the estate the right to possession

Fee simple absolute This estate provides the most complete form of ownership and bundle of rights in real property

Fee simple on condition A fee simple defeasible ownership recognized by the words "but if" in the transfer

Fixtures Improvements both on and to the land

Freehold estate Ownership for an undetermined length of time

Holdover tenant A tenant who does not leave upon expiration of the lease

Illiquidity Investments in which one's assets are not readily convertible to cash

Joint tenancy A form of co-ownership requiring all four unities of time, title, interest, and possession

Leasehold estate An estate of less than a lifetime and therefore of limited duration

Life estate Possession and control for the remainder of someone's life

Littoral rights Rights that apply to property bordering a nonflowing body of water, such as a lake or sea

Parcel A specific portion of land, such as a lot

Partition A legal proceeding dividing property of co-owners so each will hold title in severalty or directing that the property be sold and the proceeds be divided

Periodic estate An estate that renews itself for another period at the end of each period unless one party gives notice to the other during the prescribed time

Personal property Everything that is not real property

Qualified fee simple A fee simple defeasible estate recognized by the words "as long as" in the deed

Real estate Land and all improvements, whether found in nature or placed there by people

Real property Real estate plus all legal rights, powers, and privileges inherent in ownership

Reversionary interest Upon the death of a life tenant, the reversion of possession to the grantor or the grantor's heirs, if no other specification has been made

Right of survivorship When one (or more) of the co-owners of a property dies, the right of surviving co-owners to the interest of the deceased

Riparian water rights Rights that belong to owners of property bordering a flowing body of water

Severalty Title to real property held in the name of only one person or entity; the interest is severed from all others

Special purpose property Property that combines both the land and improvements for one highest and best use, such as a public park

Subsurface rights Rights to the area below the earth's surface; also called mineral rights

Tenancy in common Tenancy characterized by two or more persons holding title to a property at the same time; the only required unity is that of the right to possession

Tenants by the entirety Form of ownership limited to husband and wife; contains the right of survivorship

Trade fixtures Items installed by a commercial tenant and removable upon termination of the tenancy
Trust A fiduciary relationship between the trustee and the beneficiary of the trust

Trustee One who holds title to property for the benefit of a beneficiary

Trustor One who conveys title to a trustee

Unity of interest Co-owners who all have the same percentage of ownership in a property

Unity of possession Co-owners who have the right to possess or access any portion of a property that is owned without physical division

Unity of time Co-owners who receive title at the same time in the same conveyance

Unity of title Co-owners who have the same type of ownership, such as a life estate, fee simple, or conditional fee

Water rights Include percolating water rights, riparian water rights, and surface water rights

Key Points

1 Real property consists of land and everything attached to the land and the bundle of rights inherent in ownership.
2. Everything that is not real property is personal property.
3. Ownership in land includes the surface of the earth and the area above and below the surface, although these rights may be assigned.
4. Personal property that attaches permanently to the land or improvements and becomes part of the real property is a fixture.
5. Real property has the physical characteristics of immobility, indestructibility, and uniqueness and economic characteristics based on scarcity, permanence of investment, location, and improvements.
6. Estates in land are divided into two groups: freehold estates and estates of less than freehold (nonfreeholds or leaseholds).
7. Freehold estates are fee simple estates that are inheritable. Freehold estates are also life estates that are not inheritable.
8. The most complete form of ownership in real property is fee simple absolute.
9. Life estates may be in reversion or in remainder. The duration of a life estate may be measured by the life tenant or by the life of another *(pur autre vie).* A life tenant has the right of possession and enjoyment of the property and to derive income from it.
10. Title held in the name of one person only is ownership in severalty.
11. When two or more people or organizations hold title at the same time, it is called co-ownership or concurrent ownership. The forms of co-ownership include tenancy in common, joint tenancy, tenancy by the entirety, and community property.
12. Joint tenancy and tenancy by the entirety include the right of survivorship and require the unities of time, title, interest, and possession. Tenancy by the entirety is restricted to husband and wife and adds the fifth unity of marriage (unity of person).
13. Business organizations may receive, hold, and convey title to real property.

Legal Issues
Part II Liens and Easements

Key Terms

Appurtenances Inherent or automatic ownership rights that are a natural consequence of owning real property

Corporation franchise tax A tax calculated on the net profit of the corporation, which if not paid, becomes a lien against the corporation's assets

Dominant tenement The land that benefits from an easement appurtenant or from an easement in gross

Easement A nonpossessory interest in land owned by another; someone who owns an easement right does not own or possess the land where the easement lies, only the right to a specified use

Easement appurtenant All easements that are not easements in gross; two land owners must be involved, one receiving a benefit and the other accepting a burden

Easement by condemnation Created by the exercise of the government's right of eminent domain

Easements by grant or reservation Created by the express written agreement of the land owners, usually in a deed

Easements by implication Arises by implication from the conduct of the parties

Easements by necessity Exists when land has no access to roads and is landlocked

Easements by prescription Obtained by use of the land of another for a legally prescribed length of time

Easement for light and air A type of negative easement generally pertaining to the view of a property

Easements in gross Also called commercial easements in gross; usually owned by a government agency, or a public utility

Encroachment A trespass on the land of another created by the intrusion of some structure or object, such as a tree limb or roof overhang, across a boundary line

Encumbrance Interest in a property that secures debt or gives use and/or control to another

General liens Claims against all property of a debtor

In rem legal proceeding A legal action brought against the real property and not against an individual and his personal property

Involuntary lien A lien created by a legal proceeding when a creditor places a claim on real and/or personal property to obtain payment of a debt

Judgment A court decree resulting from a lawsuit

License Permission to do a particular act or series of acts on land of another without possessing any estate or interest in the land

Lien A claim or charge against the property of another

Lis pendens A notice that a lawsuit has been filed and a trial is pending, the judgment in which will affect title to a specific property

Materialman's lien A specific lien filed by a supplier of products required in construction or improvement of a building

Mechanic's lien A specific lien filed by a person who provides labor or furnishes material for the improvement of real property

Nonpossessory A non ownership interest in a property such as an easement

Party wall A common wall used by two adjoining structures

Possessory Either actively or constructively occupy the property which gives the possessor certain rights

Profit The right to take products of the soil from the land of another

Restrictive covenant Restrictions placed on a private owner's use of land by a nongovernmental entity or an individual

Servient tenement The land that suffers by allowing an easement use

Specific lien Claims, such as a mortgage, against a specific and readily identifiable property

Voluntary lien A lien in which individuals consent to placing a charge against their property as security for a debt; a mortgage is an example of a voluntary lien

Writ of attachment A court order preventing any transfer of the attached property during the litigation

Key Points

1. An encumbrance is a claim, lien, charge, or liability attached to and binding upon real property. Examples are encroachments, easements, leases, liens, assessments, and restrictive covenants.
2. Specific liens are claims against a specific and readily identifiable property, such as a mortgage or a mechanic's lien.
3. The lien for real property taxes is a specific lien. In New York, this lien has the highest priority for payment.
4. Mechanics' and materialmen's liens are specific liens that may receive preferential treatment for priority of liens.
5. General liens are claims against a person and all of his property, such as a judgment resulting from a lawsuit. The property of a judgment debtor is subject to execution and forced sale to satisfy an unpaid judgment.
6. Easements are nonpossessory interests in land owned by another. Easements can be in gross (commercial) or appurtenant (all other easements that are not easements in gross). Easements are created by grant (reservation), necessity, prescription, implication, and condemnation.
7. Easements appurtenant can be negative or affirmative. With an affirmative easement, the dominant tenement has the right to physically cross the servient tenement. With a negative easement appurtenant, the dominant tenement does not have the right to enter the land of the servient tenement. Instead, the dominant tenement has the right to restrict some activity or use of the servient tenement.
8. Easements are terminated by release, merger, abandonment, necessity, or expiration of the prescribed time.
9. An encroachment is a trespass on land or an intrusion over the boundary of land. A survey of a boundary provides evidence of an encroachment.
10. A profit in real property is transferable and inheritable. A license in real property is not transferable or inheritable.

Legal Issues
Part III Deeds/Conveyances

Key Terms

Accession Real property owners' right to all that their land produces or all that is added to the land, either intentionally or by mistake

Accretion The gradual building up of land in a watercourse over time by deposits of silt, sand, and gravel

Acknowledgment Public officer or notary's witnessing of signatures that make a deed or other instrument eligible for recording; the signatory must appear before a public officer, such as a notary public, and state that signing the deed was a voluntary act

Administrator (man) or Administratrix (woman) The person appointed by a court to distribute the property of a person dying intestate

Adverse possession A method of acquiring title to real property by conforming to statutory requirements; a form of involuntary alienation of title

Alluvion The land mass added to property over time by accretion; owned by the owner of the land to which it has been added

Avulsion The loss of land when a sudden or violent change in a watercourse results in its washing away

Bargain and sale deed May be with or without covenants of warranty; with covenants, the grantor claims that he is conveying substantial title and possession of the property; without covenants, the legal effect is similar to a quitclaim deed

Beneficiary or legatee The recipient of a gift of personal property by will

Bequest or legacy A gift of personal property by will

Conveyance A deed

Codicil A supplement or appendix to a will either adding or changing some bequest

Dedication A gift of land or an easement for public use; an example of an implied dedication is when the public is allowed access to a private road

Dedication by deed Used when a developer deeds to the municipality a parcel of land for a park; a cession or quitclaim deed may be used

Deed The document used to legally convey title to real property

Deed of correction Used when a deed contains an error that requires correction

Deed of gift Conveys real property without consideration; can be accomplished by any type of deed

Deed of trust A conveyance of real property that gives legal title to a trustee; not commonly used in New York, it can take the place of a mortgage because the title gives security for repayment of the debt owed on the property

Delivery and acceptance To effect transfer of title by transfer a deed, the grantor must deliver a deed to the grantee and the grantee must accept the deed

Description by monument Used in place of the metes and bounds method when describing multiple acre tracts of land that would be very expensive to survey; permanent objects such as stone walls, large trees, or boulders are used as markers

Description by reference, plat, or lot and block Legal description that references a plat of subdivision or other legal document

Devise A gift of real property by will

Devisee A recipient of the gift of real property by will

Executor (man) or Executrix (woman) A person appointed in a will to carry out its provisions

Formal or witnessed will One signed by the testator or testatrix in front of two witnesses where he declares the writing to be his last Will and Testament and states that it expresses his wishes for the disposition of his property after death

Full covenant and warranty deed Contains the strongest and broadest form of guarantee of title of any type of deed and therefore the greatest protection to the grantee

Grantee The person receiving title; does not need to have legal capacity; a minor or a mentally incompetent person can receive and hold title to real property

Granting clause The essential clause in a deed, containing words of conveyance stating that it is the grantor's intention to transfer the title to the named grantee

Grantor The one conveying the title; must be legally competent

Guardian's deed A deed executed by an individual who is legally vested with the power to manage the rights and property of another

Habendum clause A clause in a deed beginning with the words, to have and to hold, which describes the estate granted and always must agree with the granting clause

Intestate The condition of death without leaving a valid will

Involuntary alienation Occurs when an individual must relinquish title to real property against his/her will

Judicial deed Results from a court order to the official executing the deed; contain no warranties

Land patent Instrument conveying public land to a private party; can also mean the actual land conveyed

Metes and bounds description Legal description of surveyed land where the metes are the distances from point to point in the description and the bounds are the directions from one point to another

Probate Judicial determination of a will's validity by a court of competent jurisdiction and subsequent supervision over distribution of the estate

Public grant A grant of a power, license, or real property from the state or government to a private individual

Quitclaim deed Simply a deed of release; releases or conveys to the grantee any interest, including title, that the grantor may have; contains no warranties

Referee's deed An instrument executed by an individual empowered by the court to exercise judicial power, as in a court-ordered sale and conveyance of real property

Reference to a plat A valid legal description on a deed referring to a plat (map) and lot number as part of a recorded subdivision

Reliction An increase in land by the permanent withdrawal of a sea, river, lake, stream, or other body of water

Sheriff's deed Gives ownership rights in property to a buyer at a sheriff's sale

Tacking A procedure used to preserve the adverse possession claim when the possession of the property is taken over from one person to another sometimes through inheritance

Testate A person who dies having made a valid will while alive; a person may die testate as to some property and intestate as to other property

Testator A man who makes a will; a woman is a testatrix

Voluntary alienation Willing transfer of title during life; accomplished by the grantor's delivery of a valid deed to the grantee while both are alive

Key Points

1. A deed is the document used to convey title to real property. Transfer of title is termed *alienation*. Alienation may be voluntary or involuntary.
2. Examples of voluntary transfer of title during life are by sale, gift, dedication, or grant. Transfer after death is by will or New York statutes, as interpreted by the court.
3. Involuntary transfer of title occurs during the life of a property owner because of a lien foreclosure, bankruptcy, condemnation, or adverse possession. Involuntary transfer after death is escheat, which means the property goes to the state if no heirs can be found.
4. The requirements for deed validity are (1) deed in writing, (2) competent grantor, (3) competent or incompetent grantee, (4) grantor and grantee named with certainty, (5) adequate property description, (6) recital of consideration, (7) words of conveyance that sometimes contain a *habendum* clause, (8) proper execution by grantor, and (9) delivery and acceptance to convey title.
5. To be eligible for recording on the public record, a deed must be acknowledged or proved. Recording protects the grantee's title against future conveyances by the grantor.
6. Deed descriptions include metes and bounds, lot and block (plat of subdivision), and monuments.

7. A full covenant and warranty deed is the strongest and broadest form of title guarantee.
8. A quitclaim deed is a deed of release and contains no warranties. It conveys any interest the grantor may have. The quitclaim deed is used mainly to remove a cloud from a title.
9. A bargain and sale deed may be with or without covenants. When the bargain and sale deed contains covenants, it is acceptable to lenders.
10. Judicial deeds result from a court order to the official executing the deed. Forms of judicial deeds include sheriff's deed, referee's deed, tax deed, guardian's deed, and executor's or administrator's deed.
11. When a person dies and leaves no will, the laws of descent determine the order of distribution of property to the heirs.
12. When a person dies and leaves a will, the gift of real property through the will is a devise. A gift of personal property through a will is a bequest.
13. Surrogate's Court in the county where the deceased lived is the court of jurisdiction over probate matters.
14. The New York statute that defines distribution of property by the deceased is the New York Estate, Powers and Trusts Law.
15. Dedication occurs when land or an easement to land is given for public use.
16. A person other than the owner can claim title to real property under adverse possession. In New York, the possession must be continuous and uninterrupted for a period of ten years and a court must award title.
17. Natural processes of nature may give or take away land from property owners. These processes include accretion, alluvion, avulsion, and erosion.

Legal Issues
Part IV Title Closing and Costs

Key Terms

Abstract of title A condensed history of the title, summarizing all links in the chain of title plus any other matters of public record affecting the title

Actual notice Requires that the person actually knows about a document or situation

Assessments Referring to condominiums and cooperatives monies payable to the homeowner's association for maintenance of the common elements

Certificate of title opinion An attorney's written opinion as to which person or entity owns a property and the quality of title and exceptions, if any, to clear title

Chain of title The successive conveyances of title, starting with the current deed and going back an appropriate time (typically 40 to 60 years); title must be unbroken to be good and, therefore, marketable

Closing statement Sets forth the distribution of monies involved in the transaction—who is to pay what amount for each expense and who is to receive that amount

Combined Real Estate Transfer Tax Return, Credit Line Mortgage Certificate, and Certification of Exemption from the Payment of Estimated Personal Income Tax Form (Form TP 584) This form is used to transmit the NYS transfer tax and is furnished by the NYS Department of Taxation and Finance. In addition to the transfer tax information and payment, the form includes other important sections.

Constructive notice The theory that all the world is bound by knowledge of the existence of a document if evidence of the document is recorded

Credit In a closing statement, money to be received or credit given for money

Debit In a closing statement, an expense; monies that are owed

Insurable title A title that is acceptable to a title insurance company

Marketable title One that is reasonably free and clear of encumbrances

Mortgage recording tax 0.75% percent of the mortgage amount in certain counties; in counties with a public transportation system, the amount is 1 percent, with 0.25 percent paid by the lender, if there is one

New York City Real Property Transfer Tax In addition to the NYS transfer tax, New York City imposes an additional transfer tax of 1 percent of the selling price for residential property; if the selling price is over $500,000, the transfer tax is 1.425%. For other property types, the tax is 1.425% and if the consideration is more than $500,000, the tax is 2.65%

Proration A division of closing costs to ensure fair apportioning of expenses between buyer and seller

Real Estate Settlement Procedures Act (RESPA) Applies to residential federally financed properties, not to commercial properties or to owner-financed loans, and regulates lending institutions in making mortgage loans

Real property transfer tax A tax on the conveyance of title to real property paid by the seller and based on the consideration the seller receives for the property

Real Property Transfer Report Used to document the information associated with all real property transfers within New York (Form RP-5217)

Survey The process by which parcels of land are measured; the final document is a map showing measurements, boundaries, and area

Title Evidence of the right to possess property

Title closing Settlement of the obligations undertaken in the contract of sale; parties to the title transfer and other interested persons review the closing documents, execute the closing documents, pay and receive money, and receive title

Title insurance policy A contract that insures the policy owner against financial loss if title to real estate is not good

Title search Search of the records affecting real estate titles

Key Points

1. At a title closing, all interested parties meet to review closing documents and to transfer title to real estate. The deed is the document that conveys the title from seller to purchaser (grantor to grantee).

2. Recordation of a deed provides protection for the owner's title against subsequent claimants. Deeds and other closing documents are recorded in the county clerk's office of the county where the property is situated; in NYC, they are recorded in the Office of the City Register.
3. The purpose of a title examination is to determine a title's quality. An attorney or a title company makes the examination. Only an attorney can legally give an opinion about the title's quality.
4. A title insurance policy protects the insured against financial loss caused by a title defect.
5. Various types of tests and inspections of the property take place before closing. A licensed home inspector accompanied by the purchaser generally performs the "structural" before (and sometimes after) a contract is signed. A real estate agent may take a prospective purchaser to a walk-through of the property immediately before closing.
6. The Real Estate Settlement Procedures Act (RESPA) regulates lending activities of lending institutions that provide mortgages for housing.
7. The Commission Escrow Act applies to one-to four unit residential properties as well as individual condominiums and cooperatives sold by real estate brokers and sales agents. The law protects the broker's real estate commission when a seller does not pay the full commission upon closing.
8. The closing statement computes the distribution of monies involved in the transaction.
9. Seller closing costs may include the New York title transfer taxes; broker commission; attorney fees; costs of document preparation; and satisfaction of existing liens, if any.
10. Purchaser costs may include the structural inspection; title policy; survey fees; mortgage recording tax; lender fees; recording fees; and if relevant, broker commission.
11. Prorations are the division of expenses and income between the purchaser and the seller at closing.

Useful Links

Shopping for Your Home Loan-HUD's Settlement Cost Booklet
http://portal.hud.gov/hudportal/documents/huddoc?id=DOC_12617.pdf

HUD Good Faith Estimate
http://www.hud.gov/content/releases/goodfaithestimate.pdf

HUD Form No. 1
http://www.hud.gov/offices/adm/hudclips/forms/files/1.pdf

Automated City Register Information System ACRIS (New York City)
http://www.nyc.gov/html/dof/html/jump/acris.shtml

The Contract of Sale and Leases
Part I Leases

Key Terms

Actual eviction Wrongful use of self-help whereby the landlord, without the aid or control of the court system, physically removes the tenant and his belongings from the premises or takes action to prevent tenant access to the premises

Assignment Transfer of a lease from the present tenant to the assignee; the assignee then must make lease payments to the landlord

Constructive eviction Occurs when the tenant is prevented from the quiet enjoyment of the premises

Estate at sufferance Describes a tenant who is originally in lawful possession of another's property but refuses to leave after his right to possession terminates

Estate at will An estate in which the duration of the term is unknown when the estate is created because either party may terminate the lease simply by giving notice to the other party

Estate for years Exists for a fixed period, which can be as short as one day

Eviction A legal action for removal of a tenant and his belongings and a return of possession of the premises to the landlord

Graduated lease One in which the rental changes from period to period over the lease term

Gross lease Provides for the owner (lessor) to pay all expenses, such as real property taxes, owner's insurance, liability insurance, and maintenance

Ground lease A long term lease of unimproved land, usually for construction purposes

Holdover tenant A tenant who remains in possession of a property after a lease terminates

Index lease A method of determining rent on long term leases where the rent is tied to an economic indicator such as an index

Landlease Allows a lessee the right to use land for any purpose for a specified period

Lease A contract in which, for a consideration (usually rent), a property owner transfers to a tenant a property interest or possession, for a prescribed time

Lessee The tenant placed in possession of the leased premises

Lessor The landlord or owner of the leased property

Net lease The tenant (lessee) pays some or all of the expenses

Percentage lease A lease with a base rent plus an additional monthly rent based on a percentage of the lessee's gross sales

Periodic lease Automatically renews itself for another period at the end of each period unless one party gives notice to the other at the prescribed time

Periodic tenancy or estate from year-to-year The period length can be a week, a month, or any other negotiated time period

Security deposit Money paid by the tenant at the start of a lease that will be refunded at the end of the lease based upon the condition of the premises; often negotiated as one month's rent

Sublease A lease under which a tenant leases a property to a third party, the sublessee; the original tenant is still responsible to the landlord for the lease payments under the original lease contract; the sublessee pays the rent to the tenant (lessee), and the tenant pays the landlord

Triple net lease In addition to the rent, the lessee pays all expenses associated with the property

Key Points

1. Rental of property creates a leasehold estate. Types of leasehold estates include tenancy or estate for years, periodic (year-to-year) estates, estate at will, estate at sufferance.
2. A contract between the landlord of property and the tenant creates a lease. The landlord is the lessor. The tenant is the lessee.
3. The landlord and tenant are bound by contractual rights and obligations created by the lease agreement.
4. Leasehold estates (or nonfreeholds) are estates of limited duration, providing possession and control but not title, as in the case of freehold estates. Leasehold estates are estates for years, periodic tenancy, estates at will, and estates at sufferance.
5. The lessee's transfer of the entire remaining term of a lease is an assignment. A transfer of part of the lease term with a reversion to the lessee or a transfer of part of the leased premises is a subletting.
6. The Emergency Tenants Protection Act of 1974 (revised 1997) and the Rent Law of 2003 govern rent regulation. Two programs, rent control and rent stabilization, are intended to protect tenants in privately owned buildings from illegal rent increases while limiting the rights of landlords to evict tenants.
7. In a lease of residential property, the landlord's warranty of habitability must provide habitable premises to the tenant.
8. At expiration of the lease, the tenant must maintain and return the premises to the landlord in the same condition as at the beginning of the lease, ordinary wear and tear excepted.
9. The tenant can make a claim of constructive eviction when the premises become uninhabitable because of the landlord's lack of maintenance. A determination of constructive eviction terminates the lease.
10. Leases terminate by (a) expiration of lease term, (b) mutual agreement, (c) breach of condition, (d) actual eviction, (e) court-ordered eviction, or (f) constructive eviction. Actual eviction is illegal in New York.

Useful Links

The Division of Housing and Community Renewal
http://www.dhcr.state.ny.us

New York City Rent Guidelines Board
http://www.housingnyc.com

The Contract of Sale and Leases
Part II Contracts

Key Terms

Apportionment The division of expenses between seller and purchaser

Arm's length The relationship between parties to a contract; they are assumed to have equal bargaining power and are not related by business interest or familial relationship

As is Wording on an offer to purchase contract indicating that the premises is sold without warranty as to condition and the purchaser agrees to take title in the present condition subject to reasonable use, wear, and tear between the date of the contract and the closing date

Assignment A new party to a contract agrees to satisfy the former contracting party's obligation

Breach of contract Violation of the terms of a contract

Bilateral contract One in which two parties have made promises of some kind to each other

Binder In certain areas of New York, a written document for the purchase and sale of real property used by licensees instead of an offer to purchase contract; does not generally contain all the elements of a valid contract; however, if it does, it may be enforced as a contract

Caveat Latin for a warning or caution; in New York, properties that lie within an Agricultural District must have a disclosure attached stating that the property lies within an agricultural district

Caveat emptor Latin for "let the buyer beware"

Contingencies Additions, amendments or agreements annexed to the contract and incorporated into its terms

Contract An agreement between competent legal parties to do or refrain from doing some legal act in exchange for consideration

Counteroffer An acceptance that differs in any way from the offer

Earnest-money deposit Shows the sincerity of the buyer and expresses a commitment to raise the money called for in the contract

Executed contract A contract that has been fully performed

Executory contract A contract that is not fully performed

Express contract A contract in which the parties have agreed on all terms; can be written or oral

Forbearance May be granted by a lending institution; the act of refraining from taking legal action for nonpayment of a mortgage despite the fact that it is due

Implied contract One inferred from the conduct and actions of another without express agreement

Liquidated damages The parties to the contract can stipulate in the contract an amount of money to be paid upon certain breaches of the contract

Meeting of the minds When the parties to the contract reach agreement on the terms to be included in the contract

Novation A form of agreement that terminates a previous contract; the substitution of a new contract for a prior contract or the substitution of a new party for an old party

Offer to purchase contract A bilateral, express contract that is the "road map" for the real estate transaction

Option A contract in which an optionor (owner) sells a right to purchase a property to a prospective buyer, called an optionee, at a particular price for a specified time period; if no time limit is set, it may contain a clause allowing the optionee the first choice to either purchase or not purchase the property (right of first refusal) if a third party wishes to purchase the property

Power of attorney The right given by one party to another to perform certain acts in his behalf

Rescission To take back, remove, or annul; contract remedy applied when a contract has not been performed by either party and has been breached by a party

Specific performance An order from the court requiring the contract to be completed as originally agreed

Statute of Frauds In New York is the General Obligations Law; requires that real estate contracts be in writing. Leases and listing contracts for more than one year must be in writing to be enforceable in court

Statute of Limitations Law stating that, if a party to a contract fails to bring a lawsuit against a defaulting party within a time period set by statute, the injured party loses the right of remedy

"Time is of the essence" If written on the contract for purchase and sale, the closing must take place on or before the exact date stipulated in the contract

Unenforceable contract One that appears to meet the requirements for validity but would not be enforceable in court

Uniform Commercial Code Contains rules governing the financing of loans to purchase cooperative apartments; provides for the lender to retain a security interest in the personal property until the lender is paid in full

Unilateral contract When one party makes a promise in order to induce a second party to do something; the party making the promise is not obligated under the contract until the other party does what has been asked

Valid contract One that is binding and enforceable on all parties; contains all the essential elements of a contract

Voidable contract May or may not be enforceable between the parties; results from the failure of the contracting parties to meet some legal requirement in negotiating the agreement

Void contract Has absolutely no legal force or effect

Key Points

1. A contract is an agreement between competent parties, upon legal consideration, to do or refrain from doing some legal act.
2. An express contract is spoken or written. An implied contract is a contract inferred from the actions of the parties.

3. Bilateral contracts are based on mutual promises. Unilateral contracts are based on a promise by one party and an act by another party.
4. An executed contract is fully performed. An executory contract contains provisions yet to be performed.
5. A contract is created by the unconditional acceptance of a valid offer. Acceptance of bilateral offers must be communicated.
6. A voidable contract is one that may not be enforceable at the option of one of the parties to the contract.
7. The requirements for contract validity are (a) competent parties, (b) mutual agreement, (c) lawful objective, (d) consideration, and (e) written format when required to be.
8. The remedies for breach of contract are (a) compensatory damages, (b) liquidated damages, (c) specific performance, and (d) rescission.
9. A sales contract is a road map for the real estate transaction and is a bilateral express contract.
10. A binder and an offer to purchase are written outlines of the scope of a real estate transaction. They may contain all of the essential elements of a valid contract.
11. An installment land contract is a sales contract and a method of financing by the seller for the buyer. Legal title does not pass until the buyer pays all or some specified part of the purchase price.
12. An option is often tied to a lease. In some cases, all or part of the rent applies toward the purchase price of the property.
13. A broker is generally entitled to a commission when he produces a buyer who is ready, willing, and able to purchase the subject property on terms acceptable to the seller.
14. Contract preparation differs between upstate and downstate New York.

The Contract of Sale and Leases
Part III Contract Preparation

Key Terms

Attorney review or approval clause A condition making a contract subject to approval by each party's attorney.

Down payment The portion of a property's purchase price that is paid in cash and is not part of the mortgage loan. In certain upstate areas, the term used is deposit down payment; generally, when the buyer defaults, the down payment is the amount of liquidated damages to which the seller is entitled.

Lawyers' Fund for Client Protection One of its purposes is to reimburse client money that is misused in the practice of law.

Mortgage contingency clause States that the closing is contingent, or dependent upon, the purchaser's receipt of a mortgage commitment.

Key Points

1. In many upstate counties, the real estate agent fills out a preprinted contract of sale. In other places, such as the downstate area, the agent prepares a binder or an offer to purchase. An attorney prepares the contract of sale.

2. A binder is also called a receipt, a purchaser offer, and an agreement. The real estate agent may prepare a binder. Downstate, the seller's attorney sometimes prepares the binder.
3. Forms of contracts include the Contract of Sale (residential one- to four-unit property); Condominium Contract of Sale; Cooperative Contract of Sale; Commercial Contract of Sale for residential income property; Commercial Contract of Sale for retail, business property, and large tracts of land; Installment Sales Contract; and Option to Buy.
4. At the listing presentation, the agent can collect from the sellers the prior deed and title insurance policy; survey; Certificate of Occupancy (CO); and property tax, fuel, and water bills. These documents assist the attorneys who are preparing the closing documents.
5. Generally, for a residential or commercial sale of improved property, the property's common address (street address) is used. When tracts of unimproved land or lots are transferred, the deed, tax map, plat map filed, or survey may be attached to the contract.
6. The mortgage contingency clause states that the closing is contingent, or dependent upon, the purchaser's receipt of a mortgage commitment. If the purchaser complies with the terms of the clause but does not obtain a commitment, the contract may be canceled and the deposit returned.
7. It is customary for a purchaser to deposit up to 10 percent of the purchase price, in escrow, as an initial contract down payment. However, this percentage or the amount can be negotiated between the parties.
8. One of the purposes of the Lawyers' Fund for Client Protection is to reimburse client escrow money that is misused by attorneys.
9. Generally, the purchaser signs the contract of sale first because the purchaser is the party making the offer. The purchaser is stating the purchase price he wants to offer and the terms.
10. A real estate agent who prepares a fill-in-the-blanks purchase and sale contract can avoid the unlawful practice of law by including in the contract a condition making it subject to approval by each party's attorney. This condition is contained in an attorney approval clause.
11. The New York Judiciary Law prohibits the practice of law by non-attorneys. A violation is a misdemeanor. The DOS can also take action against the licensee.

Real Estate Finance/Real Estate Finance II

Key Terms

Acceleration clause A mortgage clause enabling the lender to declare the entire balance remaining immediately due and payable if the borrower is in default

Adjustable rate mortgage (ARM) A mortgage interest rate that varies, depending on fluctuations of a standard financial index

Alienation (due-on-sale) clause A clause in the note accompanying a mortgage that entitles the lender to declare the principal balance immediately due and payable if the borrower sells the property during the mortgage term; makes the mortgage unassumable without the lender's permission

Amortization Provides for paying a debt by installment payments; each payment covers current interest with the remainder applied to reduction of the principal

Balloon mortgage Provides for installment payments that are not enough to pay off both the principal and interest over the term of the mortgage; the final (balloon) payment to satisfy the remaining principal and interest is larger than any previous payment

Blanket mortgage Two or more parcels of real estate are pledged as security for payment of the mortgage debt

Bridge loan A short-term loan often used to finance projects until a permanent loan is obtained

Buydown The voluntary payment of discount points to reduce mortgage interest rates when the loan is made

Construction mortgage Interim, or temporary, short-term financing for creating improvements on land

Conventional loans Involves no participation by federal government agencies

Deed in lieu of foreclosure Conveyance of a property by a borrower in default to the lender to avoid record of foreclosure

Default Failure to perform an obligation, such as making mortgage payments

Defeasance clause A mortgage clause giving the borrower the right to defeat and remove the lien by paying the indebtedness in full

Deficiency judgment A court order stating that the borrower still owes a lender money when the proceeds of a foreclosure sale are not sufficient to satisfy the balance due the lender

Department of Veteran Affairs (VA) Federal agency offering a loan program that guarantees repayment of the top portion of the loan to the lender in the event the borrower defaults

Depression The lowest possible point in the economic cycle; the cycle encompasses all facets of the economy, including real estate and business; unemployment is generally high, the demand for goods and services is low, and production levels are down

Discount points Cash paid at the time of loan closing to reduce the interest rate on a loan; each point equals 1 percent of the loan amount

Equity of redemption After default and up to the time a foreclosure sale is held, the borrower has the right to redeem his property by paying the mortgage obligation; the foreclosure sale terminates the right

Federal Home Loan Mortgage Corporation (Freddie Mac) A federal agency that purchases mortgages on the secondary market to increase the availability of mortgage credit and provide greater liquidity for savings associations

Federal Housing Administration (FHA) A federal agency that insures mortgage loans to protect lending institutions; does not make mortgage loans, but protects lenders against financial loss; part of HUD

Federal National Mortgage Association (Fannie Mae) Fannie Mae is the oldest secondary mortgage institution and the single largest holder of home mortgages; taken over by the federal government in September, 2008, along with Freddie Mac.

Federal Home Loan Mortgage Corporation (FHLMC) (Freddie Mac) A seconding mortgage institution, it exists to increase the availability of mortgage credit and to provide greater liquidity for savings associations; purchases mortgages and packages them into securities that are sold to investors.

Flexible payment mortgage Mortgage plan based on the borrower's ability to pay

Foreclosure The process leading to the sale of real property pledged to secure mortgage debt

Government National Mortgage Association (Ginnie Mae) A federal agency that purchases FHA and VA mortgages on the secondary mortgage market

Grace period A specified time during which a mortgage payment may be made before the lender requires a penalty payment

Graduated payment mortgage A mortgage with lower payments in the early years of the term; payments increase at specified intervals until they are sufficient to amortize the loan over the remaining term

Home equity loan A loan against an owner's equity in his home

Hypothecating Pledging property as security for a loan

Inflation An increase in money and credit relative to available goods, resulting in higher prices

Installment land contract A means of buying land by making payments to the seller; when the property is paid for, title is transferred to the purchaser

Junior mortgage Describes any mortgage that is subordinate (lower in priority) to another mortgage

Loan-to-value ratio Compares the loan amount to the property value; expressed as a percentage

Margin For an adjustable rate mortgage, the amount above the designated index the lender adds to set the rate the borrower pays

Mortgage A two-party legal document pledging a property as security for the repayment of a loan under certain terms and conditions

Mortgagee The lender who receives the mortgage

Mortgagor The borrower who gives the mortgage

Open-end mortgage The borrower has the right to demand that the lender advance additional funds without rewriting the mortgage or incurring additional closing costs

Payment cap If the interest rate on an adjustable rate loan increases, a lender may allow a payment cap to keep the monthly payment the same, with the money for the higher interest rate being added to the principal

Predatory lending A practice in which a lender loans money to unqualified buyers.

Prepayment privilege or penalty clause A clause in a note accompanying a mortgage stating that the borrower may pay off the loan at any time without incurring a financial penalty or that a prepayment penalty will be imposed if the debt is paid off early

Promissory note or bond A note, in writing, required by a lender to provide evidence that a valid debt exists

Purchase money mortgage A mortgage given by a buyer to the seller to cover part of the purchase price or given to a third party lender to secure a loan, the proceeds of which are used to acquire the property

Rate caps With adjustable rate mortgages, limits on interest rates during the lifetime of the loan

Recession A moderate and temporary decline in economic activity that occurs during a period of otherwise increasing prosperity; often occurs in a recovery period following a depression

Release clause With a blanket mortgage, allows certain parcels of property to be removed from the mortgage lien if the loan balance is reduced by a specified amount

Rural Economic and Community Development (RECD) Operates federal loan programs targeted to rural areas; makes direct loans and guarantees loans

Rural Housing Service An agency of the U.S. Department of Agriculture (USDA; the service operates federal loan programs that strengthen family farms and finance rural housing; the Housing and Community Facilities Programs (HCFP) is an agency of the USDA and within the mission area of the Rural Housing Service

Satisfaction of mortgage An instrument drawn by the mortgagee (lender) when the mortgage is paid in full

Secondary mortgage market Buys and sells mortgages created in the primary mortgage market; mortgages must be assignable to qualify

Stagflation When economic growth is stagnant, but inflation persists

State of New York Mortgage Agency (SONYMA, also known as Sonny Mae) Raises money for mortgage loans from the sale of New York tax-free bonds; generally available through participating lenders at interest rates lower than most conventional loans

Straight term mortgage The borrower pays interest only for a specified term and pays the principal at the end of the term

Subprime mortgage A loan that may charge more points and have a higher interest rate than other loans; made to borrowers with lower than average credit ratings

Swing loan An interim or bridge loan usually not secured by a mortgage

Usury Laws that fix a maximum legal interest rate; the maximum rate is subject to fluctuation

Wraparound mortgage A subordinate mortgage that "wraps around" the existing first mortgage, which stays in place and is superior to the wraparound

Key Terms

1. The purpose of a mortgage is to secure the payment of a debt. A mortgage creates a lien against the property. Without the mortgage, comparatively few transactions would occur.
2. If a borrower defaults on a loan, a lender may institute foreclosure proceedings. If the sale proceeds available to the lender do not satisfy the debt, the lender may sue for a deficiency judgment.

3. The borrower's rights are (a) possession of the property before default, (b) defeat of lien by paying debt in full before default, and (c) equity of redemption.
4. The lender's rights are (a) possession of the property after foreclosure, (b) foreclosure, and (c) right to assign the mortgage.
5. A buyer assuming a seller's mortgage assumes liability on the mortgage and the note. The seller remains liable on the note unless released by a mortgage clause or by the lender. A buyer taking title subject to an existing mortgage has no liability on the note.
6. Conventional loans need not be insured if the loan amount does not exceed 80 percent of the property value. Most conventional insured loans are 90 percent and 95 percent loans. The insurance is called private mortgage insurance (PMI). The borrower pays the premium.
7. Lending institutions may charge discount points in making mortgage loans. Each point that the lender charges costs someone (either the buyer or the seller, depending upon the situation) 1 percent of the loan amount, paid at the time of closing.
8. A fully amortized mortgage requires payments of principal and interest that will satisfy the debt over the mortgage term.
9. Various types of mortgages and loans include term, adjustable or variable rate, balloon, amortized, pledged account, graduated payment, open-end, blanket, wraparound, swing (or bridge), purchase money, construction, shared equity, home equity, reverse annuity, and package.
10. Qualified lending institutions make FHA, VA, and RHS (Rural Housing Authority) loans.
11. The FHA-insured programs include 203(b). The FHA annual mortgage insurance premium (MIP) and the upfront mortgage insurance premium protect the lender from financial loss because of foreclosure. FHA establishes a maximum loan amount.
12. The Department of Veterans Affairs (VA) guarantees to the lender a maximum of 25 percent of a home loan amount up to $104,250 in case the borrower defaults. This limits the maximum loan amount with no down payment to $417,000.
13. The primary mortgage market is the activity of lending institutions making loans directly to individual borrowers. The secondary market is the activity of lending institutions selling and buying existing mortgages. The secondary mortgage market, which purchases mortgages from lenders, frees up capital so that lenders have money available for mortgages. The secondary market mortgage companies include Fannie Mae (FNMA), Ginnie Mae (GNMA), and Freddie Mac (FHLMC).
14. Methods of financing include insured and uninsured conventional mortgage loans, FHA-insured loans, VA-guaranteed loans, State of New York Mortgage Agency (SONYMA) mortgages, RHS loans, and various types of private financing.
15. Regulation Z of the Truth in Lending Act provides for disclosure by lenders and truth in advertising.
16. Lender criteria for granting a loan include investment quality of the property, sales price and appraised value, loan-to-value ratio, types of property, and purchaser's ability to pay.
17. Income, qualifying ratios, employment history, the borrower's business organization (if any), liquid assets, monthly obligations, and credit history are considered by the lender when someone is trying to qualify for a loan.
18. Commercial mortgages are extremely dependent on the financial strength of the borrower and may include personal guarantees as well as a substantial down payment. Package mortgages are used in commercial lending.
19. A provision in a convertible mortgage gives the lender the option of converting the outstanding balance into an agreed-upon percentage of property ownership
20. The real estate market is subject to cyclical changes in the economy and is often the first industry to feel the adverse effects of depressed conditions.
21. Factors such as employment levels, interest rates, the stock market, seller valuation of property, and buyers' ability to afford property affect changes in market activity.

22. The cycles in the economy can be defined by four main economic events: recession, depression, inflation, and stagflation.
23. Lender policies reflect the changing real estate climate. Some of the policies include non-income verification loans, loan-to-value and income ratios, and condominium and cooperative loans.
24. A capital-short market occurs when lenders do not have funds for underwriting.
25. Subprime mortgages are mortgages in which a lender charges a higher interest rate and high closing costs to compensate for potential losses from customers who may later default. While the loans have increased home ownership, they can increase mortgage defaults and foreclosures.
26. The New York Anti-Predatory Lending Law protects borrowers from lenders who charge excessive interest and points to high-risk borrowers.
27. The NYS Mortgage Foreclosure Law gives certain rights and protections to borrowers who face foreclosure.

Useful Links

The Federal Emergency Management Agency (FEMA)
http://www.fema.gov/business/nfip

FHA mortgage limits per county or area
https://entp.hud.gov/idapp/html/hicostlook.cfm

FHA loan information
http://www.fha.com/fha_requirements_mortgage_insurance.cfm

VA loan information
http://www.valoans.com

The Rural Housing Service
http://www.rurdev.usda.gov

SONYMA loan information
http://www.nyhomes.org/AboutUs/SONYMA/

Land Use Regulations/Development

Key Terms

Abutting land Parcels of land with a common boundary

Accessory apartment An apartment not intended for commercial rental; an example is an in-law apartment in a residential home

Accessory uses Use of a property that are incidental or subordinate to the main use of the property

Air rights Ownership right of the air space above the surface of the land; landowners may lease or sell air space to others

Area variance Permission to use land in a manner not normally allowed by the dimensional or physical requirements of the current zoning ordinance

Article 9-A Covers the sale or lease of vacant subdivided lands within and without New York only when sold through an installment land contract; covers a sale made by a salesperson, broker, owner, or any other individual empowered to sell the land

Building codes State and local rules and regulations that govern construction practices; regulate materials used in construction, electrical wiring, fire and safety standards, and sanitary equipment facilities

Building permit Local government permission to undertake construction or renovation

Census tracts Small geographical areas established by the local community and the Bureau of Census; they have numerical identification numbers

Certificate of occupancy A document permitting occupation of a structure by tenants or the owner after a satisfactory final inspection

Cluster zoning Allows a developer to place single-family houses, townhomes, apartments and other dwellings closer together in exchange for leaving parts of the development open for community enjoyment

Completion Bond Also known as a subdivision bond, it ensures the municipality that off-site improvements to the subdivision will be made upon completion of the total project.

Condemnation Actual taking of property under the power of eminent domain

Conditions Restrictions that provide for a reversion of title if they are violated

Cul-de-sacs Streets with only one outlet; dead ends

Deed restrictions In the form of covenants or conditions, they run with the land (move with the title in any subsequent conveyance) as private controls placed on real estate

Demography The study of the social and economic characteristics of a community

Density A measure of the number of people inhabiting an area of land

Doctrine of Laches If property owners do not act to enforce a restrictive covenant on a timely basis, the court will not apply the restriction against the violator and the covenant will be terminated; if landowners are lax in protecting their rights, they may lose them

Cumulative zoning A type of zoning permitting a higher-priority use even though it is different from the use intended for the area

Exclusive-use zoning Zoning regulations that state that property may only be used in the ways specified in a specific zone

Eminent domain The right or power of government and its agencies to take private property for public use; must be for the public good

Environmental impact statement The process that describes and analyzes a proposed action that may have a significant effect on the environment

Escheat The power of the state to take title to a deceased person's property when no one else is qualified to receive the title

Family According to New York law, any of the following: a group of up to three people who are not married, blood relatives, or adopted living together as a single housekeeping unit; an individual or two or more persons related by blood or marriage or adoption living together in one dwelling; one or more persons living as a single housekeeping unit, as distinguished from a group occupying a hotel, club fraternity, or sorority house

Group home A residential facility for five or more adults who have been institutionalized for various reasons and then released

Home occupation Use of residential property by an owner or lessee for a small business; may be conducted only by the residents of the dwelling and must be incidental and secondary to the use of the dwelling

Infrastructure Support systems of a community such as water, wastewater treatment, utilities, schools, roadways, medical services, police, and fire departments

Lead agency The agency that oversees the environmental assessment process and makes the final decisions

Moratorium Imposed by a municipality, it is a delay in allowing property development in the municipality

Nonconforming use ("grandfathered in") A preexisting use of property different from that specified by the current zoning code

NYS Office of Parks, Recreation and Historic Preservation Administers federal and state preservation programs authorized by federal law and by the New York Historic Preservation Law

Outlots Land that is outside of the main area of development

Police power Enables government to fulfill its responsibility to provide for the public health, safety, and welfare

Public land use control Regulation of land use by government organizations in the form of zoning laws, building codes, subdivision ordinances, and environmental protection laws

Restrictive covenants Restrictions placed on a private owner's use of land by a nongovernmental entity or individual.

Setback Specified distances from the front property line and from the interior property lines to the building line

Special use permit A use not permitted in the zone except with the special permission of the planning board or other legislative body

Spot zoning Rezoning of a specific property to permit a use different from the zoning requirements for that area; illegal in New York

Subdivision Land that is divided into lots for development purposes

Subdivision plat A map of a subdivision dividing or platting the land into lots; recorded on the public record

Subdivision regulations Public control of residential subdivision development

Survey The measurements of the boundaries and the total physical dimensions of the property

Taking The act of a government body obtaining a property under its power of eminent domain

Topography The physical features and contours of the land

Transfer of development rights (TDR) Programs that encourage a shift in growth away from agricultural, environmentally sensitive, or open space regions of a municipality to more appropriate areas; the exchange of zoning privileges from areas with low population needs, such as farmland, to areas of high population needs, such as downtown areas

Use variance Permission to use the land for a purpose prohibited under current zoning restrictions

Variance A permitted deviation from zoning ordinance requirements

Zoning board of appeals Local government body that has the power to review administrative rulings made by the planning board or other legislative body, to grant or deny exceptions and special permits, and to process applications for variances

Zoning ordinance A statement setting forth the type of use permitted under each zoning classification and specific requirements for compliance

Key Points

1. Individual owners have the right to place private controls on their own real estate. The purpose of a deed restriction is to limit the use or appearance of a property.
2. Cities, counties, and other local governing units may impose land use regulations and building codes.
3. A subdivision is a tract of land divided into lots or plots for future building purposes. Local planning boards coordinate the site plan review and approval process.
4. Subdivision regulations protect owners within a subdivision, as well as protecting taxpayers from undue tax burdens resulting from the additional services that a subdivision requires.
5. The development process includes a feasibility study, application to a municipality and/or other appropriate agencies, an environmental review, financing, construction, and marketing.
6. To obtain financing for a subdivision project, the developer may have to raise funds through a combination of sources.
7. Developers generally place restrictive covenants on their entire subdivision to maintain quality and consistency
8. In New York, the State Environmental Quality Review Act (SEQRA) controls environmental impacts. An environmental impact statement (EIS) evaluates the effect the environment has on the property.
9. Public land use controls include police power, taxation, eminent domain, and escheat.
10. The Interstate Land Sales Full Disclosure Act regulates the sale of unimproved lots in interstate commerce to prevent fraudulent schemes in selling land sight unseen.
11. The NYS Uniform Fire Prevention and Building Code provides minimum standards for all types of buildings.

12. The New York building code requires that a property owner obtain a building permit from the appropriate local government authority (usually the building department) before constructing or renovating a commercial building or residential property.
13. If an individual dies without a will and there are no heirs or creditors, his property reverts to the state through the power of escheat.
14. Types of zones include residential, commercial, industrial, vacant land, agricultural, public open space, parklands, recreation areas, and institutional.
15. In New York, local planning boards oversee the type of land use within the municipality and have the authority to review site plans.

Construction and Environmental Issues
Part I Construction/Subdivision

Key Terms

Amperage The amount of electricity flowing though a wire

Balloon framing An alternative to platform framing; uses wall studs that run from the foundation through the first and second floors to the ceiling support; rarely used in residential construction

Bearing walls Walls, including the outside wall frame, that support the ceiling and/or the roof

British Thermal Unit (BTU) A measure of heat energy; the amount of heat required to raise the temperature of one pound of water by one degree Fahrenheit

Building plan A detailed architectural rendering of a structure; blueprint

Building specifications Written narratives that describe the building plan and materials

Circuit breakers Devices that that switch off electrical power for a given circuit if the current increases beyond the capacity of the system

Infrastructure Support systems of a community such as water, sewers, utilities, schools, roadways, medical services, and police and fire departments

Distribution panel Metal box containing electrical circuit breakers or fuses; where outside power enters a structure to be distributed inside

Double top plate Also known as a flitch beam, used to tie walls together and provide support for the ceiling and roof system

Energy Conservation Construction Code of New York State (ECCCNYS) A New York law that sets minimum efficiency requirements for the design of new buildings and renovations and additions to existing buildings.

Eave The lowest part of the roof which project beyond the walls of the structure

Fascia The material facing the outer edge of the soffit; if guttering is installed on a roof, it is fastened to the fascia

Flashing Metallic material used in certain areas of the roof to prevent water from seeping into the structure

Footing The most important foundation building block; the concrete base below the frost line that supports a structure's foundation

Foundation walls Generally composed of poured concrete, masonry block, or sometimes brick; the height of the foundation wall determines whether the structure will have a full basement or a crawl space

Frieze board A component of the roof overhang fastened directly under the soffit against the top of the wall; both decorative and functional

Fuse A device that melts to open a circuit and cut off electrical power when overheating occurs

Girder A main carrying beam, either a steel beam or several wooden members fastened together, that spans the distance from one side of a foundation to the other

Headers Also known as lintels; framing members that reinforce door and window openings

Joists Framing members used for floor and ceiling framing

Lally columns Support the main carrying beam of the structure; round steel columns filled with concrete that rest on a base plate, which is the column-footing pad

National Electric Code A national standard for electrical installation and service written to safeguard people and property from hazards arising from the use of electricity

Pitch Slope of the roof

Platform framing Framing in which the structure rests on a subfloor platform; the most common type of framing for residential construction

Post-and-beam framing Framing in which studs are much larger than ordinary studs (they may be four or six inches square); the larger posts are placed several feet apart; seldom used in residential construction

R-factor The degree of a wall's resistance to heat transfer; used to rate insulation: the larger the R-factor, the greater the degree of insulation

Rafters Long wood members fastened to the ends of the ceiling joists to form roof gables

Ridge beam The highest part of the framing; forms the apex, or top line, of the roof

Septic system A household wastewater treatment system consisting of a house sewer, septic tank, distribution box, and absorption field or seepage pit

Sheathing A plywood covering placed over exterior framing members; sheetrock or wallboard may be used

Sill plate The first wooden member of a structure; used as the nailing surface for the floor system

Slab-on-grade construction A concrete slab used instead of a foundation wall; the slab is poured directly on the ground, eliminating the crawl space or basement

Soffit The area under the roof extension; made of wood, aluminum, or vinyl

Sole plate A horizontal base plate that serves as the foundation for the wall system

Studs Wood framing members are lumber with a nominal dimension of 2 inches thickness

Urea Formaldehyde Foam Insulation (UFFI) Widely used in homes from 1970s to the 1980s; a hot, viscous mixture sprayed inside the sheathing where it solidifies

Voltage The electrical pressure that pushes through a wire

Key Points

1. In New York, residential and commercial structures must comply with state and local building codes. The NYS Uniform Fire Prevention and Building Code dictates minimum requirements. The Energy Conservation Construction Code of New York (ECCCNYS) governs building energy efficiencies.
2. It is not the duty of the broker to verify all representations by the owner, but if the broker uses those representations as a selling point, the broker could incur liability. If the broker knows or has reason to know that the owner has made a false representation or has not disclosed a material defect, the broker must disclose this information or terminate the agency.
3. Brokers must disclose any material defects that they have knowledge of to a prospective purchaser. Liability may be imposed upon the agent for concealing defects or failing to disclose the existence of defects.
4. New York has laws and regulations that govern on-site well regulations and on-site sanitary waste systems. The sanitary waste or drainage system of a structure carries wastewater and used water from the structure and deposits it in the public sewer system or private wastewater treatment system.
5. Other site considerations in the planning stage include drainage, landscaping, shading, and walkways.
6. Framing is the wooden skeleton of a structure. Framing members are lumber with a nominal dimension of 2 inches thick.
7. The floor system starts with the sill plate nailed to the foundation system. Wood joists support the subfloor material.
8. Wall framing is usually 2″ × 4″ studs placed 16 inches on center. The most common wall-framing system is the platform method. Alternative methods are balloon and post-and-beam framing.
9. The main purpose of insulation is to resist the flow of heat from one area to another. Insulation is rated on an R-factor; the larger the R-factor, the greater the degree of insulation.
10. HVAC stands for heating, ventilation, and air conditioning. Some systems use fuel oil or natural gas for energy, while others use electricity.
11. Heating systems found in the home are usually hot water, steam, forced warm air, or electric. The heat pump is another type of heating system.
12. Forced-air heating and cooling systems use a central fan or blower to distribute the heated or cooled air throughout the structure. Hot water heating systems use circulator pumps to propel the heated water through pipes to the convectors.
13. Air conditioning units are placed inside or outside a structure. Components of an air conditioner include liquid refrigerant, an evaporator, a compressor, and a condenser.

14. The plumbing system consists of two systems: the water supply system for drinking, cooking, and washing and the drainage system for wastewater.
15. Hot water systems commonly found in residential construction include gas and electric water tanks as well as other systems that are connected to the heat source.
16. Electric power is brought to a structure through outside cables and is delivered through conductors (wires) to the building wiring system.
17. The New York General Business Law provides for a one-year builder's warranty against construction defects and a six-year warranty against material defects.
18. In New York, every one- and two-family dwelling as well as apartments in multiple dwellings, including residential condominiums and cooperatives, must have an installed operable single-station smoke alarm.
19. A carbon monoxide detector must be installed in one- and two-family homes, residential condominiums or cooperatives, and multiple dwellings, regardless of the date of construction or sale. Because of Amanda's Law, carbon monoxide detectors are required in nearly all residential structures in New York. When a one- or two-family property or a residential condominium or cooperative property is transferred, a smoke alarm and carbon monoxide detector affidavit is required.

Useful Links

NYS Department of Health
http://www.health.state.ny.us

NYC Home Improvement Contractor license information
http://www.nyc.gov/html/dca/html/licenses/100.shtml

Construction and Environmental Issues Part II Environmental Issues

Key Terms

Asbestos A fibrous mineral found in rocks and soil throughout the world; used in construction because it is strong, durable, fire retardant, and an efficient insulator; improper handling of asbestos products results in lung disease

Chlordane A chemical insecticide and termiticide banned in the early 1980s because of its toxicity

Chloro-fluoro-carbons (CFCs) Manmade chemical substances used in hundreds of applications, including refrigerators and air conditioners, styrofoam products, aerosol dispensers, and cleanings agents; a danger to the ozone layer

Clean Air Act (1972) A comprehensive federal law intended to control air pollution; a 1990 amendment bans the release of CFCs and HCFCs during the service, maintenance, and disposal of air conditioners and other equipment that uses these refrigerants

Comprehensive Environmental Response, Compensation and Liability Act (CERCLA) A federal law enacted to correct environmental problems created by uncontrolled waste disposal

Due diligence Because liability for environmental problems passes to new owners in the sale of large tracts of land or commercial property, lenders, purchasers, and tenants often conduct environmental reviews of the property

Electromagnetic fields Magnetic fields created by electricity flowing through a wire

Friable Flaky or crumbly texture of asbestos when hand pressure is applied

Hydro-chloro-fluoro-carbons (HCFCs) Also known as Freon, a non toxic chemical substance formerly used in most home air-conditioning units; when released poses a danger to the ozone layer; in recent years, Freon has replaced with another safer gas.

Kilovolt A measure of voltage flowing through a power line

Lead A metallic element found worldwide in rocks and soils; can be present in drinking water, house paint, dust, and soil around a home; toxic

PCB A manmade, odorless, liquid organic compound; PCBs are used to cool and insulate electrical transformers; known to appear in ground water and soil; a carcinogen

Radon A colorless, odorless, tasteless, radioactive gas present in soil and well water; enters homes through openings such as cracks in concrete, floor drains, sump pump openings, wall/floor joints in basements, and the pores in hollow block walls

Sick building syndrome Occurs when many people in a commercial building fall ill with a variety of complaints ranging from allergic reactions to flu-like symptoms to more serious complaints; may be blamed on poor air quality inside the building

State Environmental Quality Review Act (SEQRA) Calls for the preparation of an environmental impact statement on any actions that may affect the environment; this action may be proposed by a governmental body, private individuals, or entities whose projects require governmental approval

Superfund Amendments and Reauthorization Act (SARA) An amendment to CERCLA imposing stringent clean-up standards and expanding the definition of persons liable for clean-up costs

Wetlands Marshes, swamps, bogs which are protected areas as they provide flood and storm water control, surface and groundwater protection, erosion control, pollution treatment, fish and wildlife habitats and natural beauty

Key Points

1. Long-standing environmental issues relative to real estate include drinking water, wastewater treatment, and pest infestation. Contemporary issues include the use of chemical contaminants such as asbestos, lead, radon, and PCBs. Other present and future concerns include underground storage tanks, electromagnetic fields, mold, and the release of chlorofluorocarbons.
2. Federal and state legislation provide regulations and guidelines for environmental policy.
3. The federal Safe Drinking Water Act is New York's guideline for drinking water regulations. The NYS Department of Health oversees the safety of drinking water in New York.
4. A federal law, The Residential Leadbased Hazard Reduction Act mandates that in the sale or lease of pre-1978 residential properties, sellers or their agents must distribute a lead hazard pamphlet and disclose any known information to the buyers or their agent concerning lead paint. The parties must agree to a ten-day period for a lead paint assessment before a purchaser becomes

obligated under the contract. Sales and lease contracts must include specific disclosure and acknowledgment language.

5. The NYS Department of Environmental Conservation (NYSDEC) oversees and protects wetlands. Construction can take place on or near a wetland. Builders must obtain approval for regulated activities from the state through local and federal governments.
6. One source of air pollution in the home may be urea-formaldehyde foam insulation (UFFI), which contains large amounts of formaldehyde.
7. Another source of home air pollution is insecticides. Chlordane is a chemical insecticide and termiticide that has been banned since the early 1980s.
8. Bacteria are a source of air pollution in homes and buildings. Sometimes large numbers of people in a commercial building fall ill from a chemical illness called sick building syndrome.
9. An environmental impact statement (EIS) describes and analyzes a proposed action that may have a significant effect on the environment.
10. Because of liability for environmental cleanup, lenders, purchasers, and tenants often conduct due diligence reviews of property before transfer.
11. The NYSDEC regulates the bulk storage of chemicals and petroleum both aboveground and underground. These tanks must be monitored for leakage.

Useful Links

EPA radon prevention in construction information
http://epa.gov/radon/construc.html

NYS Department of Environmental Conservation
http://www.dec.state.ny.us

Valuation Process and Pricing Properties

Key Terms

Appraisal An unbiased estimate of the nature, quality, value, or utility of an interest in or aspect of identified real estate and related personality, based on factual data; it is an opinion of the market value of a property, as of a given date, supported in writing with collected data and logical reasoning

Comparative market analysis (CMA) An analysis of the competition that a property offered for sale will face in the marketplace; not an appraisal

Cost The total expenditure for labor, materials, legal services, architectural design, financing, taxes during construction, interest, contractor's overhead and profit, and entrepreneurial overhead and profit

Cost Approach Appraisal method for evaluating properties that have few, if any, comparables and are not income producing

Depreciation Loss in value from any cause

Direct costs Also called hard costs, they include the cost of labor and materials

Evaluation The study of the nature, quality, or utility of certain property interests in which a value estimate is not necessarily required; examples are studies of land utilization, highest and best use, marketability, feasibility, and supply and demand

External Obsolescence Changes in surrounding land use patterns resulting in increased traffic, air pollution, and other hazards and nuisances

Functional Obsolescence Flawed or faulty property rendered inferior because of advances and change in such items as wiring, equipment or design

Highest and best use The use of land that will preserve its usefulness, provide the greatest income, and result in the highest land value

Income Approach Appraisal method used to estimate the present value of properties that produce income

Indirect costs The costs that create and support the project include architectural and engineering fees, professional fees such as surveyors, attorneys, and appraisers, financing costs, administrative costs, costs, filing fees and other costs

Insured value The cost of replacing or reproducing a structure in the event of a total loss due to an insured hazard

Investment value Value based on the amount of financial return that a property would produce

Market value The most probable price, as of a specific date, in cash, or in terms equivalent to cash, or in other precisely revealed terms, at which the specified property rights should sell after reasonable exposure in a competitive market, under all conditions requisite to a fair sale, with the buyer and seller each acting prudently, knowledgeably, and for self interest, and assuming that neither is under duress

Mortgage value Value based on what a lender believes the property will bring at a foreclosure sale or subsequent resale

Plottage Small plots of land are combined to form a larger plot

Price The amount a purchaser agrees to pay and a seller agrees to accept under the circumstances surrounding the transaction

Residential market analysis A careful study of the individual property being listed as it stands on its own and in light of current market conditions

Sales comparison approach Primary appraisal method for estimating the value of single-family, owner-occupied dwellings and vacant land

Valuation Establishes an opinion of value utilizing a totally objective approach; it is the process of estimating the value of an identified interest in a specific property as of a given date

Value in use Property considered more for its value to the owner and not for its value if placed on the market

Key Points

1. An appraisal is an estimate of value based on factual data as of a specific date for a particular purpose on a specified property.
2. Valuation is the process of estimating the value of an identified interest in a specific property as of a given date. Besides market value, other types of value include value in use, insurance value, investment value, assessed value, and mortgage loan value.
3. Market value is the amount of money a typical buyer will give in exchange for a property.
4. Evaluation, as compared with valuation, is a study of the quality or utility of a property without reference to a specific estimate of value.
5. Various evaluation studies include marketability, feasibility, supply and demand, land utilization, and highest and best use. In the context of market value, highest and best use is the most probable use. It may or may not be the present use of the property.
6. Price is the amount a purchaser agrees to pay and a seller agrees to accept under the circumstances surrounding the transaction.
7. Cost is composed of a number of factors that equal the total dollar expenditure to construct the improvements. Included are direct costs, such as labor and materials, and indirect costs, such as professional fees, filing fees, and other items in the construction process.
8. A comparative market analysis (CMA) is an analysis of the competition in the marketplace that a property encounters upon sale attempts.
9. A residential market analysis consists of a study of recently sold properties, currently competing properties, recently expired properties, buyer appeal, market position, assets and drawbacks, area market conditions, recommended terms, and price range.
10. The degree of competence, diligence, documentation, and effective communication skills by the licensee is integral to effective marketing.
11. Highest and best use refers to the use of land aimed at preserving its usefulness, providing the greatest income, and resulting in the highest land value. To achieve the highest and best use, land is improved through the use of capital and labor to make the land productive.
12. A first step in site valuation is to conduct a feasibility study. Factors reviewed are site development costs (including environmental factors), financing costs (including prevailing interest rates), tax considerations, rates of return on similar types of investments, and the benefit to and acceptance by the community.
13. A site is generally valued using the sales comparison approach.
14. Appraisals commonly use three approaches to value: the sales comparison, cost, and income approaches. The sales comparison approach most closely resembles the comparative market analysis.
15. Part of the listing process involves recommending to the owner a market price that will be the listing price.
16. A comparison of the property with similar properties that have sold recently (within the last six months), other currently listed properties, and evaluation of expired listings determines the price.

Human Rights and Fair Housing

Key Terms

Americans with Disabilities Act (1992) Protects the rights of individuals with disabilities with regard to access to commercial facilities, public accommodations, and new housing developments with at least four units

Blockbusting Occurs when real estate salespersons induce owners to list property for sale or rent by telling them that persons of a particular race, color, national origin, sex, religion, disability, or familial status are moving into the area; also when real estate firms sell a home in a neighborhood to a person from one of the protected classes with the sole intent to cause property owners to panic and place their property for sale at reduced prices

Cease and desist zone Established by the NYS DOS after determining that some homeowners within certain geographic areas have been subject to intense and repeated solicitation by real estate agents; upon establishment of a cease and desist zone, homeowners in the zone may be placed on a list indicating that they do not desire to sell, lease, or list their residential property or be solicited by real estate agents

Civil Rights Act of 1866 The first significant statute affecting equal housing opportunity; it is interpreted to prohibit all racial discrimination

Department of Housing and Urban Development (HUD) A federal regulatory agency through which civil rights violations can be reported

Disability Legally defined as a physical or mental impairment that greatly limits one or more of a person's major life activities

The Fair Housing Amendments Act of 1988 Prohibits discrimination based on mental or physical handicap or familial status

Fair Housing poster A poster that an amendment to the Fair Housing Act of 1968 requires to be prominently displayed in real estate brokerage offices

Familial status Legally defined as an adult with children under 18, a person who is pregnant, or one who has legal custody of a child or who is in the process of obtaining custody

Federal Fair Housing Act (Civil Rights Act of 1968) Prohibits discrimination in housing on the basis of race, color, religion, or national origin

Filtering down Properties in neighborhoods that were once middle or upper income decline in value, allowing people with lower incomes to purchase them

Housing and Community Development Act of 1974 Federal law prohibiting discrimination based on gender

Human Rights Law Known as Article 15 of the NYS Executive Law, prohibits discrimination in the rental and leasing of housing, land, commercial space, and other non-real estate related activities

Jones v. Alfred H. Mayer Co., The U.S. Supreme Court applied the older Civil Rights Act of 1866 to prohibit any racially based discrimination in housing. This court ruling is important because the Federal Fair Housing Act provides exemptions under certain circumstances. Because of the court's determination in Jones v. Mayer, exemptions in the Fair Housing Act cannot be used to allow racial discrimination under any circumstances

Marital status Individuals who are either married or single

Multiple dwellings Residences that contain three or more family units

Nonsolicitation order An order from the NYS DOS prohibiting licensees from soliciting listings for the sale or purchase of real property in certain areas of the state

Redlining Term applied to lending institutions' refusing to make loans to purchase, construct, or repair dwellings by discriminating on the basis of race, color, religion, sex, national origin, handicap or familial status

Steering Illegal practice of directing prospective minority purchasers to presently integrated areas to avoid integration of nonintegrated areas

Testers Volunteers or employees of federal and state agencies as well as private civil rights groups who visit real estate offices posing as prospective home seekers to see if race influences the information or services provided

Key Points

1. The Civil Rights Act of 1968, known as the Fair Housing Act, prohibits discrimination in housing because of race, color, religion, sex, national origin, age, handicap, or familial status.
2. Discrimination is prohibited in the (a) sale or rental of housing, (b) advertising of the sale or rental of housing, (c) financing of housing, and (d) provision of real estate brokerage services. The act forbids blockbusting.
3. The Federal Fair Housing Act has certain exemptions, but New York laws that are more restrictive preempt these exemptions.
4. 4.The Civil Rights Act of 1964 prohibited discrimination in any housing program receiving federal money but did not cover privately financed housing.
5. The Civil Rights Act of 1866 prohibits discrimination based only on race. The prohibition is not limited to housing, but includes real estate transactions. The act may be enforced only by civil suit in federal court. This law has no exemptions.
6. Supreme Court decisions such as *Plessy v. Ferguson* (1896), separate but equal; *Buchanan v. Warley* (1917), disallowing block-by-block segregation; and *Brown v. Board of Education* (1954), separate but unequal shaped much of U.S. policy.
7. Enforcement of Title VIII of the 1968 Civil Rights Act was amended in 1988. Enforcement procedures include (a) administrative procedure through the Office of Equal Opportunity of HUD that attempts voluntary conciliation first and then possible referral to an administrative law judge, who can impose financial penalties of $10,000 to $50,000; (b) civil suit in federal court; and (c) action by the U.S. Attorney General, who may file a suit in federal court and impose penalties of up to $50,000 on the first offense for a "pattern of discrimination."
8. The Americans with Disabilities Act provides that individuals with disabilities cannot be denied access to public transportation or any commercial facility or public accommodation. Barriers in existing buildings must be removed if readily achievable. New buildings must be readily accessible and usable by individuals with disabilities.
9. New York is governed by Article 15 of the Executive Law, called the Human Rights Law. This law adds four protected classes not included in federal law—marital status, age, sexual orientation, and military status. It covers the lease and sale of commercial space and land as well as residential housing.
10. The human rights agency in New York is the Division of Human Rights (DHR). Complaints must be filed with the DHR within one year of an alleged discriminatory act.
11. The New York City Commission on Human Rights is the enforcement agency for antidiscrimination policy in the five boroughs that compose NYC. NYC law includes four more protected classes to those covered by New York law: citizenship or alienage, lawful occupation, partnership status, and lawful source of income.

Useful Links

National Association of REALTORS® (NAR)
http://www.realtor.org

Department of Housing and Urban Development (HUD)
http://www.hud.gov

HUD New York
http://www.hud.gov/local/index.cfm?state=ny

NYS DHR Human Rights Poster
http://www.dhr.state.ny.us/doc/poster.pdf

NYS Division of Human Rights
http://www.dhr.state.ny.us

New York City Commission on Human Rights
http://www.nyc.gov/html/cchr

Fair Housing Guide
http://www.dhr.state.ny.us/Basic_guide/basicguide.pdf

Real Estate Mathematics

Key Terms

Acre 43,560 square feet

Commission A percentage of the sales price

Front foot A linear foot of property frontage on a street or highway

Gross Income Income received without subtracting expenses

Income The amount of money one receives

Interest Calculated by multiplying the rate as a percentage times the principal balance

Net Operating Income Gross income less operating expenses

Point Fee charged by a lender equal to 1% of the loan amount

Rate A percentage

Tax Rate Determined by the amount of the tax levy and expressed either in dollars per $100 of assessed value or in mills, (one mill is one-tenth of a cent) per $1,000 of assessed value

Value The total amount of worth or cost of the unit

Key Points

1. In the real estate business, many calculations involve percentages which is a number divided by 100.
2. An increase in property value is known as appreciation; a decrease in value is known as depreciation.
3. A hectare is equal to 2.47 acres.
4. The perimeter is the entire outer boundary of a figure such as a plot of land or the measure around a figure, such as a house or building.
5. Debt service is the annual amount to be paid to retire or regularly reduce a loan or mortgage balance.
6. Many mortgages are paid through a type of installment plan each month known as amortization.
7. A balloon mortgage provides for installment payments that are not enough to pay off the principal and interest over the term of the mortgage. A balloon mortgage is also known as a partially amortized mortgage because the loan does not amortize out at the due date.
8. Prorations at closing involve the division between the seller and the buyer of annual real property taxes, rents, homeowner's association dues, and other items that may have been paid or must be paid.
9. Profit or loss is always based upon the amount of money invested in the property.
10. The capitalization rate is the percentage of the investment the owner will receive back each year from the net income from the property. The rate is based upon the dollar invested and the annual net income from the property.

Municipal Agencies

Key Terms

Architectural review boards Composed mostly of people with expertise in art, architecture, and planning, oversees building design

Building department Enforces the building code; protects the public by ensuring that code restrictions are followed

Conservation Advisory Council Advises in the development, management, and protection of the municipality's natural resources

County health department Cooperates with the NYS Department of Health; these local agencies may have laws that are more restrictive than state law

Historic Preservation/Landmark Commission Identifies and protects historic landmarks

Planning boards On all government levels, plans for the future of the region; the boards consider the available natural and supplied resources of the community

Receiver of taxes The collecting officer for each city and town who receives real property taxes and assessments during a specified collection period

Tax assessor An elected or appointed local official or officials who have the legal authority to independently estimate the value of real property in an assessing unit

Village board of trustees The governing body of villages

Key Points

1. The city charter and town or village ordinance; the county, city, town, and village handbooks; information officers; and websites are sources of information regarding the agencies within a municipality.
2. A legislative body creates an administrative government agency. These agencies are empowered by the state legislature as well as by the legislative bodies of cities, counties, towns, and villages.
3. The legislative power of a city is vested in its city council or common council. The town council or board is the governing body of towns. The village board of trustees is the governing body of villages. All members of these government bodies are elected.
4. Planning boards work with the master plan of the municipality or region.
5. The local legislative body of any city, town, or village can appoint a conservation advisory council to advise in the development, management, and protection of its natural resources. The council can conduct research regarding environment projects.
6. The New York regulatory agency that oversees wetlands is the Department of Environmental Conservation. Under New York law, local governments also can manage wetlands. The Conservation Advisory Council and/or the Wetlands Commissions performs local management.
7. The Historic Preservation/Landmark Commissions in cities, towns, villages, and counties regulate special conditions and restrictions for the protection of places and objects that have a special character, historical, or aesthetic interest.
8. Building departments enforce the building code. This department provides building permits and certificates of occupancy. Building inspectors visit construction sites to ensure that construction complies with all applicable building codes.
9. The tax assessor is a local government official who estimates the value of real property within a city, town, or village's boundaries. All properties are assessed at a uniform percentage of value. The tax assessor maintains tax maps and tax records for the municipality.
10. The city or town engineer estimates the costs of paving, sewers and sidewalks, and other public works projects. The engineer supervises streets and other public works activities.
11. County departments of health oversee drinking water safety, including standards for private and community well construction and well water safety and regulation, septic system approval, and certain wastewater treatment approval.

Property Insurance

Key Terms

Actual cash value (ACV) A type of insurance in which the insured is reimbursed for the replacement cost minus the physical depreciation of the lost or damaged property

Deductible The amount the insured must pay toward a claim before receiving any policy benefits

Liability insurance Insurance coverage to protect against claims alleging that one's negligence or inappropriate action resulted in bodily injury or property damage

Package policy A policy that includes several different types of coverage, such as property insurance and liability insurance

Property insurance Protects a home or income/business property against any physical damage or loss of assets in the case of fire, theft, or vandalism

Replacement cost A type of insurance in which the insured is covered and reimbursed for the actual cost of replacing the damaged property

Umbrella policy An excess liability policy that provides additional coverage above that offered by primary policies

Key Points

1. Property insurance protects a home, a business, or income property against any physical damage or loss of assets in the case of fire, theft, or vandalism. The typical homeowners policy has two main sections: Section I covers the property of the insured; Section II provides personal liability coverage to the insured.
2. Generally, if the insured purchases coverage on a replacement cost basis and insures the home for at least 80 percent of its replacement cost, the insurance is automatically issued on a replacement cost basis.
3. The New York Property Insurance Underwriting Association (NYPIUA) is a pool of all insurance companies writing fire insurance in New York. It offers fire and extended coverage as well as coverage for vandalism, malicious mischief, and sprinkler leakage to consumers who are unable to purchase this type of insurance from individual insurance companies.
4. The Federal Emergency Management Association (FEMA) administers the National Flood Insurance Program. Insurance coverage for losses resulting from floods is generally not provided in any homeowners or tenants policies.
5. Section 3445 of the New York Insurance Law requires that insurers provide proper disclosure to their insureds of any windstorm deductibles attached to their homeowners policies.
6. Under New York law, an insurance company may cancel a homeowners or tenants policy by issuing a cancellation notice during the first 60 days it is in effect as long as the cancellation notice states the specific reason or reasons for the cancellation.
7. Specific insurance is available for rental/income property. Commercial General Liability (CGL) insurance is a basic business liability policy that covers four forms of injury: bodily injury that results in actual physical damage or loss, property damage that results in actual physical damage or loss, personal injury, and advertising injury.
8. Real estate agents should counsel their buyers as to the importance of obtaining property insurance, lender requirements, and the escrow account for property insurance premiums

Useful Links

NYS Insurance Department
http://www.dfs.ny.gov/

NY Property Insurance Underwriting Association
http://www.nypiua.com

National Flood Insurance Program
http://www.fema.gov/business/nfip

Taxes and Assessments

Key Terms

Ad valorem Latin for according to value; in New York, the real property tax is based on the fair market value of real property

Apportionment Division of property and school tax monies so that school districts, counties, towns and cities in the different municipalities all pay their fair share of the tax levy

Appropriation Occurs when a government agency sets aside funds for a certain purpose.

Approved assessing unit One that has completed a property reevaluation and is certified by the NYS Office of Real Property Tax Services (NYSORPTS)

Assessed value The value of a property as determined by a tax assessor

Assessing units Counties, cities, towns, villages, school districts, and special districts that raise money through real property taxes

Assessment A percentage of a property's market value; this figure is used for property tax purposes and ultimately determines how the total tax is shared among property owners

Assessment roll Usually in section, block/lot order, it lists all real property in the taxing jurisdiction, with information about each parcel, including its assessed value and exempt status

Board of Assessment Review (BAR) An appointed body consisting of three to five members that hears and decides upon grievances from taxpayers

Equalization rate Represents the average percentage of market value at which a municipality's assessment is set

Exemptions Full exemptions or partial reductions in property taxes available to certain people, institutions, and organizations

Grievance A written complaint filed with the local board of assessment review protesting a property tax assessment

Homestead Properties that are completely or partially used as the owner's residence and are classified as such for tax purposes

Non-homestead All properties not classified as homesteads; includes commercial, industrial, special franchise, utility properties, and some vacant land

Residential assessment ratios (RARs) A indication of the level of assessment for residential real property in a municipality; a measurement of the overall ratio of the total assessed value of residential property in the municipality compared to the full market value of that residential property.

Special assessment A tax levied by the taxing unit to collect payment for a share of the cost of improvements made to areas nearby or adjoining the property; constitutes a specific lien against the property until paid

Special assessment districts Localities that raise money through real property taxes

Tax certiorari proceeding A New York Supreme Court review of cases requested by taxpayers who protest their assessment and are still dissatisfied with the decision of the board of assessment review

Tax exemptions Taxing authorities may grant full or partial exemptions from tax obligations to certain groups

Tax levy The amount that a municipality must raise to meet budgetary requirements by taxing real property

Tax lien An encumbrance against a property filed by the taxing jurisdiction for delinquency in paying real property taxes

Tax rate The amount of money needed by a municipality to meet budgetary requirements divided by the taxable assessed and nonexempt value of all the real property within that jurisdiction

Taxable status date The ownership and physical condition of real property are assessed according to price fixed as of the valuation date; all applications must be filed with the assessor by this date

Uniform percentage Each assessing unit sets the percentage of market value to be used as the assessment standard and must apply this percentage uniformly to all properties within its boundaries

Key Points

1. In New York, property is taxed on an *ad valorem* basis, that is, according to the market value of the property.
2. A tax bill is determined by a formula that includes two items: the property's assessment and the tax rate of the taxing jurisdiction.
3. A property's assessment is a percentage of its market value; in most areas outside of New York City and Nassau County, the assessment must be a uniform percentage of the property's market value throughout the taxing jurisdiction.
4. All property is subject to assessment; however, not all property is taxed. Property tax exemptions may be full or partial.
5. An approved assessing unit is a taxing jurisdiction that has completed a property reevaluation and is certified by the NYS Office of Real Property Tax Services.
6. The assessment roll that describes all properties and their assessed value is published each year. Taxpayers who disagree with their assessment may file a complaint called a grievance.
7. If taxpayers are still dissatisfied with the decision of the board of assessment review, they may file a complaint with the New York Supreme Court, called a tax certiorari proceeding, or be heard by specially appointed small claims hearing officers.
8. The tax rate must be sufficient to provide the amount of revenue to accomplish the budgetary requirements of the local governmental unit.
9. The equalization rate represents the average percentage of market value at which assessments in a municipality are set at a given point in time.
10. If a property owner is delinquent in paying property taxes, his taxing jurisdiction may impose a lien against the property.

Useful Links

NYS Office of Real Property Tax Services (ORPTS)
http://www.tax.ny.gov/

The NYC Tax Commission
http://ww nyc.gov/html/taxcomm/html/home/home.shtml

Nassau County Department of Assessment
http://www.nassaucountyny.gov/agencies/Assessor

Nassau County Assessment Review Commission
http://www.nassaucountyny.govagencies/ARC/index.html

Condominiums and Cooperatives

Key Terms

Alteration agreement Describes the terms under which the cooperative gives permission to a shareholder before making any changes or improvements to the unit the shareholder occupies

Board package Documents of a proposed purchaser reviewed by a cooperative board

Bylaws The shareholder's rights and obligations for a condominium

Common Elements Ownership of areas and utilities in a condominium or cooperative building shared by owners

Condominium A form of ownership of real property that consists of individual ownership of some aspects and co-ownership in other aspects of the property

Condop A building that includes condominium and cooperative ownership in the same structure

Cooperative A form of ownership in which stockholders in a corporation occupy property owned by the corporation under a lease

Covenants, conditions, and restrictions (CCRs) In a condominium, the document that sets forth all of the rights, duties, and obligations of the unit owners

Declaration A master deed containing a legal description of the condominium facility, a plat of the property, plans and specifications for the building and units, a description of the common areas, and the degree of ownership in the common areas available to each owner

Flip tax Sometimes imposed by the board of directors of a cooperative; this is a revenue-producing device for the cooperative corporation; usually paid by the seller at closing

Flipping Investors buy a property at a certain price, then immediately sell the property at a higher price.

House rules Rules in a cooperative that cover issues as garbage disposal, maintenance, noise, and conflict resolution.

Letter of intent An agreement to purchase a condominium; may or may not be binding

Maintenance Monthly payment by shareholder to the cooperative corporation

Offering plan or statement The document filed with the New York Attorney General detailing the setup and rules for a condominium or cooperative

Proprietary lease A lease for a cooperative apartment

Recognition agreement Describes the relationship between the cooperative and other entities

Share loan A type of loan in which stock is the collateral; used for cooperative purchases

Sponsor The developer of a condominium or cooperative

Key Points

1. The main difference between cooperatives and condominiums is the form of ownership. With a cooperative, a cooperative corporation usually owns the land, buildings, and property rights and all interests in the corporation.
2. The purchaser of a cooperative becomes a shareholder of the corporation and a tenant in the building. The tenant-shareholder has the right of occupancy. A cooperative purchaser does not obtain a deed; instead, he receives a proprietary lease issued by the cooperative corporation.
3. A financial statement of a condo or co-op development should include a balance sheet describing assets and liabilities, an income and expense statement, and a cash flow statement. For a cooperative, the status of the underlying mortgage is very important.
4. Cooperative ownership documents typically include the articles of incorporation, bylaws, proprietary lease or occupancy agreement, subscription agreement, and house rules.
5. The developer that constructs or converts a building into a cooperative or condominium must file a declaration and disclosure statement with the New York Attorney General's office.
6. The co-op members develop house rules for the operation of the cooperative. House rules cover such issues as garbage disposal, maintenance, and noise and conflict resolution. They are generally more detailed than items in the proprietary lease addressing behavior of the tenants and general operations.
7. Two processes can by used by a cooperative to approve a purchaser: (1) acceptance of the purchaser's package by the board of directors and (2) a private interview between the prospective purchasers and the board of directors.
8. To keep subletting from overtaking the building, most cooperatives that allow subletting limit the time frame of the sublet.
9. A condop is a building that includes condominium and cooperative ownership in the same structure. The creation of a condop allows property owners to collect a sizable portion of rent from a nonshareholder building tenant and not violate the IRS 80-20 rule.
10. To create a condominium, the owner/developer of the property (the declarant) records a condominium declaration. The declaration includes certain provisions required by statute. The sponsor records the declaration with the county clerk and the offering plan with the New York Attorney General.
11. The shareholder's rights and obligations are in the condominium's bylaws. A board of managers (or directors) oversees the finances and decision-making policy regarding the property.

12. The sponsor is the owner or developer of the condominium. He must appoint the board of directors and the managing agent and place a limitation on sponsor control of the board.
13. A letter of intent is an agreement to purchase a condominium. The letter is a written offer to reserve a specific unit that may be under construction. Certain sections of the letter may be nonbinding, such as the unit's final price.
14. A lender normally requires at least a temporary CO before it will close the loan. If a temporary certificate of occupancy (TCO) expires and is not renewed, a new buyer may find it difficult or impossible to renew homeowners' insurance policies or sell or refinance the unit.
15. Flipping may be a problem because it can drive up prices. The investor attempts to buy low and sell high. It can cause major losses for people who buy the flipped property from the investor and end up paying more than if they bought it from the developer.
16. The title company completes a title search before purchase. The search reveals any defects in the title of the unit along with any problems or liens against the condominium building or the complex.
17. Condominium contracts are similar to other fee simple interest real estate contracts. However, they may contain a right of first refusal clause for the board of managers of a condominium association.
18. Closing costs for the seller include the NYC Real Property Transfer Tax (if applicable) and NYS Real Property Transfer Tax, broker's commission, managing agent's fees, UCC-3 filing fee, and attorney's fees. The cooperative corporation may charge a flip tax and a stock transfer fee. Closing costs for the buyer include the UCC-1 filing fee, mortgage recording tax, title search and title policy, managing agent's fees, credit report fees, attorney's fees, and Mansion Tax (if applicable).

Commercial and Investment Properties/ Real Estate Investments

Key Terms

After-tax cash flow The profit from income-producing property, less income taxes, if any, attributable to the property's income

Anchor tenant A well-known commercial retail business, such as a national chain store or regional department store, placed in a shopping center to generate the most customers for all stores in the shopping center

Capitalization rate The annual return that an investor expects to receive; the primary method to estimate the present value of income producing properties

Cash flow The net proceeds after all expenses are met; may be measured before or after taxes are considered

Cash-on-cash return The ratio of annual before-tax cash flow to the total amount of cash invested, expressed as a percentage.

Common areas Includes the lobby, elevators, corridors, restrooms, and utility closets; tenants may pay a pro rata share for the common areas in addition to their own space

Debt service Mortgage principal and interest payments

Effective gross income Total potential income, less deductions for vacancy and credit losses, plus other income

Feasibility study A detailed economic analysis that considers the cost of site development, construction, financing, tax considerations, rates of return on similar investments, and the benefit to the community

Gross income Income received without subtracting expenses

Lease escalation clauses Increased costs to the tenant for different reasons at specified times during the lease term

Leasehold mortgage An instrument that pledges a leasehold estate rather than a freehold estate to secure payment of a note; leaseholds acceptable to lenders are usually long-term estates for years

Joint venture An organization formed by two or more parties for the purpose of investing in real estate or other assets

Leverage The use of borrowed funds in addition to an investor's own funds

Net operating income Gross operating income minus operating expenses and debt service (cash flow)

Operating statement A report of rental property receipts and disbursements, resulting in net income

Participation mortgage A mortgage in which two or more lenders participate in making the loan or one in which the lender participates in the profits generated by a commercial property that secures the mortgage loan

Porter's wage escalation formula Provides that the rent will increase a specific amount per square foot for a specified increase in the porter's hourly wage

Pro-forma schedule An operating statement that reflects a property's income and expenses based upon the investor's expectations about the real estate market

Rate of return Percentage of income that the investor gets back on an investment

Rentable square footage Equals the entire space including the usable square footage and the tenant's pro-rata share of the building common areas, such as the lobby, hallways, and restrooms

Sensitivity analysis A study of how a change in one factor can affect a property's income

Sole proprietorship A business owned by an individual in his/her own name or doing business as (d/b/a) a trade name

Short sale A transaction in which the sale proceeds fall short of the balance owed on the property; used when a borrower cannot pay back the mortgage and the lender decides that selling the property at a loss is better than going after the borrower for the full indebtedness

Tax shelter A method of protecting income from taxation; for example, by accelerating allowable depreciation

Time value of money The principle that the passage of time affects the value of a given sum by earning interest and by being eroded by inflation

Usable square footage The area contained within the space that the tenant occupies

Key Points

1. The primary purpose of the investor is to generate income (cash flow) without higher than expected risk. An investor must consider the time value of money in determining the return on dollars invested over a given period of time.
2. Types of investment property include unimproved land, residential building, multi-use buildings, retail centers, and offices.
3. The primary purpose of the investor is to generate income (cash flow) without taking a substantial risk.
4. Leverage is the use of borrowed funds. Leverage allows the investor to accumulate the maximum amount of real estate with the minimum amount of personal funds.
5. Before investing, an investor must consider the time value of money, that is, where his investment funds will bring the greatest return on dollars invested for a given period.
6. The rate of return, or percentage of income per dollar amount invested, that the investor receives back on an investment includes a risk factor. The greater the risk of loss, the greater the potential rate of return the investor can expect.
7. A ground lease is a long-term lease on unimproved land. It is generally for construction purposes.
8. An operating statement for a property includes the income and expenses for a property. The costs of business or investment property are tax-deductible.
9. Forms of property ownership include sole proprietorship, partnership, corporation, limited liability company, limited partnership, syndication, and joint venture.
10. A property profile includes the analysis of risk and return; special risks; timing; pricing; rate of return; portfolio development and securitization; sensitivity analysis; and special financing.
11. The result of deducting operating expenses is net operating income.
12. There are two types of income to consider: cash flows during the holding period of the investment and cash generated when the property is sold at the end of the holding period.
13. Cash-on-cash return is a value measurement for a property that considers the equity in the property measured against the cash flow. The method looks at the amount of cash required to purchase the equity interest in a property—the difference between the sales price and the mortgage loan. It also measures the cash flow.
14. A capitalization rate is the annual return that an investor expects to receive. The capitalization rate is used in the appraisal income approach. It is the primary method used to estimate the present value of income-producing properties. The capitalization formula is value × capitalization rate = annual net income.
15. The rentable square footage of most commercial space includes square footage that cannot be used or sometimes seen, but that the tenant pays rent for anyway. Rentable square footage includes the usable square footage plus the tenant's pro rata share of the building common areas, such as the lobby, hallways, and restrooms.
16. Tenant costs may include common area maintenance (CAM) costs for areas such as the lobby, elevators, corridors, restrooms, and utility closets.
17. A business client is generally committed to a longer lease term and a more costly lease. Unlike residential leases, there is no standard commercial lease agreement. Each lease conforms to the particular space and tenant.
18. Generally, there are four types of leases for commercial space: gross lease, net lease, percentage lease, and operating stop or expense stop lease.

19. Leases based on arrangement for payment are the gross lease and the net lease. Under a gross lease, the landlord pays the real property taxes, insurance, and costs for maintaining the property. Under a net lease, the tenant pays some or all of these expenses.
20. Lease clauses include use clauses; subordination, nondisturbance, and attornment clauses; estoppel certificates; sublease/assignment clauses; and electric service clauses.
21. Lease escalation clauses call for increased costs to the tenant for different reasons at specified times during the lease term. These clauses protect the property owner against increases in operating costs.
22. Lease escalation clauses include definitions for proportionate share of occupancy and base year, operating stop and tax stop clauses, real property tax clauses, direct operating costs, the Porter's Wage Escalation formula, and fixed percentage increases.
23. Properties can be purchased below market value through foreclosure, other bank owned property, government owned property, or a short sale. These types of purchases offer the real estate investor opportunities to acquire properties at substantial discounts.

Useful Links

Government owned properties for sale
http://www.homesales.gov/homesales/ContactUs.jsp

Income Tax Issues in Real Estate Transactions

Key Terms

Active income Salaries or income from a business in which the taxpayer materially participates

Adjusted basis Value of property used to determine the amount of gain or loss realized by an owner upon sale of the property; equals acquisition cost plus capital improvements minus depreciation taken

Appreciation An increase in value

Basis Usually the cost of a property

Boot Cash received in a tax-deferred exchange

Capital gain The profit realized from the sale of real estate or other investment

Capital loss Occurs when an investment property or other type of investment is sold

Cost recovery A type of income tax deduction available for real estate and personal

Deductible expenses Cost of operating a property used in business or held as an investment; these expenses are subtracted from gross income to arrive at net income

Depreciated value The basis of a depreciable asset, used to compute the taxable gain from its sale; the basis is acquisition cost, plus capital improvements, less accrued depreciation

Economic depreciation Loss of value from physical deterioration of property caused by normal use, damage caused by natural and other hazards, and failure to maintain the property adequately

Passive activity A trade or business in which the taxpayer invests but does not materially participate Passive activity income Income from funds invested in passive activities

Portfolio income Interest, annuities, dividends, royalties, and profits from the sale of portfolio assets

Recaptured depreciation When a property owner disposes of the property, a tax on the income or gain realized because of the allowed depreciation is recaptured as ordinary income up to the amount of the depreciation; recapture means to be included as taxable income.

Straight-line depreciation A type of income tax depreciation that allows investment property to be deducted in installments over a number of years

Tax basis Consists of the price paid for the property, plus expenses incurred in acquiring the property (other than those incurred in arranging financing), plus the costs of any capital improvements

Tax depreciation A deduction from a property's income when determining taxable income

Tax-deferred exchange Trading of like-kind properties held as an investment or for business use.

Key Points

1. There are six tax for federal income tax: 10, 15, 25, 28, 33, and 35 percent. Most taxpayers fall between the 15 and 28 percent tax brackets.
2. The "Age 59½ Rule" allows first-time homebuyers to use IRA distributions to fund up to $10,000 of their new home cost. They do not have to pay the 10 percent early distribution penalty. But even though the penalty is waived, the taxpayer is still required to pay taxes (as applicable) on the traditional IRA withdrawal itself.
3. Property taxes may be deducted on any type of real property including a personal residence, a second home, a time-share, vacant land, income property, and inherited property.
4. A mortgage must be a secured debt on a qualified home for a taxpayer to take out a home mortgage interest deduction. Interest paid on investment property is generally fully deductible.
5. Capital gain is the profit realized from real estate investment. Capital loss occurs when an investment sells at a loss. The long-term capital gain tax is 15 percent when the taxpayer's rate is above the 15 percent income bracket. The gain is taxed at 5 percent when the taxpayer is in the 15 percent bracket or below.
6. According to the tax code, single taxpayers may take up to a $250,000 exclusion from taxation on gain in the sale of their homes. Married taxpayers may take up to a $500,000 exclusion.
7. The adjusted basis of a property consists of the price paid for the property. It also includes expenses incurred in acquiring the property and the cost of any capital improvements (less depreciation if applicable).
8. There are three classifications of income: active income earned through salaries or in a business in which the taxpayer actively participates; portfolio income, which includes interest, annuities, dividends, and royalties; and passive activity income, that includes invested funds.
9. A passive activity involves conducting any trade or business in which the taxpayer does not actively participate. This includes rental activities and limited partnerships.
10. When a taxpayer disposes of property, a tax on the income or gain realized because of the allowed depreciation is recaptured as ordinary income up to the amount of the depreciation. Real estate sold is recaptured at a 25 percent rate.

11. To qualify as a tax-deferred exchange, like-kind property must be exchanged. The property exchanged must have been held for use in business (other than inventory) or as an investment.
12. When an exchangor receives cash or some other type of nonqualifying property in addition to like-kind property, the transaction may still partially qualify as a tax-deferred exchange. The cash in the exchange is called the boot.
13. Interest may be deducted for home acquisition and home equity financing, home improvement loans, and construction financing.
14. A buyer can deduct points charged for mortgage financing in the year paid or over the life of the mortgage depending on whether the points charged meet certain IRS tests. Prepayment penalty charges may be tax-deductible. Other closing expenses are not generally tax-deductible.
15. Tax losses from investment property are allowed to offset income only from passive activities.
16. Deductible allowances from property income to arrive at taxable income, and tax losses allowed to offset passive and active income, are income shelters for investors.
17. Tax depreciation is a deductible allowance from net income used to arrive at taxable income. It provides a tax shelter for the property owner.
18. Depreciation enables the owner of a business or an investment property to recover the cost or other basis of the asset. Land is not depreciable—only structures on the land.

Useful Links

IRS publication 530
http://www.irs.gov/pub/irs-pdf/p530.pdf

IRS publication 936
http://www.irs.gov/pub/irs-pdf/p936.pdf

New York State Division of Housing and Community Renewal
(DHCR) http://www.dhcr.state.ny.us

Mortgage Brokerage

Key Terms

Mortgage bankers Individuals and entities licensed by the NYS Department of Financial Services to make residential mortgage loans.

Mortgage brokers Individuals and entities registered by the NYS Department of Financial Services to solicit, process, place, or negotiate residential mortgage loans for others; applies to one- to four-unit properties

Mortgage Broker Dual Agency Disclosure Form A banking department form required when a person is acting as a mortgage broker and a real estate broker in the same transaction

Mortgage commitment A promise made by a lending institution to make a certain type of mortgage loan

Mortgage loan originators (MLO) Individuals who are licensed by the NYS Department of Financial Services who, for compensation or gain, takes a residential mortgage loan application or offers or negotiates terms of a residential mortgage loan

Mortgage loan servicers (MLS) Individuals and entities registered by the NYS Department of Financial Services who service residential mortgage loans by receiving any scheduled periodic payments from a borrower for a mortgage

Nonconforming loan A loan that does not meet Federal Reserve Bank criteria for funding. The reason may be that the loan amount is a higher dollar amount than the conforming loan limit

Preapplication and Fee Agreement According to the Banking Law, a mortgage broker or mortgage banker must provide certain disclosures to each applicant for a mortgage loan, at or before the time of application. These disclosures include the fees payable at the time of application, the conditions for refunding the fee, and if the mortgage broker is using three or fewer lenders; this form complies with the Banking Law

Preapproval A step above pre-qualification; involves verifying a purchaser's credit, down payment, and employment history

Prequalification Not a commitment by the lender; after the loan officer determines that a purchaser prequalifies, he issues a pre-qualification letter that is used to make an offer on a property and show the seller that the purchaser qualifies to buy the property

Rate lock A mortgage loan cannot be closed without locking in an interest rate

Service release premium A form of compensation that a lender may pay to a broker for delivering a loan; each loan comes with a servicing right to collect the mortgage payments

Underwriting The process in which the lender evaluates all of the borrower's financial data and determines if the borrower will obtain the loan

Yield spread premium (also known as a lender rebate) is the rate at which a mortgage broker is compensated for the difference between the interest rate on a par loan and the interest rate on an above par loan that a mortgage broker can deliver to the lender; this is expressed in the number of points paid to a mortgage broker

Key Points

1. In New York, a mortgage broker must register with the NYS Department of Financial Services (NYSDFS).
2. A licensed real estate broker may use his broker license as experience for the mortgage broker registration. The real estate broker license must be current. Licensed salespersons must have actively participated in the residential mortgage business for two years.
3. A mortgage loan servicer is a sole proprietorship or company registered by the NYSDFS to service loans for residential property in New York.
4. A mortgage loan originator is an individual licensed by the NYSDFS who for compensation, takes a residential mortgage loan application or offers or negotiates terms of a residential mortgage loan. MLOs are employed by mortgage brokers.
5. To obtain a mortgage loan originator license, the applicant must complete 20 hours of prescribed education and pass an exam.

6. According to New York banking regulations, when a mortgage broker representing the buyer/borrower also is the real estate broker representing the seller in the same residential real estate transaction, that information must be disclosed at the first substantive contact between the mortgage broker and the purchaser/borrower.
7. A mortgage broker acting as a real estate broker in the same transaction must use the disclosure form for real estate transactions and the disclosure form for mortgage broker transactions for covered properties.
8. A mortgage banker is an individual or a company licensed by the NYSDFS to engage in the business of making residential mortgage loans. Mortgage bankers, also called mortgage companies, make mortgage loans for housing construction and the purchase of existing housing.
9. The requirements for a mortgage banker license include having a net worth of at least $250,000 and having an existing line of credit of at least $1 million provided by a banking institution, an insurance company, or a similar credit facility approved by the superintendent of banking.
10. The role of the mortgage broker is to find appropriate financing at the most favorable interest rate and terms for a borrower.
11. A mortgage broker may arrange for a prequalification or preapproval letter. He suggests the best financing options, coordinates the appraisal, and helps obtain the mortgage commitment.
12. Mortgage brokers analyze and find mortgage products that may be applicable to a certain borrower. These products include amortized mortgages, adjustable rate mortgages, construction loans, and conforming and nonconforming loans.
13. Some mortgage brokers process loans and close loans in their own name. However, at or about the time of settlement, they transfer these loans to lenders that simultaneously advance funds for the loans. This transaction is known in the lending industry as table funding.
14. Mortgage brokers assist with other closing details such as assuring the loan is available, the certificate of occupancy is issued, and bank conditions are satisfied.
15. A mortgage broker chooses from a variety of available lenders to secure a deal for the borrower. For example, when a purchaser obtains a mortgage loan, it may be possible to lock in a certain interest rate. This lock-in can be achieved with traditional lenders as well.
16. The mortgage broker's commission is paid by the borrower or more likely by the lender. The fee increases the loan balance and is paid through a lender's rebate (yield spread premium or service release premium). The mortgage broker's fee must be disclosed to the borrower.

Useful Links

NYS Department of Financial Services
http://www.dfs.ny.gov

The Nationwide Mortgage Licensing System
http://mortgage.nationwide/licensingsystem.org

Mortgage Loan Originator Application Instructions
http://www.dfs.ny.gov/banking/iambmloins.htm

NYSDFS requirements for all licenses and registrations, NMLS checklist
http://mortgage.nationwidelicensingsystem.org/slr/Pages/DynamicLicenses.aspx?StateID=NY

Information on the mortgage banker application
http://www.banking.state.ny.us/iambla.htm

National Association of Mortgage Brokers
http://www.nyamb.org

Property Management

Key Terms

Anchor store A well-known commercial retail business, such as a national chain store or regional department store, placed in a shopping center to generate the most customers for all stores in the shopping center

Actual eviction The removal of a tenant by the landlord because the tenant breached a condition of a lease or other rental contract

Capital expense Capital expenses are those required to improve or maintain a building

Capital reserve budget A projected budget over the economic life of the improvements of the property set aside to cover variable expenses such as repairs, decorating, remodeling, and capital improvements

Constructive eviction Results from some action or inaction by the landlord that renders the premises unsuitable for the use agreed to in a lease or other rental contract

Corrective maintenance Work performed to fix a nonfunctioning item that the tenant has reported; example, repair of a leaky faucet

Eviction A landlord's action that interferes with the tenant's use or possession of the property; eviction may be actual or constructive

Fixed expenses Expenditures such as property taxes, license fees, and property insurance; subtracted from effective gross income to determine net operating income

Insurable interest The legitimate financial interest an insured has in a property that provides eligibility for insurance coverage of any type

Management agreement A contract that creates an agency relationship in which the owner is the principal and the property manager is the agent for the purposes specified in the agreement

Management proposal A document that sets forth the duties of the manager if employed by the owner

Operating budget An annual budget that includes only the items of income and expense expected for week-to-week operation

Planned Unit Development (PUD) A form of cluster zoning providing for both residential and commercial land uses within a zoned area

Preventative maintenance Requires a periodic check of mechanical equipment on the premises to minimize wear and tear; for example, changing air filters on air conditioners and furnaces

Property management report A periodic (usually monthly) accounting of all funds received and disbursed; contains detailed information of all receipts and expenditures for the period covered (plus the year-to-date) and relates each item to the operating budget for the period

Property management The leasing, marketing, managing, maintenance, and accounting functions necessary to operate a commercial property

Property manager A person who manages properties as an agent of the owner

Public liability insurance Covers the risks an owner assumes when the public enters his premises

Resident manager A person living on the premises who is a paid employee of the owner

Risk management Embodies the concern for controlling and limiting risk in property ownership

Stabilized budget A forecast of income and expenses reasonably projected over a short term, typically five years

Variable expense An expense that is not specifically predictable and is subject to the needs of a property at any given time

Key Points

1. The property manager strives to produce the greatest net return possible for the owner.
2. When an individual is employed by one owner of real property on a salaried basis to perform any of the functions of a real estate salesperson or broker defined in the New York Real Property Law, he does not require a real estate license.
3. If an individual or a company works for more than one owner, the individual or company should have a real estate license. If the individual or company has a broker license, the people working for the company would have salesperson licenses.
4. A building manager may work for a property management firm or have his own company.
5. A resident manager lives on the premises and is a salaried employee of the owner. A real estate broker, a management firm, or an owner of a building may employ the resident manager.
6. Real estate asset managers act as the property owner's advisor for the property. They plan and direct the purchase, development, and sale of real estate on behalf of the business and investors. They focus on long-term financial planning rather than on day-to-day operations of the property.
7. The property manager acts as the owner's agent and fiduciary in managing renting, leasing, and perhaps selling the property.
8. When a property manager enters into a management agreement, a general agency is created. The manager owes a fiduciary (undivided loyalty) to the owner-principal.
9. Risk management describes the concern for controlling and limiting risk in property ownership. A manager's written specifications to competing agents ensure comparable quotes.
10. Property managers formulate the management plan; handle rentals, tenant relations, and employees; oversee the budget; pay bills; and supervise maintenance.
11. The property manager must be skilled in a number of areas, including accounting, budgeting, construction and building systems, and owner-tenant relations. Real estate-related knowledge is essential.
12. Properties that may require management are condominiums, cooperatives, apartments, single-family rental houses, mobile home parks, office buildings, shopping malls, industrial property, and farms.
13. The overall goals of the property manager are to (a) produce the best possible net operating income from the property and (b) increase the value of the principal's investment.
14. The property manager must continuously evaluate rents, budgets, and markets to ensure the best future return on the investment.

15. An operating budget, capital reserve budget, and stabilized budget should be established before rental of a project is organized and structured. The budgets are subject to adjustments, mostly in the first months of a project.
16. The operating statement is a method that property owners use to project net operating income for a property. Net operating income (NOI) is the gross income minus the operating expenses.
17. Public relations serves two roles in the property management office. A management company uses public relations to market itself, and to market client properties.
18. Many individuals from diverse backgrounds are attracted to the property management profession. Formal education and training are available through various entities, and different professional designations are awarded to individuals demonstrating competence through education and field activity.

Useful Links

The Institute of Real Estate Management
http://www.irem.org

New York City Chapter of IREM
http://www.iremnyc.org

Rochester-Western New York Chapter of IREM
http://www.irem58.org

The BOMI Institute
http://www.bomi.org

General Business Law (Broker course only)

Key Terms

Administrative law Laws that address administrative directives in the form of rules, regulations, and orders to carry out regulatory powers

Arbitration A form of resolving a dispute that includes two or more opposing parties and a neutral third party; the neutral third party makes a judgment after hearing both sides

Automatic stay Bankruptcy court order that suspends certain actions of creditors against the debtor or the debtor's property

Case law Legal precedent derived through court decisions

Certificate of deposit Note containing an acknowledgement by a bank that a sum of money has been received; the bank must repay the money together with interest at an agreed upon rate when the CD expires

Chapter 7 Bankruptcy Liquidation form of bankruptcy in which the debtor's nonexempt property is sold for cash

Chapter 11 Bankruptcy Reorganization form of bankruptcy that provides for a method for reorganizing the debtor's financial affairs under the supervision of the bankruptcy court

Chapter 13 Bankruptcy A consumer debt adjustment form of bankruptcy which permits the court to supervise the debtor's plans for the payment of unpaid debts by installments
Check A type of draft and three-party negotiable instrument containing an order to pay

Civil Law Laws which address the private rights of citizens to sue and seek remedies through the courts for a wrongful action against them

Commercial law Laws that are applicable to the rights and relations of persons engaged in commerce or trade carried on for profit

Constitutional law Laws which address the role of the Supreme Court and its authority as it relates to the President, Congress, and the states; also deals with the powers of Congress and the executive branch

Corporation A taxable legal entity recognized by law, with tax rates separate from individual income tax rates

Corporation law Laws that address federal and state formation and operation of corporations

Criminal law Laws that declare what conduct is criminal and prescribes the punishment to be imposed for such conduct

Draft A three-party negotiable instrument containing an order to pay

Drawee A person ordered in a draft to make payment

Drawer A person who signs a draft and is identified as the one ordering payment

Due process Mandate that anyone involved in a legal matter is entitled to a legal proceeding according to established rules and regulations

Equitable distribution Theory which governs the division of marital property in New York

General partnership The partners are personally liable for partnership debts exceeding partnership assets

Holder in due course Holder of a negotiable instrument who takes an instrument for value, in good faith, and without notice that it is defective or overdue

Endorsee The person who is the payee on an endorser

Endorsement A signature other than a maker, drawee, or an acceptor, that is placed on an instrument to negotiate (or transfer) it to another

Endorser The person who transfers or endorses a negotiable instrument to another

Limited partnership An organization consisting of one or more general partners and several partners with lesser roles

Litigation A lawsuit

Marital property Property acquired during the marriage and distributed equitably taking into account various factors

Mediation The use of a neutral third party to discuss and attempt to resolve a dispute

Negotiable instrument An unconditional promise or order to pay a fixed amount with or without interest

Notice of pendency A statement on the public record warning all persons that a title to real property is the subject of a lawsuit and any lien resulting from the suit will attach to the title held by a purchaser from the defendant

Partnership/partnership law Laws that address the form of business organization composed of two or more individuals

Payee A recipient of money

Personal property law Laws that relate to ownership other than real property

Private placement exemption Allows issuers of securities to raise capital from an unlimited number of accredited investors without having to register with the Securities Exchange Commission

Procedural law Laws that address the rules as to how a lawsuit proceeds through the court system and also deals with the functions of administrative agencies

Real property law Laws that address the acquisition, transfer, and possession of an interest in real estate, and the rights attached to it

Registration statement A filing statement required by the Securities Exchange Commission containing pertinent information about the securities offering

Secured creditor One who has filed a financing statement or who possesses a written security agreement as security for extending credit to a debtor

Statutory law A body of law which addresses everyday behavior

Tort Wrongful act that is committed either intentionally or unintentionally

Trustee One who holds title to property for the benefit of another, called a "beneficiary"

Trustor One who conveys title to a trustee

Trusts and wills Laws which address the succession to the ownership of an estate by inheritance or any act of law

Uniform Commercial Code A state statute enacted by New York and, in substantially the same form, by most other states, to simplify, clarify, and modernize the laws governing commercial transactions

Key Points

1. The U.S. Constitution is the supreme law of our country. Federal, state, or local laws that conflict with the Constitution are unenforceable.
2. Negotiable instruments include checks and drafts (three-party instruments) as well as promissory notes and certificates of deposit (two-party instruments).
3. Negotiable instruments must comply with the following: be in writing; be signed; contain an order or promise to pay a fixed sum of money; and be payable on demand or by a definite date. If no date is specified, it is payable on demand.
4. In a general partnership, the partners are personally liable for partnership debts exceeding partnership assets. Partners are jointly (together) and severally (separately) liable for these debts. A limited partnership consists of one or more general partners who are jointly and severally liable, and one or more silent, or limited, partners who contribute money or other assets of value to the extent of their ownership interest.
5. Corporations have the power to receive, hold, and convey title to real property. Shareholders are owners of the corporation to the extent of their shareholdings.
6. A subchapter S corporation is a type of corporate organization that is permitted to function as a corporation but is taxed as a partnership
7. A C corporation must pay corporate income tax to the IRS and the shareholders are also taxed on their dividends that are profits of the corporation. Therefore, a double tax is paid, both at the corporate level and at the shareholder level.
8. The Securities Act of 1933 regulates securities offered by corporations, general or limited partnerships, unincorporated associations, or individuals.
9. Organizations offering securities must register with the Securities Exchange Commission (SEC). Registration includes a registration statement and prospectus.
10. Securities that do not involve a public offering are exempt from the SEC registration requirement. This exemption is known as the private placement exemption.
11. No more than 35 nonaccredited investors may purchase shares of stock in a private offering. Advertising to the public is not permitted.
12. In New York, companies offering securities to the public must register with the Department of Law, including an offering of plans to sell condominiums or cooperatives.
13. Real estate investment trusts (REITs) allow small investors to pool their money to participate in larger real estate transactions. REITs make financing available for large real estate developments.
14. The U.S. Supreme Court is the nation's highest court. It is composed of nine justices appointed by the president with the approval of the Senate.
15. The federal court system includes federal trial courts. There is at least one federal district court in each state.
16. Special federal courts hear only certain types of lawsuits. They include the U.S. Tax Court; U.S. Claims Court; U.S. Court of International Trade; and the U.S. Bankruptcy Court.
17. The U.S. Courts of Appeals are the federal court system's intermediate appellate courts. There are 13 circuits in the federal court system. Circuits refer to the areas where the court serves.
18. The unified court system in New York is composed of city, town, and village courts; county courts include county court, family court, and surrogate's court.
19. The New York Supreme Court hears civil cases and the New York supreme court appellate division reviews cases from the supreme court and county courts as well as administrative boards such as the Workers' Compensation Board. The court of appeals is the highest court in the state.
20. New York City's court system is divided into two courts: a civil court that decides matters up $25,000, including small claims and housing matters; and a criminal court that rules on misdemeanors and traffic violations.
21. Laws can be categorized into substantive laws dealing with everyday behavior and procedural laws dealing with rules and regulations.

22. Bodies of law include, but are not limited to, agency law, real property law, administrative law, commercial law, contract law, corporation law, trusts and wills law, civil law, criminal law, personal property law, partnership law, torts, and civil procedure.
23. Litigation (lawsuit), mediation, and arbitration are methods to resolve disputes.
24. The theory of equitable distribution is applied by the New York courts as to the division of marital property.
25. Bankruptcies must adhere to the federal bankruptcy code and New York bankruptcy laws, and are filed in the federal district court. Bankruptcy options include Chapter 7, Chapter 11, and Chapter 13 of the bankruptcy code.
26. If a person receives money or property from another, the donor may be subject to a federal gift tax. Money and property owned upon death may be subject to an estate tax.
27. In December 2010, Congress passed the Tax Relief, Unemployment Insurance Reauthorization and Job Creation Act of 2010 (HR 4853). This extends the existing tax rate structure that was set to expire in 2010 for two more years, until 2012. As of January 1, 2011, both the federal gift tax exemption and federal estate tax exemption amounts are $5 million.
28. A decedent's estate must file a NYS estate tax return if the total of the federal gross estate plus the federal adjusted taxable gifts and specific exemptions exceed $1 million. The New York estate tax is limited to the maximum amount allowed on the federal estate tax return as a credit for state death taxes. There is no New York gift tax.
29. The Statute of Limitations imposes time limits within which litigation may be commenced. In New York, the time limit by statute to bring legal action against a party based on contract is six years.
30. The Statute of Frauds states that contracts involving the creation of an interest in real property or the conveyance of an interest in real property must be written to be enforceable.
31. A mechanic's lien for a single-family dwelling must be filed with the clerk of the county where the property is situated within four months from the date of completion of the contract. For other types of property, the liens must be filed in the public records within eight months after the completion date of the contract.

Quick View Tables

The following quick view tables contain important study information from each of the subjects in the salesperson 75-hour course and the broker 45-hour course.

License Law and Regulations/ The Broker's Office-Operation, Management, and Supervision

Table 1. A Summary of License Requirements

Requirement	Salesperson	Broker/ Associate Broker
Age	18	20
Citizenship/permanent residency	Yes, other choices	Yes
Qualifying course	75 hours	120 hours total
Experience	None	2 years as salesperson or 3 years' equivalent
Fee/term of license	$50/2 years	$150/2 years
Continuing Ed	22.5/every 2 years	22.5/every 2 years
Licensing agency	Dept of State	Dept of State
License Law	Article 12-A of the Real Property Law	Article 12-A of the Real Property Law

Table 1.B Broker's Responsibility

Form/Online Application	Kept by	Displayed	DOS fee
Broker license	Broker	Yes	$150
Change of address form	N/A	No	$10
New branch office	N/A	No	$150
Salesperson's license	Broker	No	$50
Termination or new association	N/A	No	$10

Law of Agency/ Real Estate Agency Disclosure

Table 2.A Types of Agents

Type of Agent	Representation	Definition	Limitations
1. Single agent	Buyer or seller	The agent works for the buyer or seller.	The agent never represents both. Firms that represent solely the buyer or seller may reject subagency and dual agency. The broker should counsel, but not advise the principal as to the limitations of this relationship. If a situation arises to compromise the relationship, the broker could suggest that another broker from a referral firm be utilized.
2. Seller agent	Seller	A listing agent who acts alone or cooperates with other agents as a sub-agent or broker's agent.	The agent works in the best interests of the seller but must deal fairly and honestly with buyers.
3. Subagent	Seller or buyer	An agent of the principal under the agency relationship of the primary broker.	The agent must be hired with the principal's informed consent. The principal may be vicariously liable for the acts of the subagent.
4. Buyer agent	Buyer	The agent represents the buyer as principal and enters into a listing agreement with the buyer. Locates a property and negotiates for the buyer.	The agent works in the best interests of the buyer but must deal fairly and honestly with sellers.
5. Dual agent	Buyer and seller	Represents both buyer and seller in the same transaction; undisclosed dual agency is a breach of fiduciary duty and violation of license law.	This arrangement is allowable only with disclosure and written informed consent. The agent cannot give undivided loyalty to either party.

6. Brokers agent	Broker (who may represent either buyer or seller)	A broker's agent cooperates with or is engaged by a listing agent, buyer's agent, or tenant's agent. The seller, buyer, landlord, or tenant does not have vicarious liability for the acts of the broker's agent.	The broker's agent does not have a direct relationship with the seller, buyer, landlord, or tenant.
7. Cooperating Agent	Buyers or sellers	Representation includes seller agents, subagents, buyer agents, and broker's agents. These agents work to assist the listing broker in the sale of the property. Cooperating agents may or may not work through MLS.	The principal can designate those agents that work as broker's agents, subagents, or buyer agents. The principal may choose to reject subagency arrangements.

Table 2.B Express and Implied agency

Type of Agency	How Communicated	Form
Express	In writing/orally	Listing agreement/conversation
Implied	Action of parties	Ratification/estoppel*

***Agency by estoppel** exists when a principal does not stop an individual from representing his interests, therefore creating an agency relationship between the two.

Agency by ratification confirms an earlier implied agency agreement such as when a principal signs a contract of sale.

Independent Contractor/Antitrust

Table 2.C Requirements for Salesperson Independent Contractor Status

Requirement	Parties involved
NYS salesperson or broker license	Regulated by NYS Department of State
Independent contractor agreement	Between salesperson and broker
Termination of relationship	Agreement between salesperson and broker at any time

Table 2.D Antitrust Violations

Violation	When it occurs	Laws it violates
Price fixing	Competitors in the same industry conspire to charge the same or similar price for goods and services	Sherman and Clayton Antitrust Acts; NYS Antitrust Laws
Group boycott	A person or group is persuaded to not do business with another person or group	Sherman and Clayton Antitrust Acts; NYS Antitrust Laws
Market Allocation Agreement	Agreement between competitors who divide or assign a certain territory for sales	Sherman and Clayton Antitrust Acts; NYS Antitrust Laws
Tie-in Arrangements	Agreement between a buyer and seller that as a condition of sale, the buyer will do business with another	Sherman and Clayton Antitrust Acts; NYS Antitrust Laws

Legal Issues

Estates and Interests

Table 3.A Types of ownership

Type	Owners	Right of Survivorship
In severalty	One owner	No
Tenancy in common	Two or more	No
Joint tenancy	Two or more	Yes

Liens and Easements

Table 3.B Types of Liens

Type	Specific/General	Voluntary/Involuntary
Mortgage	Specific	Voluntary
Real property tax	Specific	Involuntary
Mechanic's	Specific	Involuntary
Judgment	General	Involuntary
Income tax	General	Involuntary

Table 3.C Types of Easements

Type of easement	Purpose	Owner
Easement in gross	Utilities	Government/public company
Easement appurtenant	Ingress/egress	Private parties
Negative easement appurtenant	View easements	Private parties

Deeds/Conveyances

Table 3.D Forms of Deeds

Type	Description
Full covenant and warranty	Fullest guarantee of title
Quitclaim	No warranties of title
Bargain and sale with covenants	Contains warranties of title
Judicial deed	Results from a court order

Table 3.E A Valid Deed or Conveyance

Requirement	Clarification
In Writing	Required by the Statute of Frauds
Competent grantor	Grantee need not be competent but must be living
Legal description	Must have formal legal description
Consideration	Something of value; minimum nominal consideration ($1.00)
Words of conveyance	Demonstrates grantor's intent to convey title
Acknowledgement	Grantor's signature before a notary to allow recording
Delivery and Acceptance	Grantor must deliver the deed; and grantee must accept

Title Closing and Costs

Table 3.F Closing Preparations

Required for Closing	Definition
Closing statement	Prepared by attorneys for buyer, seller, and lender
Licensee assistance	Inspection of property with purchaser before closing
Marketable title	Includes title search, check for chain of title, abstract of title
Payment of broker commission	Paid at closing; may include all or part of deposit
Perc, soil, water flow tests	New construction and other property that have wastewater treatment or well
Place of closing	Lender, attorney office, title company, county clerk
Structural inspection	Performed by NYS licensed home inspector, other professionals
Title Insurance	Insures the policy owner against financial loss if title is not good

Table 3.G Closing Costs

Seller Closing Costs	Purchaser Closing Costs
Real property transfer tax	Appraisal and credit report fees
Broker commission	Mortgage recording tax
Discharging liens	Lender fees
Discount points	Mortgage and homeowner's insurance
Survey (may be buyer)	Pest inspection

Contract of Sale and Leases

Leases

Table 4.A Lease Agreements

Term	Definition
Assignment	Full transfer of lease by lessee to another who pays owner
Sublease	Sublessee pays leaseholder who pays owner
Actual eviction	Illegal forcible eviction of tenant
Constructive eviction	Tenant may withhold rent if necessary services not provided (requires court order)
Eviction	Legal proceeding to evict a tenant

Table 4.B Types of Leasehold Estates

Type of Estate	Definition	Inheritable
Tenancy for years	Exists for a fixed time period	Yes
Periodic estate	Automatically renews itself for another period unless notice is given	Yes
Estate at Will	Lease terminates at any time	No
Estate at Sufferance	Tenant who refuses to leave after right to possession ends	No

Contracts

Table 4.C Types of contracts

Express	Oral or written agreement
Implied	Inferred from behavior of the parties
Unilateral	One party is obligated under the contract
Bilateral	Two parties are obligated under the contract
Executory	Not fully performed contract
Executed	Fully performed contract
Valid	Binding and enforceable
Void	No legal force or effect
Voidable	May or may not be enforceable

Contract Preparation

Table 4.D Data Required for Contract Preparation

Data	Supplied By
Certificate of Occupancy	Building Department
Personal Data	Buyer , Seller, Real Estate Agent
Prior Deed	Seller
Prior Title Insurance Policy	Seller, Lender
Survey	Seller or Buyer (new survey may be required)
Tax , water, fuel bills	Seller through his agent

Real Estate Finance/Real Estate Finance II

Table 5.A Mortgage Summary

Mortgage Type	Definition	Participants
Primary mortgage market	Mortgages obtained from lender	Any bank or other lending institution
Secondary mortgage market	Mortgage purchased from lender by secondary market agencies	Fannie Mae, Ginnie Mae, Freddie Mac
Conventional loans	Loans not insured by a government agency	Any bank or other lending institution
Government loans	Loans insured by a government agency	Lenders that process FHA, VA, RHS, SONYMA loans
Conforming loans	Loan application that conforms to secondary market guidelines	Fannie Mae, Ginnie Mae, Freddie Mac
Seller financing	Seller takes a mortgage for all or part of the purchase price	Sellers that participate in purchase money, wraparound mortgages, installment land contracts, or sale leaseback

Table 5.B Types of seller financing

Type of financing	Title transfer	Payment arrangement
Installment land contract	Remains with seller until full payment is made	Down payment may be required; monthly installment payments
Purchase money mortgage	Conveyed to buyer	Title used as security for loan; monthly amortized loan
Wraparound	Conveyed to buyer	Buyer takes title subject to existing first mortgage; monthly amortized loan payment to seller
Sale leaseback	Buyer takes title; leases property back to seller	Seller makes lease payments to buyer

Land Use Regulations/Development

Table 6.A Public Control of Land

Control	Definition	Method
Eminent domain	Government right to take property for public good	Condemnation-act of taking
Taxation	Levy against property value	Lien against property
Police Power	Right of government to act for public welfare	All public laws, regulations, and agencies
Escheat	Right of government to seize property if there are no heirs	Government follows protocol to locate heirs

Table 6.B Types of Zoning

Type of Zoning	Definition	Legal?
Cluster	Cluster development that allows for open space	Yes
Exclusive use	Property to be used only as designated in zone	Yes
Cumulative use	May permit higher priority uses that are not designated for that zone	Yes
Nonconforming use	When a preexisting use is different from that specified by the zoning code	Yes
Spot	A property is rezoned to permit a different use than the zoning requirements	No
Transfer of development rights	A transfer of zoning rights from one property to another property	Yes

Construction and Environmental Issues

Construction

Table 7.A Main Building Systems Defined

System	Purpose
Electrical system	Begins outside with service entrance cables that connect to the main panel board. Branch circuit wires bring electrical power to receptacles.
Heating system	Consist of either hot water, steam, forced warm air, or electric furnaces. Fueled by oil, gas, solar, or electricity.
HVAC system	Heating, ventilating, and cooling system
Insulation System	Insulation is applied to the warm (inside) of exterior walls such as roofs, ceilings, floors, and foundation walls.
Plumbing system	Actually two piping systems; one delivers clean water into the structure; the other processes waste-water
Private wastewater system	Also called a septic system, it processes and treats wastewater on site.
Private water supply system	Consists of well or wells pumping water from the ground to a pressurized holding tank

Environmental Issues

Table 7.B The Residential Leadbased Paint Hazard Reduction Act

Main Point	Explanation
Property types	Sale or lease of residential properties built before 1978
Who must comply	Sellers and seller agents
Forms needed	Lead hazard pamphlet, reports of leadbased paint, contingency for 10-day lead paint assessment, disclosure form
Penalty for non compliance	Payment of up to 3 times the amount of damage incurred by lessor or purchaser; up to $10,000 fine

Valuation Process and Pricing Properties

Table 8 Comparing Market Value, Price, and Cost

Type of Value	Definition
Market value	The price a property will bring in a competitive market with neither party under duress
Price	The amount of money a purchaser and seller agrees upon
Cost	The dollar expenditure for labor, materials, other items

Human Rights and Fair Housing

Table 9 Human Rights Law Violations

Violation	Definition	Possible Violator
Blockbusting	Behavior that causes panic selling by announcing that people of certain protected classes are moving to the neighborhood; an attempt to gain listings	Salespersons, Brokers
Steering	Behavior that encourages prospects either toward or away from certain communities based on membership in certain protected classes	Salespersons, Brokers
Redlining	Certain neighborhoods are targeted as ones that are not eligible for mortgages or other home loans based on the community's membership in certain protected classes	Lenders

Real Estate Mathematics

Table 10 Table of Important Measures and Formulas

Measure	Formula
Acre	43,560 sq. ft.
Area of rectangle	Width x depth
Area of a triangle	1/2 base × height
Interest	Loan balance × interest rate = annual interest
Commission	Sales price paid x percentage of commission = commission

Municipal Agencies

Table 11 List of Municipal Agencies

Agency	Level of Government
Architectural Review Board	City, Town, Village
Building Department	City, Town, Village
City/Town Council	City/Town
Conservational Advisory Council/	County, City, Town,
Wetlands Commission	Village
Engineer	City, Town, Village
Health Department	City, County
Planning Board	Town, City, Village, County
Tax Assessor	City, Town, Village
Village Board of Trustees	Village
Zoning Board of Appeals	City, Town, Village

Property Insurance

Table 12 Types of Insurance

Type of Insurance Policy	Purpose
Commercial	Liability and property insurance and possible business suspension insurance
Contents	Issued on an actual cash basis, must pay extra for replacement cost
Flood	Issued to property owners in coastal and other flood prone areas
Homeowners	Varying levels of coverage insuring the home and contents
Tenants	Generally applies to improvements within the unit, not the building
Umbrella	Excess liability policy for additional coverage above primary policy

Taxes and Assessments

Table 13.A When Reassessment May Occur

Reassessment	Explanation
Community wide reassessment	Periodically to restore fairness within the community
Illegal/ legal assessment	Taxpayer may protest unequal or unlawful assessment
Obtaining a building permit	Improvement made to property, finished basement, pool, garage
Reassessment upon sale	Property may not be reassessed immediately upon purchase but at a later date for fairness
Undeclared improvements discovered	Assessor cross-checks building permits

*Table 13.B Grounds for Protesting Residential Property Assessments**

Grounds	Definition
Unequal assessment	Owner believes that property is assessed at higher percentage of value than others
Excessive Assessment	Owner believes that assessed value of property is greater than full value of property
Unlawful Assessment	Property is fully exempt from property taxation
Misclassification of homestead and nonhomestead classes	Property designated in the wrong class or the allocation of the total assessed value between the homestead and nonhomestead is incorrect

*Protests are by the property owner or a representative such as an attorney.

Condominiums and Cooperatives

Table 14 Ownership Differences and Similarities between a Condominium and a Cooperative

Cooperatives	Condominiums
Leasehold ownership	Fee simple ownership
Board package and interview	Purchaser documents and interview but may not be as strict as coop
By-laws and house rules	Covenants, conditions, and restrictions, and bylaws
Common areas owned by cooperative cooperation	Common area owned in common by owners of individual units
Monthly maintenance fee to cooperative for underlying mortgage, other expenses	Common charges for upkeep, insurance, and salaries
Offering plan must be approved by attorney general	Offering plan must be approved by attorney general
Possible flip tax at closing	No flip tax
Proprietary lease and shares of stock in cooperative corporation	Deed

Commercial and Investment Real Estate/Real Estate Investments

Table 15.A Commercial Lease Clauses

Lease Clause	Purpose
Building amenities	Moving allowances, parking, other incentives
Escalation clauses	Various types of clauses indicating terms of lease payment increases
Estoppel certificate	Tenant's statement pertaining to the lease term, rent, security, and other issues
Lease Duration	Short-term leases generally 3-5 years; long term, 5 or more years
On-site management	Degree of maintenance coverage
Subordination, nondisturbance, and attornment agreement	Legal agreements pertaining to the lease
Tenant mix	Variety of businesses in the building
Type of lease	Triple net, net, gross, percentage
Use clause	Limitations as to how space can be used

Table 15.B Types of value

Type of Value	Definition
Investment	Amount of return produced
Value in Use	Based on usefulness to investor
Assessed value	Value to which a tax rate is applied
Mortgage loan value	Amount a lender believes a property will bring in a foreclosure sale

Income Tax Issues in Real Estate Transactions

Table 16 Like-Kind (Tax Deferred) Exchange

Issues for a like-kind exchange	Explanation
Any cash (boot) received in the transaction	Transaction may still partially qualify as a tax deferred exchange
Closing of new property	Must close within 180 days from the date exchangor sold the original property
Must be business or investment property	Personal residences, stocks, cars, not allowed
Purchase of replacement property	Investor must contract for replacement property within 45 days
Qualified Intermediary (QI)	The QI accepts funds and handles contracts

Mortgage Brokerage

Table 17 The Differences and Similarities between a Mortgage Broker and a Mortgage Banker

Mortgage Broker	Mortgage Banker
Cannot act as a mortgage banker	Can act as a mortgage broker
Does not collect payments	May collect payments
Finds financing	Provides financing
Receives a fee for finding financing (through borrower, mortgage banker)	Receives payment (points, interest) for providing financing (from borrower)
Registered by NYS Department of Financial Services	Licensed by NYS Department of Financial Services

Property Management

Table 18.A Property Manager's Obligations to the Owner

Obligations	Explanation
Budget	Operating budget, capital reserve budget, variable expenses, stabilized budget
Future of the project	Analyze business trends
Maintenance	Preventative maintenance, corrective maintenance, construction
Rents space, collects rent, pays expenses	Basic functions
Reporting	A periodic accounting of all funds received and disbursed
Tenant relations	Tenant problems, evictions, subletting

General Business Law

Table 19 Substantive and Procedural Law

Substantive Law-Every day behavior	Procedural Law-How a lawsuit proceeds through the courts	Definition
Agency law		Relationship of parties to an agreement
Real property law		Acquisition, transfer, and possession of real property
	Administrative law	Directives, rules, regulations
Commercial law		Commerce or trade for profit
	Constitutional law	Role of Supreme Court
Contract law		Promises made by different parties
Corporation law		Formation and operation of corporations
Trusts and wills		Ownership of an estate
Civil law		Citizens seeking remedy for wrongful acts
Criminal law		Definition of crime and subsequent punishment
Personal property law		Ownership rights other than real property
Partnership law		Form of business for two or more
Torts		Civil lawsuits due to wrongful acts
	Civil Procedure	Steps to be followed in a lawsuit

Table 20 Remembering the "ors" and "ees" and what they mean

There are many "ors" and "ees" in real estate law. If the word ends in *or*, think of this party as the *giver*, the *seller*, or the *initiator* of something.

If the word ends in *ee*, think of the party as the *receiver*, the *purchaser*, or the *taker* of something. Examples:

"or"	**"ee"**
Grantor—gives deed	Grantee—receives deed
Lessor—gives lease	Lessee—receives lease
Optionor-gives option	Optionee—receives option
Mortgagor—or borrower gives mortgage (note)	Mortgagee—or lender receives mortgage (note)
Vendor—sells item	Vendee—receives or purchases item

Marcia's List

A Study Guide Summary

The following is a quick abbreviated overview of the most important key terms and concepts from each of the topics in the 75-hour salesperson and the 45-hour broker qualifying courses. Check off the items you are unsure of and look them up in this *Cram*, **New *York Real Estate for Salespersons, 5th e*** or ***New York Real Estate for Brokers, 5th e***. Check out the comments for helpful explanations for certain key concepts.

License Law and Regulations/The Broker's Office: Operation, Management and Supervision

Article 12-A
Blind Ad
Commingling
eAccessNY
Exemptions to licensure
Kickback
Mandatory Seller Property Condition Disclosure Form
Misdemeanor
Net listing
Requirements for licensure
Relationship and supervision responsibilities for salespersons and associate brokers
Salesperson/broker/associate broker
Types of business organizations for broker licensure

Comment: **Article 12-A** of the New York Real Property Law addresses the licensure of salespersons and brokers. Also, NYSDOS regulations govern the licensure process.

***Comment*:** **Commingling** of funds is prohibited by the New York license law. Brokers must keep personal and business accounts separate to avoid *commingling* personal and business monies.

Comment: There are several **exemptions to licensure.** An important one is that NYS licensed attorneys admitted to the New York Bar may also serve as real estate brokers. Should the attorney want to open an office and hire salespeople, the attorney must obtain a real estate broker license from the NYSDOS (but does not have to take a course or exam).

Comment: A **net listing** contract is illegal in New York. It can occur if a broker arranges to keep as a commission any money obtained from the property sale above a price specified by the seller. Commissions for the sale of real property are generally a percentage of the entire selling price.

Law of Agency/Real Estate Agency Disclosure (includes Independent Contractor and Antitrust)

Advance informed consent to dual agency
Agency Disclosure Form for Buyer/Seller and Landlord/Tenant (two separate forms)
Broker's agent/ seller's agent /buyer's agent/ dual agent /subagent/ designated agent client/principal/customer
Fiduciary
First substantive contact or meeting
Group boycott/ market allocation agreement/ price fixing/ tie-in arrangement
Independent contractor/independent contractor agreement
Internal Revenue Code Section 3508 (a) (b)

Comment: **Advance informed consent to dual agency** allows buyers or sellers to consent to dual agency on the NYS agency disclosure form in advance of it occurring. *Dual agency* occurs when a real estate broker or salesperson attempts to represent the buyer and seller in the same transaction. It is allowable in New York with disclosure and informed consent.

Comment: The **first substantive contact** occurs when some detail and information about the property is shared with parties who express interest in the real estate transaction. Examples of this contact include the signing of the listing agreement with the seller or a showing of the property with the buyer.

Comment: A **group boycott**, **market allocation agreement**, **price fixing** or **tie-in arrangement** are all illegal restraints of trade activities and violations of antitrust law that are counter to free competition in the marketplace.

Meaning and difference between exclusive agency and exclusive-right-to-sell
Open listing
Special agent/general agent
Sherman and Clayton Antitrust Acts
Undivided loyalty
Vicarious liability

Comment: The difference between an **exclusive agency** and an **exclusive right to sell** listing agreement is that with an exclusive agency contract, the broker is legally entitled to the commission if the exclusive broker or another broker effects sale of the property, but not if the owner sells the property without the assistance of any broker. With the exclusive right to sell contract, the exclusive broker is entitled to the commission no matter who effects the sale, including the owner.

Comment: A real estate agent is a **special agent** who has narrow authorization to act on behalf of the principal or client. An example is a listing broker who represents a client for the sale of his or her property. A **general agent** is one who is authorized to handle all affairs of the principal concerning a specified matter or property. An example is a property manager who has varied duties to perform for his or her principal or client.

Comment: As part of their fiduciary duties, agents must remain loyal to the principal and work in the best interest the principal. It is important to note that when a real estate agent enters into a dual agency relationship with the buyer and seller, the client or principal must give up the fiduciary duty of **undivided loyalty** which is not possible in a dual agency relationship.

Legal Issues
Part I Estates and Interests

Fee simple absolute
Fixture/Trade Fixture
Difference between joint tenancy and tenancy in common
Leasehold estate
Life estate
Severalty

Comment: The fee **simple absolute estate** in real property provides the most complete form of ownership and bundle of rights in real property. There are other estates in real property that do not provide this complete form of ownership and are known as *defeasible estates.*

Comment: Ownership in **joint tenancy** requires all four unities of time, title, interest, and possession, Should one of the owners die, the other owners acquire the decedent's rights to the real property. This is known as the *right of survivorship.* With a **tenancy in common**, the only unity is that of possession. The tenant in common can devise this ownership right to another outside of the tenancy in common. There is no right of survivorship for the other owners.

Comment: **A leasehold estate** is one for a limited time. It is useful to think of a leasehold estate as a rental of real property.

Comment: **Severalty** means that the title to real property is held in the name of only one person or entity. Do not think of the word "several," but rather that the interest is severed from *all others.*

Part II - Liens and Easements

Easement appurtenant
Easement in gross
Encroachment
Encumbrance
Judgment
Lien
Lis pendens
Mechanic's lien

Comment: All easements that are not *easements appurtenant* are **easements in gross** which are commercial easements. They are usually owned by government agencies or utility companies. Think of electrical or cable lines.

Comment: ***Lis pendens*** is a Latin term meaning a notice that a lawsuit has been filed and litigation may be pending. Sometimes a property cannot transfer if a *lis pendens* has been filed.

Part III - Deeds/Conveyance of Real Property

Accession/alluvion/avulsion rights
Adverse possession
Deed/Conveyance
Dedication
Delivery and acceptance
Executor/Executrix
Full covenant and warranty deed
Grantor/grantee
Metes and bounds description
Quitclaim deed
Testate/intestate
Voluntary and involuntary alienation

Comment: To transfer title by a deed, the grantor (seller) must **deliver** a deed to the grantee (buyer) and the grantee must **accept** the deed.

Comment: A **full covenant and warranty deed** contains the strongest and broadest form of guarantee of title of any type of deed and the greatest protection to the grantee. Most residential title transfers use this type of deed.

Comment: A **quitclaim deed** releases or conveys to the grantee any interest, including title, that the grantor may have and contains no warranties of title. It is sometimes used when there is a "cloud on the title" and the seller cannot warrant clear title to the buyer.

Comment: **Voluntary** and **involuntary alienation** may occur during the life of an owner. *Voluntary alienation* occurs when there is a willing transfer of title during life. An example is if a grantor transfers title to a grantee while both are alive such as with a deed. *Involuntary alienation* occurs when an individual must give up title to real property against his/her will because of bankruptcy, adverse possession, or foreclosure.

Part IV-Title Closing and Costs

Abstract of title/chain of title/marketable/title search
Commission Escrow Act
Debits/credits
HUD Form No. 1
Flip tax
Good Faith Estimate (GFE)
Proration
Real Estate Settlement Procedures Act
Survey

Comment: An **abstract of title** is a condensed history of the title that summarizes all links in the **chain of title (**continuous title with no breaks**)** plus any public records affecting the title. This process is called a **title search** and is performed before a real estate closing. If there are no problems found during the title search, a property is said to have **marketable title**, that is, the property is reasonably free and clear of encumbrances.

Comment: **The Real Estate Settlement Procedures Act** applies to real estate closings for residential federally financed properties, not commercial properties or owner-financed loans. The law regulates lending institutions in making mortgage loans and requires a **Good Faith Estimate (GFE)** of all costs of settlement (closing) within three days of a buyer making a mortgage application.

The Contract of Sale and Leases
Part I Leases

Assignment/Sublease
Eviction/actual eviction/constructive eviction
Estate at sufferance/estate at will/tenancy for years/periodic estate
Gross/net lease
Lessor/lessee
Quiet enjoyment

Comment: An **assignment** involves the transfer of a contract such as a lease from the present tenant to the assignee. The assignee (the person who is now responsible for the contract) then must make lease payments to the landlord. With a **sublease,** a tenant leases a property to a third party, the sublessee. The original tenant, however, is still responsible to the landlord for the lease payments under the original lease.

Part II Contracts

Caveat emptor
Contingencies
Counteroffer
Executory/executed contract
Offer and acceptance
Statute of Frauds
Statute of Limitations
Time is of the essence
Void/voidable/ valid contract

Comment: ***Caveat emptor*** is a Latin term meaning "buyer beware." Although brokers have certain duties and responsibilities toward buyer customers, in New York, the theory of buyer beware may apply in certain situations.

Comment: An **executory contract** is one that is not fully completed. An example would be a listing contract in which the property is still be marketed. An **executed contract** is one that has been performed and the terms of the contract have been met.

Comment: In New York, the **Statute of Frauds** is in the General Obligations Law. The law requires that real estate contracts such as contracts for purchase must be in writing to be enforceable in court. Leases and listing contracts for more than one year must also be in writing.

Part III Contract Preparation

Attorney review clause
Binder
Down payment
Lawyer's Fund for Client Protection
Mortgage contingency clause

Comment: In certain areas of New York, a written document called a **binder** is used by real estate agents for the purchase and sale of real property instead of an *offer to purchase contract*. Generally, when a binder is used, the attorney for the buyer will use the information in the binder to create a contract of sale.

Real Estate Finance/Real Estate Finance II

Adjustable rate mortgage/fixed rate mortgage
Amortization
Balloon/ blanket/construction/wraparound mortgage
Buydown
Conventional mortgage
Discount points
Fannie Mae/Ginnie Mae/FreddieMac/ secondary mortgage market
FHA and VA insured loans
Foreclosure

Comment: An **adjustable rate mortgage** includes a mortgage interest rate that varies, depending on fluctuations of a standard financial index. With a **fixed rate mortgage,** the interest rate stays the same throughout the mortgage term. When interest rates are low, fixed rate mortgages are generally predictable and preferable.

Comment: The terms **mortgagor** and **mortgagee** can be misleading. The *mortgagor* or borrower is *giving* the lender a note or promise to pay back the mortgage monies (therefore the mortgag*or)*. The *mortgagee* is the lender, the party who is *receiving* payment on the mortgage note (therefore the mortgag*ee*).

Loan-to-value ratio
Mortgagor/mortgagee
Mortgage
Note or bond
Prepayment penalty
Regulation Z of the Truth in Lending Act
Satisfaction of mortgage
Sales leaseback
Subprime lenders/predatory lending practices

Comment: **Regulation Z of the Truth-in-Lending Act (TILA)** addresses the accurate advertising of credit terms to consumers by lenders or others advertising credit terms including real estate brokers. TILA requires that consumers receive disclosures regarding credit terms and costs.

Comment: **Subprime lenders** are companies that provide loans to homebuyers who do not have good credit histories or who are risky candidates for loans because of their incomes. Subprime lenders engage in **predatory lending practices** such as providing mortgage loans to unqualified buyers and also encouraging borrowers to increase their debt as the equity in their homes increase.

Land Use Regulations/Development

Article 9-A of the Real Property Law
Condemnation/eminent domain/escheat
Feasibility study
Infrastructure
Interstate Land Sales Full Disclosure Act
Moratorium
Nonconforming use
Police power
Spot zoning
Transfer of development rights
Zoning/Zoning Board of Appeals
Variance/area variance/use variance

Comment: Government may act to acquire private property. **Eminent domain** is the right or power of government and its agencies to take private property for public use. **Condemnation** is the actual taking of property under the power of eminent domain. **Escheat** is the power of the state to take title to a deceased person's property when no one else is qualified to receive the title.

Comment: **Police power** is a very encompassing right of government to fulfill its responsibility to provide for public health, safety, and welfare. Police power enables government to enact laws and regulations in the name of the public good.

Comment: **Spot zoning** is illegal in New York. It occurs when local government allows rezoning of a specific property to permit a use different from the zoning requirements for that area. This sometimes is done to raise property tax revenues for the municipality. An example might be an industrial spot zone that allows an industrial plant in a residential community.

Construction/Subdivision

Carbon monoxide/smoke alarm affidavit
Headers
Flashing
Footing/foundation
Joist
NYS General Business Law-Warranties on new home sales and home improvements
Outlots
Platform and slab-on-grade construction
Roofing terms- eave/fascia/frieze board/ pitch/ridge beam/ sheathing/soffit
Voltage/amperage

Comment: According to Article 36-B of the New York General Business Law, implied in all contracts of sale for new housing is a one-year builder's warranty against defects in construction; a two-year warranty for all plumbing, electrical, and heating and air conditioning systems; and a six-year warranty covering material defects.

Comment: See **Marcia's List Figure 1** that illustrates roof components and where they are located on the structure of a typical residential house. Look up any of the terms that you are unsure of in the subject review (key terms) section of this *Cram* under the heading, *Construction.*

Marcia's List Figure 1 Roof components

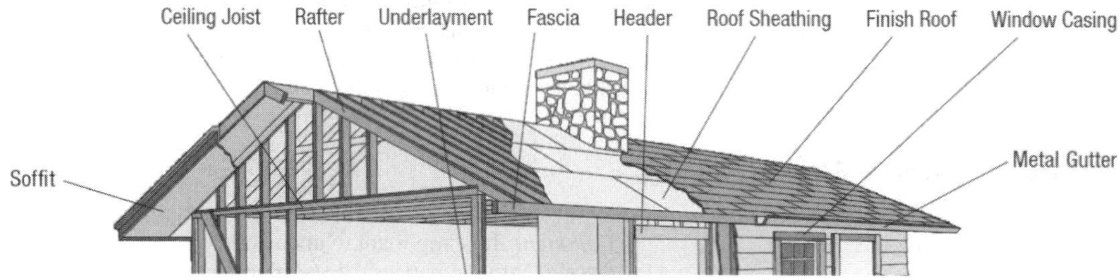

Source: The Home Inspection Book: A Guide for Professionals by Marcia Darvin Spada. © 2008. Reprinted with permission of Cengage Learning.

Environmental Issues

Asbestos/friability
Comprehensive Environmental Response, Compensation and Liability Act (CERCLA) (1980)/Superfund Amendment (1986)
Due diligence
Environmental impact statement
Lead
Radon
Residential Lead-based Paint Hazard Reduction Act
Responsibilities of the NYS Departments of Health and Environmental Conservation
State Environmental Quality Review Act
Urea formaldehyde foam insulation (UFFI)

Comment: In older building construction, **asbestos** was widely used because it is strong, durable, fire retardant, and an efficient insulator. The problem with asbestos is its **friability** or its ability to crumble when it is displaced. The asbestos particles can cause lung disease in those who handle it without training and proper protection. It is no longer used in building products.

Comment: The **Comprehensive Environmental Response, Compensation and Liability Act (CERCLA)** is a federal law to correct environmental problems created by uncontrolled waste disposal. The **Superfund Amendments and Reauthorization Act (SARA),** enacted later, strengthened CERCLA by imposing stringent clean-up standards and expanding the definition of persons liable for clean-up costs including the "innocent landowner" defense.

Comment: The federal **Residential Leadbased Hazard Reduction Act** calls for a mutually agreeable 10-day period for a lead paint assessment before a purchaser becomes obligated under a contract. The Act applies to target properties built before 1978. Disclosure is the key. Buyers can still purchase a property that has leadbased paint with disclosure by the seller and agreement by the buyer.

Valuation Process and Pricing Properties

Difference between a comparative market analysis (CMA) and an appraisal
Direct/indirect costs/price
Evaluation
Market value
Sales comparison, income, cost approaches to value
Supply and demand

Comment: A **comparative market analysis (CMA)** is not an appraisal. Rather, it is an analysis of the competition in the market place that a property will face upon sale attempts and uses current competing listings, sold properties, and expired listings to analyze the market and arrive at a price. An appraisal is an unbiased estimate of a property's value as of a certain date. The sales comparison approach is an appraisal approach that most closely resembles a CMA.

Comment: **Direct costs** are also called *hard costs* and include the cost of labor and materials for construction of the building. **Indirect costs** support the project including architectural and engineering fees, professional fees such as surveyors, attorneys, and appraisers, and financing costs. The **price** that is paid for the property may be above or below the cost depending on the market and whether or not the building costs exceed the market value of the building because of delays or other construction problems.

Comment: An **evaluation** does not necessarily find a price for a property. It is a study of the nature, quality, or utility of certain property interests in which a value estimate is not always required. Evaluations include land use, highest and best use, and feasibility studies and look at the supply and demand in the community.

Human Rights and Fair Housing

Americans with Disabilities Act
Blockbusting, steering, redlining
Testers
Cease and desist list
Civil Rights Act of 1866
Jones vs. Meyer Supreme Court decision
NYS Human Rights Law
Non solicitation order
Protected classes

Comment: It is important to understand the meaning of these illegal discriminatory practices. Illegal **blockbusting** occurs when real estate salespersons induce owners to list property for sale or rent by telling them that persons of a particular protected class are moving into the area. This may cause panic selling giving the broker new listings and eventually new sales. Illegal **steering** occurs when brokers or others direct prospective minority purchasers to presently integrated areas to avoid integration of nonintegrated areas. Illegal **redlining** occurs when lenders refuse to make loans to purchase, construct, or repair a dwelling by discriminating against any of the protected classes.

***Comment*:** **Protected classes** are groups of individuals for whom it is illegal to discriminate against under federal, state, and local laws. Protected classes in New York State include discriminatory practices against individuals because of race, color, religion, national origin, sex, disability, familial status, age, marital status, military status, and sexual orientation. Municipalities may have other protected classes such as in New York City.

Real Estate Mathematics

Acre
Appreciation/Depreciation
Area formulas
Interest
Income, Rate, Value (IRV) formula
Percentage formulas

Comment: An **acre** is 43,560 square feet. You will not be able to compute an acreage question if you do not know the square footage of an acre.

Comment: **Area formulas:**
Formula for rectangle: area = length × width, or A = L × W
Formula for square: area = side × side, or A = S × S
Formula for triangle: area = (0.5 × base) × height

Comment: See **Marcia's List Figure 2** that explains how to use the IRV formula.

Marcia's List Figure 2 IRV Formula

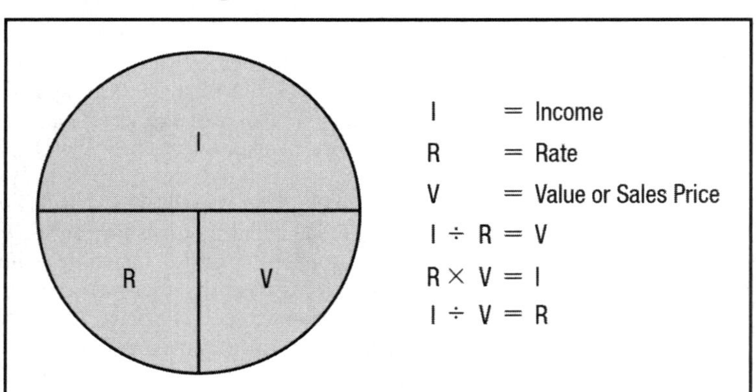

Source: New York Real Estate for Brokers 4th edition by Marcia Darvin Spada, © 2009, Cengage Learning, Mason, Ohio.

Comment: **Percentage formulas**

Commission: sales price × rate of commission = total commission
Mortgage and interest: principal × rate = annual interest
Appreciation and depreciation: original value × % of appreciated value = new value
Points: loan × number of points (%) = dollars in points

Municipal Agencies

Architectural Review Board
Conservation Advisory Council
Historic Preservation/Landmark Commission/ Planning board
Receiver of Taxes
Village Board of Trustees

Property Insurance

Actual cash value/replacement cost
Deductible
Liability insurance
Package policy
Umbrella policy

Comment: The **actual cash value (ACV)** for insurance purposes means that the insured is reimbursed for the replacement cost *minus* the physical depreciation of the lost or damaged property. In contrast, the **replacement cost** means that the insured is covered and reimbursed for the actual cost of replacing the damaged property. For instance, if a refrigerator is destroyed in a fire, the replacement cost will be the cost of buying another refrigerator.

Taxes and Assessments

Ad valorem/in rem
Assessment/assessor
Assessing unit/ approved assessing unit
Assessed value
Board of Assessment Review (BAR)
Grievance
Homestead
NYS Office of Real Property Tax Services
Residential Assessment Ratio (RAR)
Special assessment/special assessment districts
Tax levy/tax rate
Tax certiorari proceeding

Comment: *Ad valorem* and *in rem* are Latin terms. ***Ad valorem*** means according to the value. In New York, the real property tax is based on the fair market valueof real property. ***In rem*** refers to a legal proceeding brought against the real property and not against an individual and his personal property. An example is a property tax lien.

Comment: The **tax levy** is the amount that a municipality must raise to meet budgetary requirements by taxing real property. The **tax rate** is determined by the amount of the tax levy and expressed either in dollars per $100 of assessed value or in mills, (one mill is one-tenth of a cent) per $1,000 of assessed value. The formula for computing a property tax bill is: Assessed value x tax rate = annual taxes.

Condominiums and Cooperatives

Alteration agreement
By-laws
Common elements
Condominium/cooperative
Covenants, Conditions and Restrictions (CCRs)
Declaration
House Rules

Comment: **Common elements** are areas and utilities in a condominium or cooperative building shared by the owners. They can include the elevators and hallways as well as recreational facilities.

Comment: Instead of a deed at transfer of a cooperative apartment, the seller delivers to the buyer a **proprietary lease,** a long-term lease creating an estate for years to the apartment. A cooperative ownership is not a fee simple ownership. The shareholders do not own real estate, but a proportionate number of **shares of stock** in a cooperative corporation.

Maintenance
Offering statement
Proprietary lease/shares of stock
Sponsor

Commercial and Investment Properties/Real Estate Investments

Capitalization rate
Cash flow
Cash-on-cash return
Common areas
Debt service
Lease escalation clauses and other lease clauses
Leverage
Net operating income/gross income
Proforma statement
Rate of return
Sensitivity analysis
Short sale
Tax shelter
Time value of money
Usable square footage/rentable square footage/loss factor

Comment: **Lease escalation clauses** call for increased costs to the tenant for different reasons at specified times during the lease term. These clauses protect the property owner against increases in operating costs. During the past several decades, especially when vacancy rates are low, escalation clauses can generate a hidden profit for the owner, often at a large and not always justified cost to the tenant. There are **other lease clauses** including those that address sublease and assignment.

Comment: A **short sale** is a transaction in which the sale proceeds fall short of the balance owed on the property. It is used when a borrower cannot pay back the mortgage and the lender decides that selling the property at a loss is better than going after the borrower for the full indebtedness. In a short sale, the lender agrees to discount the balance due on the mortgage because of a financial hardship on the part of the borrower.

Comment: The **usable square footage** is the area contained within the space that the tenant occupies. Property owners quote rent in terms of rentable, not usable, square footage. The **rentable square footage** equals the entire space including the usable square footage and the tenant's pro rata share of the building's common areas such as the lobby. A property owner views the difference between the rentable and usable area in a commercial space as the **loss factor** such as hallways and other common areas.

Income Tax Issues in Real Estate Transactions

Active income/passive activity income/portfolio income
Age 59 ½ rule
Basis/adjusted basis
Capital gain/$250,000/$500,000 IRS law special exclusion
Deducting mortgage interest and points paid at closing
Recaptured depreciation
Tax depreciation
Tax-deferred exchange/like-kind property/boot

Comment: The **basis** of a property, for income tax purposes, is usually its cost. The **adjusted basis** is the original cost of the property or other basis plus certain additions and minus certain deductions such as depreciation and casualty losses (some kind of damage).

Comment: **Capital gain** is the profit realized from the sale of any capital investment including real estate. A capital gain occurs when an investor sells the asset for more than the basis. For income tax purposes, capital gain may be taxed at a lower rate than other income. For example, a **special exclusion in the IRS law** gives home sellers a tax break on capital gains when they are selling their home. Home sellers may be eligible to exclude up to **$250,000** if single, or up to **$500,000,** if married, of the capital gain on the sale of their residence.

Comment: Performing a 1031 **tax-deferred exchange** allows an individual to defer capital gains taxes on real estate bought and sold for investment purposes and does not include the exchange of personal residences. To qualify as a tax-deferred exchange, the properties must be *"***like-kind.***"* This involves exchanging personal property for other personal property or real property for other real property. If an exchangor receives cash or some other type of nonqualifying property in the exchange, this is called the **boot**.

Mortgage Brokerage

Difference between mortgage banker/ mortgage broker/mortgage loan originator
Lender rebate
Mortgage Broker Dual Agency Disclosure Form
NYS Department of Financial Services (NYSDFS)
Prequalification/preapproval
Rate lock

Comment: A **mortgage broker** is an individual or a company registered by the NYSDFS that is in the business of offering or soliciting, processing, placing or negotiating mortgage loans for others. *A mortgage broker does not make loans.* **A mortgage loan originator (MLO)** is an individual licensed by the NYSDFS who *works for* a mortgage broker or banker, and for compensation or gain, takes a residential mortgage loan application or offers or negotiates terms of a residential mortgage loan. A **mortgage banker** is an individual or a company licensed by the NYSDFS to engage in the business of *making* residential mortgage loans.

Property Management

Capital expense/variable expense
Corrective maintenance/preventive maintenance
Management agreement
Management proposal
Operating budget/capital reserve budget/ stabilized budget
Property management report
Resident manager

Comment: The property **management agreement** or contract creates a general agency relationship in which the owner is the principal and the property manager is the agent for the purposes specified in the agreement.

Comment: The **property management report**, provided by the property manager to the owner, is a periodic (usually monthly) accounting of all funds received and disbursed. The report contains detailed information about receipts and expenditures for the period covered (in addition to the year-to-date figures).

General Business Law (Broker course only)

Arbitration/mediation/litigation
Chapter 7, Chapter 11, Chapter 13 of the Bankruptcy Code
Corporation/general partnership/limited partnership/S corporation
Drawer/drawee
Due process
Endorsement
Litigation
Negotiable instruments
Equitable distribution
NYS Unified Court System
Trustor/Trustee
U.S. Supreme Court
Uniform Commercial Code

Comment: A **corporation** is a taxable legal entity, with tax rates separate from individual income tax rates. A corporation is formed in New York by the filing of a certificate of incorporation. A **general partnership**, formed by agreement, is made up of partners who are personally liable for partnership debts exceeding partnership assets. With a **limited partnership**, there are one or more partners who are liable for partnership debts, and one or more silent, or limited, partners who contribute money or other assets to the extent of their ownership interest. An S corporation is taxed like a partnership.

Comment: A **negotiable instrument** is an unconditional promise or order to pay a fixed amount with or without interest. It must satisfy the requirements of negotiability defined in the Uniform Commercial Code (UCC). Negotiable instruments include drafts, checks, promissory notes, and certificates of deposit.

Comment: The **U.S. Supreme Court** is our nation's highest court. It is composed of nine Justices appointed by the President with the approval of the Senate. One of the justices is appointed by the President as the Chief Justice.

Comment: The **Uniform Commercial Code (UCC)** is a number of uniform acts adopted individually by the states including New York to simplify, clarify, and modernize the laws governing commercial transactions including laws and regulations regarding negotiable instruments.

Questions for Your Review

This section provides 20 review questions for topics that appear in the salesperson and broker qualifying courses and 10 review questions for each topic that appears only in either course. There are 360 questions.

Tear out the Answer Sheet on the following pages, and use it to record your responses to the Review Questions. You may want to photocopy the blank answer sheet so that you can use it to review the questions a second time.

To complete the review questions, choose the letter that best answers the question and record that answer on the Answer Sheet. Check your responses using the "Answer Key for Review Questions" at the back of this guide. The explanation for the correct answer is in the Answer Key. Carefully review all incorrect answers. For a complete study experience, use the footnoted references in the Answer Key to find and review the content in the textbooks *New York Real Estate for Salespersons, 5th e* and *New York Real Estate for Brokers 5th e.*

Answer Sheet for Review Questions

1. ______________
2. ______________
3. ______________
4. ______________
5. ______________
6. ______________
7. ______________
8. ______________
9. ______________
10. ______________
11. ______________
12. ______________
13. ______________
14. ______________
15. ______________
16. ______________
17. ______________
18. ______________
19. ______________
20. ______________
21. ______________
22. ______________
23. ______________
24. ______________
25. ______________
26. ______________
27. ______________
28. ______________
29. ______________
30. ______________
31. ______________
32. ______________
33. ______________
34. ______________
35. ______________
36. ______________
37. ______________
38. ______________
39. ______________
40. ______________
41. ______________
42. ______________
43. ______________
44. ______________
45. ______________
46. ______________
47. ______________
48. ______________
49. ______________
50. ______________
51. ______________
52. ______________
53. ______________
54. ______________
55. ______________
56. ______________
57. ______________
58. ______________
59. ______________
60. ______________
61. ______________
62. ______________
63. ______________
64. ______________
65. ______________
66. ______________
67. ______________
68. ______________
69. ______________
70. ______________
71. ______________
72. ______________
73. ______________
74. ______________
75. ______________
76. ______________
77. ______________
78. ______________
79. ______________
80. ______________
81. ______________
82. ______________
83. ______________
84. ______________
85. ______________
86. ______________
87. ______________
88. ______________
89. ______________
90. ______________
91. ______________
92. ______________
93. ______________
94. ______________
95. ______________
96. ______________
97. ______________
98. ______________
99. ______________
100. ______________
101. ______________
102. ______________
103. ______________
104. ______________
105. ______________
106. ______________
107. ______________
108. ______________

Answer Sheet for Review Questions cont.

109. ____________
110. ____________
111. ____________
112. ____________
113. ____________
114. ____________
115. ____________
116. ____________
117. ____________
118. ____________
119. ____________
120. ____________
121. ____________
122. ____________
123. ____________
124. ____________
125. ____________
126. ____________
127. ____________
128. ____________
129. ____________
130. ____________
131. ____________
132. ____________
133. ____________
134. ____________
135. ____________
136. ____________
137. ____________
138. ____________
139. ____________
140. ____________
141. ____________
142. ____________
143. ____________
144. ____________
145. ____________
146. ____________
147. ____________
148. ____________
149. ____________
150. ____________
151. ____________
152. ____________
153. ____________
154. ____________
155. ____________
156. ____________
157. ____________
158. ____________
159. ____________
160. ____________
161. ____________
162. ____________
163. ____________
164. ____________
165. ____________
166. ____________
167. ____________
168. ____________
169. ____________
170. ____________
171. ____________
172. ____________
173. ____________
174. ____________
175. ____________
176. ____________
177. ____________
178. ____________
179. ____________
180. ____________
181. ____________
182. ____________
183. ____________
184. ____________
185. ____________
186. ____________
187. ____________
188. ____________
189. ____________
190. ____________
191. ____________
192. ____________
193. ____________
194. ____________
195. ____________
196. ____________
197. ____________
198. ____________
199. ____________
200. ____________
201. ____________
202. ____________
203. ____________
204. ____________
205. ____________
206. ____________
207. ____________
208. ____________
209. ____________
210. ____________
211. ____________
212. ____________
213. ____________
214. ____________
215. ____________
216. ____________

Answer Sheet for Review Questions cont.

217. ______
218. ______
219. ______
220. ______
221. ______
222. ______
223. ______
224. ______
225. ______
226. ______
227. ______
228. ______
229. ______
230. ______
231. ______
232. ______
233. ______
234. ______
235. ______
236. ______
237. ______
238. ______
239. ______
240. ______
241. ______
242. ______
243. ______
244. ______
245. ______
246. ______
247. ______
248. ______
249. ______
250. ______
251. ______
252. ______
253. ______
254. ______
255. ______
256. ______
257. ______
258. ______
259. ______
260. ______
261. ______
262. ______
263. ______
264. ______
265. ______
266. ______
267. ______
268. ______
269. ______
270. ______
271. ______
272. ______
273. ______
274. ______
275. ______
276. ______
277. ______
278. ______
279. ______
280. ______
281. ______
282. ______
283. ______
284. ______
285. ______
286. ______
287. ______
288. ______
289. ______
290. ______
291. ______
292. ______
293. ______
294. ______
295. ______
296. ______
297. ______
298. ______
299. ______
300. ______
301. ______
302. ______
303. ______
304. ______
305. ______
306. ______
307. ______
308. ______
309. ______
310. ______
311. ______
312. ______
313. ______
314. ______
315. ______
316. ______
317. ______
318. ______
319. ______
320. ______
321. ______
322. ______
323. ______
324. ______

Answer Sheet for Review Questions cont.

325. ____________
326. ____________
327. ____________
328. ____________
329. ____________
330. ____________
331. ____________
332. ____________
333. ____________
334. ____________
335. ____________
336. ____________
337. ____________
338. ____________
339. ____________
340. ____________
341. ____________
342. ____________
343. ____________
344. ____________
345. ____________
346. ____________
347. ____________
348. ____________
349. ____________
350. ____________
351. ____________
352. ____________
353. ____________
354. ____________
355. ____________
356. ____________
357. ____________
358. ____________
359. ____________
360. ____________

Review Questions

License Law and Regulations/The Broker's Office: Operation, Management and Supervision

1. Which of the following would NOT result in license suspension or revocation?
   a. Engaging in fraudulent practices
   b. Accepting compensation from more than one party in a transaction without making a full disclosure to all parties
   c. Licensees who are not attorneys giving legal advice
   d. Licensees accepting a commission from their sponsoring broker

2. Which of the following require a real estate license to engage in real estate practices?
   a. Building superintendent for one owner
   b. Public officers representing government interests
   c. Attorneys licensed in New York
   d. Auctioneers selling real property

3. A licensee who deposits an earnest money deposit in his personal checking account instead of in the broker's trust account is guilty of:
   a. conversion
   b. commingling
   c. escheat
   d. prescription

4. A major purpose of the real estate license law is to:
   a. protect the profitability of the real estate brokerage profession
   b. establish minimum standards for multiple listing services
   c. protect the public
   d. protect licensees from dishonest real estate investors

5. How many hours of qualifying education must a broker complete?
   a. 75
   b. 90
   c. 120
   d. 150

6. The regulatory agency that oversees the licensure process in New York is the:
   a. Department of Law
   b. Department of State
   c. Department of Housing and Urban Development
   d. Attorney General's Office

7. The minimum age for salesperson licensure is:
   a. 16
   b. 18
   c. 19
   d. 21

8. Which of the following is NOT a mandatory requirement for salesperson licensure in New York?
   a. Successful completion of the 75-hour qualifying course
   b. Broker sponsorship
   c. U.S. citizenship
   d. Passing the state license examination

9. When transacting real estate business, which of the following documents must be carried by the licensee?
   a. A listing form
   b. Driver's license
   c. Pocket card
   d. Business card

10. Licensees must complete continuing education requirements:
    a. every two years upon license renewal unless exempt
    b. every four years upon license renewal
    c. only if they are salespersons
    d. only if they have been in business for less than 10 years

11. Casey, a real estate broker, hired Jamie to help with activities such as answering the phone, making appointments, and typing contract forms. What type of license does Jamie need? A(n):
    a. salesperson license
    b. associate broker license
    c. broker license
    d. no license

12. Bill decides to open his own brokerage firm. Which of the following must he do first?
    a. Join a multiple listing service
    b. Decide what type of business organization he wants
    c. Join the local board of REALTORS®
    d. Hire at least two sales associates

13. Which of the following is NOT a legal requirement for the operation of a broker's office?
    a. A sign visible from the sidewalk or in the lobby stating that the individual or company is a licensed real estate broker
    b. A separate bank account for escrow deposits
    c. Submission of all contract forms for DOS approval
    d. DOS approval of a firm name

14. The NYS Department of State's occupational licensing management system is called:
    a. RESPA
    b. *eAccessNY*
    c. the Mortgage Nationwide Licensing System
    d. TILA

15. If a broker moves a principal or branch office, DOS must be notified online within how many days?
    a. 5
    b. 10
    c. 15
    d. 20

16. To obtain exam results from the either the salesperson or broker NYS licensure exam, applicants should:
    a. call the DOS
    b. wait for a "passed" slip to arrive in the mail
    c. view exam results through their accounts in *eAccessNY*
    d. obtain immediate exam results upon completion of the licensure exam

17. Andy, a broker, negotiated the sale of a single-family house. Both buyer and seller signed the contract of sale, the contract was reviewed and approved by attorneys for both parties, and financing was approved. A day before closing, the buyers wanted to back out of the deal. Andy:
    a. must now forfeit his commission because it is unearned
    b. take a lesser commission than arranged because of the new circumstances
    c. is entitled to the full commission as originally agreed upon
    d. must forfeit his commission because the deal involves residential real estate, and if it doesn't close, the broker cannot be compensated

18. The Harrisons were working with a buyer broker and decided to purchase an income property they were shown. However, they did not like the form used for the contract of sale presented by the seller's broker. The buyer broker decided to draw the contract of sale. Which of the following is CORRECT?
    a. The buyer broker can legally do this
    b. The buyers must agree to the contract form presented to the sellers
    c. The seller's broker can offer to rewrite the contract form
    d. Neither the seller broker nor buyer broker can write or rewrite any form of contract

19. A broker wrote a newspaper ad stating: Spacious house, 1 acre, $100,000, vicinity Catskill Mountains, John Jones, Broker, (914) 777-7777. This ad violates DOS guidelines because it does not mention:
    a. the name of the geographical area in which the property is located
    b. the terms of available financing
    c. the broker's address
    d. enough detail about the house itself

20. Much of the New York Real Property Law relating to real estate licenses is in which of the following sections? Article:
    a. 9-A
    b. 12-A
    c. 19-B
    d. 14-A

Law of Agency/ Real Estate Agency Disclosure

Includes Independent Contractor and Antitrust

21. A broker's commission is determined by:
    a. reference to maximum guidelines established by the Division of Licensing Services
    b. agreement between the broker and principal
    c. reference to the multiple listing service fee schedule
    d. reference to the Department of State's fee schedule

22. In the sale of one- to four-unit residential real estate and condominiums and cooperatives in any size building, a listing agent must first disclose her status to a prospective buyer:
    a. when a buyer calls the office
    b. only when instructed to by her broker
    c. when the parties enter into a contract of sale
    d. at the first substantive meeting

23. A person empowered to act on behalf of another is called a(n):
    a. a middleman
    b. agent
    c. principal
    d. party of the first part

24. Danielle listed her home with broker Robert. Danielle, however, sold her home without any assistance from broker Robert. A court ruled that Danielle owed Robert a full commission on the sale of her home. This is because Robert:
    a. had an exclusive agency listing agreement
    b. was a seller broker rather than a buyer broker
    c. had an exclusive right to sell listing agreement
    d. had an open listing agreement.

25. A buyer broker CANNOT receive compensation for services through which of the following methods? As:
    a. a subagent of the seller
    b. a flat fee from the buyer
    c. a commission split from a listing broker
    d. a combination of a partial flat fee from the buyer and a commission split from the listing broker

26. The agency relationship:
    a. requires the principal to compensate the agent
    b. must be the result of a written agreement
    c. makes the agent responsible for all acts of the principal
    d. is consensual

27. The most common agency relationship between brokers and principals are:
    a. special
    b. general
    c. universal
    d. power of attorney

28. In the sale of one- to- four unit residential property, and residential condominiums and cooperatives in any size building, which situation does NOT require the presentation of a disclosure form to a buyer or seller:
    a. when a buyer makes an appointment to see a property
    b. when entering into a listing agreement with a seller
    c. when a seller agent shows a property to a prospective buyer
    d. when prospects walk through an open house without any specific contact with the agent

29. If Sell-It-Quick Real Estate makes a deal with Country Lane Realty to charge the same commission to all prospective sellers, this is called an illegal:
    a. group boycott
    b. price-fixing agreement
    c. market allocation agreement
    d. tie-in arrangement

30. If Give You A Mortgage Company and Sell It Now Realty arrange that customers who purchase a home from Sell It Now will be required to apply for a mortgage through Give You A Mortgage Company, this is called an illegal:
    a. group boycott
    b. price fixing agreement
    c. market allocation agreement
    d. tie in arrangement

31. In general, most real estate agents are:
    a. independent contractors
    b. employees
    c. free agents
    d. statutory employees

32. In an independent contractor relationship:
    a. salespersons only receive their commissions twice yearly
    b. salespersons can work for any number of different brokers at the same time without permission of the other sponsoring broker
    c. salespeople are compensated according to hours worked
    d. an associate broker-independent contractor can be an office manager

33. Which of the following regarding the duties of the independent contractor is FALSE? Independent contractors may:
    a. work any hours they choose
    b. terminate the relationship at any time
    c. work from their homes
    d. not show a property without the presence of the sponsoring broker

34. In order to comply with federal and state independent contractor law, what must the broker and salesperson do?
    a. Enter into a written independent contractor agreement
    b. Enter into an oral independent contractor agreement
    c. Sign a disclosure statement
    d. The salesperson must show the broker evidence that he does not have other outside employment

35. In order to qualify under the independent contractor relationship, which of the following is necessary? The agent must:
    a. be a broker or associate broker
    b. be licensed
    c. have been licensed for at least one year
    d. work at least 25 hours per week

36. Which IRS form must a broker prepare if an independent contractor earns more than $600 per year?
    a. Form 1040
    b. Schedule C
    c. Form 1099 misc.
    d. Form 3508 (a) (b)

37. An independent contractor who earns over $600 per year must file:
    a. yearly federal tax returns only
    b. yearly state tax returns only
    c. no tax returns as the broker will take care of the filing
    d. yearly federal and state tax returns

38. How many years must a broker keep records as to the sale or mortgage of one-to-four unit properties?
    a. One year
    b. Two years
    c. Three years
    d. Four years

39. If a salesperson is classified as an independent contractor, which of the following is TRUE? The broker:
    a. has no duty to supervise the salesperson's activities
    b. has a duty to supervise the salesperson's activities
    c. can only supervise those salespersons who are classified as employees
    d. can only supervise work that is performed in the real estate office

40. If a salesperson is classified as an independent contractor, who pays withholding (social security taxes)? The:
    a. broker as it is withheld from the salesperson's commission
    b. seller who pays the commission
    c. salesperson' s pension plan
    d. salesperson must take care of his withholding and other tax obligations

41. A broker engaged to act on behalf of a principal as a listing agent for a property is what type of agent?
    a. General
    b. Universal
    c. Special
    d. Unilateral

42. Which of the following is FALSE regarding an exclusive agency listing agreement? The:
    a. property is listed with one broker only
    b. owner does not have to pay the broker a commission if the owner sells the property
    c. broker has a right to his commission if he sells the property
    d. property is listed with one or more brokers

43. In the rental of one- to-four unit residential properties and condominiums and cooperatives in any size building, at the first substantive contact, which of the following is TRUE?
    a. An agent must present the disclosure form to prospective tenants when showing the premises
    b. No disclosure form is needed at the time that the property is being shown
    c. The disclosure form need only be presented when signing the lease and at no other time
    d. The disclosure form need only be used in rental properties that have more than four units

44. Katy lists her condominium with Broker Beth for $150,000. Broker Beth tells a prospective buyer to submit a low offer because seller Katy is going through a divorce. Broker Beth:
    a. violated the fiduciary relationship
    b. did nothing wrong since an offer came through that Katy was happy with
    c. acted properly as long as Katy does not complain
    d. was correct to tell the buyers this information under her duty to disclose

45. One who is hired through a broker to work for that broker, and the principal is not vicariously liable for the acts of that agent, is called a:
    a. dual agent
    b. broker's agent
    c. subagent
    d. facilitator

46. In New York, dual agency is:
   a. illegal under all circumstances
   b. legal only in commercial transactions
   c. legal with timely disclosure and informed consent
   d. legal only with regard to sales but not rentals

47. What do subagents, listing agents, seller agents, and single agents have in common? They:
   a. are all dual agents
   b. all represent the seller
   c. all must belong to MLS
   d. are all cooperating agents

48. In an exclusive right to sell contract, under what conditions is the listing broker entitled to a commission?
   a. Only when the broker sells the property
   b. When the broker or the owner sells the property, but no one else
   c. When anyone including the broker, owner or other brokers sell the property
   d. Only if the listing broker's firm sells the property

49. Excluded from Section 443 of the Real Property Law covering the use of the disclosure form is:
   a. single-family home sales
   b. rentals in one- to four-unit properties and condos and coops in any size building
   c. vacant land
   d. sales of duplex property

50. Sellers, buyers, landlords and tenants may consent to dual agency:
   a. only at a first substantive contact
   b. under no circumstances
   c. only in the sale or rental of single-family homes
   d. in advance of it occurring

Legal Issues

Part I Estates and Interests

51. The term, estate *pur autre vie*, refers to a(n):
   a. estate of a former tenant
   b. estate owned by the government
   c. estate managed by an agent
   d. life estate measured by the life of someone other than the life tenant

52. Which of the following is NOT a characteristic of real property?
   a. Indestructibility
   b. Uniqueness
   c. Mobility
   d. Limited availability

53. Ownership as tenants by the entirety is limited to:
   a. families with children
   b. husband and wife
   c. any two individuals whose names appear on a deed
   d. ownership of commercial properties

54. Public parks and historical monuments are examples of which type of real property?
   a. Agricultural
   b. Residential
   c. Commercial
   d. Special purpose

55. A life estate can be defined as:
   a. ownership or possession for someone's lifetime
   b. a measure of profit of the estate
   c. the absorption of one estate into another
   d. a leasehold estate

56. Which of the following is NOT a freehold estate?
   a. Fee simple absolute
   b. Leasehold
   c. Fee simple defeasible
   d. Fee simple on condition

57. A grantor conveys 100 acres to his daughter, but if the daughter uses the property for a commercial purpose, her ownership terminates. This is an example of a(n):
    a. fee simple on condition
    b. estate *pur autre vie*
    c. leasehold estate
    d. fee simple absolute

58. Ownership in severalty refers to:
    a. ownership by one owner
    b. co-ownership
    c. a financing charge
    d. purchase of optioned property

59. Chattel refers to:
    a. property pledged as security for payment of a debt
    b. personal property
    c. field for cattle to graze
    d. a wife's interest in her husband's real property

60. An interest in land allowing for possession for a definite and limited time is called:
    a. an estate for years
    b. long-term estate
    c. joint tenancy
    d. usury

Legal Issues

Part II Liens and Easements

61. A lien is:
    a. a privilege to do a particular act
    b. the right to enter a parcel of land
    c. a claim that one person has against the property of another for a debt
    d. money paid for compensation to use one's land

62. An easement is a(n):
    a. parcel of land
    b. nonpossessory use of land by another
    c. easier route through a property
    d. structure that facilitates drainage

63. The meaning of the term, *lis pendens*, is:
    a. that a lawsuit is pending
    b. Latin for "lease period"
    c. a lien against a property
    d. the extent of authority of a court

64. Mortgages are:
    a. involuntary general liens
    b. voluntary general liens
    c. voluntary specific liens
    d. involuntary specific liens

65. A mechanic's lien is a(n):
    a. involuntary general lien
    b. voluntary general lien
    c. voluntary specific lien
    d. involuntary specific lien

66. Although certain types of liens have priority over other types, what other factor determines the priority of payment of the lien? The:
    a. dollar value of the lien
    b. time and date of filing
    c. credit history of the person who is responsible for payment
    d. type of property to which the lien is attached

67. Utility companies generally must obtain which type of easement to run electrical cables or pipe through a property?
    a. Easement in gross
    b. Easement appurtenant
    c. Easement by prescription
    d. Easement by grant

68. The land that benefits from an easement appurtenant is called the:
    a. servient tenement
    b. easement in gross
    c. dominant tenement
    d. encumbered property

69. Tree branches that extend over the boundary of one property into another's are called:
    a. easements
    b. created nuisances
    c. acts of nature
    d. encroachments

70. A characteristic of a license to use another's land is that it is:
    a. similar to a lien
    b. the same as an easement
    c. a temporary privilege
    d. a permanent privilege

Legal Issues

Part III Deeds/Conveyances

71. A deed is:
    a. a note payable on demand
    b. an agreement between parties to do certain things
    c. a document in writing, executed and delivered, that conveys title to real property
    d. to bequeath by a will

72. The *habendum* clause in a deed is the:
    a. forfeiture clause
    b. defeasance clause
    c. "to have and to hold" clause
    d. mortgaging clause

73. A deed that conveys to a grantee an interest in real estate with no warranty of title is called a(n):
    a. full covenant and warranty deed
    b. executor's deed in the form of a full covenant and warranty deed
    c. deed of trust
    d. quitclaim deed

74. When a deed is executed, this means that it is:
    a. delivered
    b. acknowledged
    c. signed by the grantor
    d. corrected

75. The party that conveys title to real property is called the:
    a. grantee
    b. grantor
    c. trustee
    d. party of the second part

76. The legal term for the transfer of property is called:
    a. alienation
    b. subrogation
    c. *lis pendens*
    d. execution

77. Which of the following is NOT a judicial deed?
    a. Sheriff's deed
    b. Correction deed
    c. Executor's deed
    d. Referee's deed

78. A deed description that starts with a point or place of beginning is called a:
    a. description by monument
    b. description by reference
    c. metes and bounds description
    d. description by lot and block

79. When a landowner donates a parcel of land for public use, this is called:
    a. dedication
    b. adverse possession
    c. the right of accession
    d. forced grant

80. A person appointed in a will to carry out its provisions is called the:
    a. testator
    b. legatee
    c. devisor
    d. executor

81. Alienation after death is by:
    a. deed
    b. will
    c. adverse possession
    d. bankruptcy

82. Which of the following is NOT a type of involuntary alienation?
    a. Adverse possession
    b. Dedication
    c. Lien foreclosure sale
    d. Bankruptcy

83. The law requires that all deeds be in writing is the:
   a. Statute of Frauds
   b. Statute of Limitations
   c. Sullivan Law
   d. Real Property Law

84. A person may NOT receive title under adverse possession in New York unless the individual:
   a. is at least 25 years of age
   b. has been in possession of the property for a period of at least five years
   c. has secretly lived on the property for eight years
   d. has met all legal requirements and a court confirms what has already taken place

85. If a person dies and leaves a valid will, he is said to die:
   a. intestate
   b. devised
   c. testate
   d. probate

86. To make a gift of real property by will is to:
   a. devise
   b. administer
   c. assign
   d. legate

87. The term "accretion" refers to the:
   a. taking of private property for public use
   b. dedication of land by a developer
   c. gradual build up of land in a water course
   d. the wearing away of land by water, wind, or other processes of nature

88. A quitclaim deed is most generally used when:
   a. the strongest form of guarantee of title is required
   b. an attorney is not involved in the transaction
   c. there are only two parties to the transaction
   d. the grantor's rights or interests and nothing more are conveyed

89. A tenancy in common:
   a. does not require the unity of possession
   b. requires that each tenant holds an undivided interest in the entire property
   c. includes the right of survivorship
   d. is the same as a joint tenancy

90. Evidence that something of value is present in a deed is known as:
   a. earnest money
   b. consideration
   c. chattel
   d. devise

Legal Issues

Part IV Title Closing and Costs

91. Title to real estate is transferred:
   a. when a contract for purchase and sale is executed by buyer and seller
   b. when financing for the purchaser is approved by the lending institution
   c. upon execution and delivery of a valid deed
   d. after all existing liens are satisfied

92. Generally, in the closing process, attorneys for a lender represent the best interests of the:
   a. lending institution
   b. purchaser
   c. seller
   d. real estate licensee

93. A federal statute that regulates disclosure and closing requirements relative to a mortgage loan on residential property is the:
   a. Truth in Lending Act
   b. Interstate Land Sales Act
   c. Fair Credit Disclosure Act
   d. Real Estate Settlement Procedures Act

94. An unbroken transfer of successive titles to real property is called:
   a. movable title
   b. conveyable title
   c. chain of title
   d. attorney's opinion of title

95. The document which shows the measurements, boundaries, and area of property is called a(n):
    a. feasibility study
    b. survey
    c. architectural rendering
    d. plat

96. A condensed history pertaining to the title of a property is called a(n):
    a. abstract of title
    b. chain of title
    c. title insurance
    d. intestate succession search

97. One of the most important roles of a licensee just before closing is to:
    a. examine the deed to make sure it is valid
    b. prepare the closing statement
    c. examine the abstract of title
    d. arrange and accompany a prospective purchaser through a final inspection of the property

98. A New York tax on the conveyance of title to real property is called the:
    a. mortgage recording tax
    b. real estate transfer tax
    c. capital gains tax
    d. sales tax

99. Which of the following is NOT a buyer debit at closing?
    a. Unpaid utility bills
    b. The purchase price
    c. Discount points
    d. Homeowner's insurance

100. Which of the following is NOT a seller debits at closing?
    a. Delinquent property taxes
    b. Existing mortgage
    c. Mortgage insurance
    d. Purchase money mortgage taken back from buyer

101. When all interested parties to a title closing meet, their main purpose is to:
    a. remove all clouds on title to the property
    b. transfer title to real property from seller to buyer
    c. arrange financing
    d. draw the deed and other legal documents

102. A deed for a given property is recorded in January, 20xx. A subsequent deed is drawn on the same property in June, 20xx in the same year, but is not recorded. Which of the following is TRUE?
    a. The June 20xx deed takes priority over the January deed
    b. The January 20xx takes priority over the June 20xx deed
    c. The June 20xx deed would only take priority over the January deed if it were a quitclaim deed
    d. Priority of deeds is not established by the date they are filed

103. The Commission Escrow Act is a law that protects compensation for a(n):
    a. seller
    b. buyer
    c. real estate broker
    d. board of REALTORS®

104. Grantor A conveys a certain property to Grantee B; Grantor B then conveys this same property to Grantee C; Grantor D then conveys this same property to Grantee E. Based on this information, which of the following applies?
    a. There is a break in the chain of title
    b. There is no break in the chain of title
    c. The chain of title is not a valid method of searching records pertaining to a property's history
    d. The above illustrates a clear title to the property

105. A title insurance policy:
    a. is only issued upon receipt of an acceptable abstract or title opinion
    b. is not generally required by lenders
    c. is routinely issued even without an acceptable abstract of title
    d. can only be issued by the state insurance department after an examination of all records pertaining to the property

106. The Real Estate Settlement Procedures Act:
    a. provides guidelines to protect sellers with regard to the sale of residential property
    b. requires disclosure of settlement costs before closing
    c. protects banks from lending to individuals who are questionable credit risks
    d. ensures that banks do not have an overabundance of mortgages in their portfolios

107. Which of the following is NOT a buyer debit on a closing statement?
    a. Purchase price
    b. Loan origination fee
    c. Discount points
    d. Earnest money deposit

108. Which of the following is NOT a seller debit on a closing statement?
    a. Delinquent real property taxes
    b. Purchase money mortgage taken back from buyer
    c. Purchase price
    d. Broker commission

109. A federal tax on capital gains derived by foreign people from the sale of their U.S. property is called:
    a. FIRPTA
    b. a flip tax
    c. the sales tax
    d. the escrow tax

110. A type of purchase that involves the transfer of shares of stock rather than conveyance through a deed is that of a(n):
    a. condominium
    b. industrial property
    c. cooperative
    d. vacant land

The Contract of Sale and Leases

Part I Leases

111. Which of the following is a key feature of a periodic lease?
    a. It automatically renews for another period unless notice is given to terminate
    b. It is never for more than one year's duration
    c. It is only used for commercial leases
    d. At the death of the landlord or tenant, the heirs of the deceased are not bound by the terms of the lease

112. Which of the following defines the nature of a leasehold estate? It:
    a. provides title to real property
    b. provides possession, but not title to real property
    c. is conveyed by deed
    d. never exists for a fixed period

113. When the duration of the lease is completely unknown when the lease is signed, this is called a(n):
    a. fixed estate
    b. periodic estate
    c. estate at will
    d. freehold estate

114. A tenant who was originally in lawful possession of a premises but refuses to leave after his right to possession terminates is legally called a:
    a. tenant at will
    b. holdover tenant
    c. squatter
    d. trespasser

115. A lease is most generally a type of:
a. deed
b. promissory note
c. contract
d. option agreement

116. Which of the following is NOT a standard lease provision?
a. Identification of the premises
b. Competency of the parties to contract
c. Specification of rent and payment
d. Specification of a minimum one-year term

117. When Heath looked over the lease to his apartment, it had so many legal terms and unclear language that he had to take it to his attorney for interpretation. This lease:
a. is perfectly acceptable
b. should always be read by an attorney before signing
c. should appear in at least two languages
d. should be written in a clear and coherent manner using everyday terminology

118. Which of the following is a right of a landlord and does not have to be specified in the lease?
a. Automatic right to inspect the leased premises for any reason
b. Right to remove a tenant from a premises at any time during the lease
c. Right to enter the premises in an emergency such as a fire
d. Right to send repair persons to the premises without permission from the tenant.

119. If a tenant must leave a leased premises because of lack of heat, he may be able to forfeit his lease obligations and claim:
a. constructive eviction
b. actual eviction
c. forfeiture
d. *lis pendens*

120. If a landlord sells a building containing rental properties, the new owner may:
a. evict any of the current tenants without cause
b. raise the rents on the leased premises before termination of the lease
c. inspect all of the leased premises without permission from the lessees
d. none of the above

The Contract of Sale and Leases

Part II Contracts

121. Consideration is:
a. a promise of quiet enjoyment
b. the giving of something, which need not be monetary value, as an inducement to contract
c. always expressed as a dollar value
d. a power of attorney

122. Which of the following is NOT an essential requirement for a real estate contract?
a. Competent parties
b. Consideration
c. Financing contingency
d. Offer and acceptance

123. The law that places a time limit on the years allowed to commence a lawsuit is the:
a. Statute of Limitations
b. Real Estate Settlement Procedures Act
c. Statute of Frauds
d. Uniform Commercial Code

124. A contract between two parties who have definitely agreed to the contract terms is called a(n):
a. express unilateral contract
b. express bilateral contract
c. implied bilateral contract
d. implied unilateral contract

125. Under an installment land contract, which of the following does NOT apply?
   a. The purchaser has immediate legal title to the property
   b. It is an express bilateral executory contract
   c. The purchaser is given possession of the property
   d. The purchaser must maintain the property

126. The substitution of a new contract for a prior contract is called:
   a. sublet
   b. assignment
   c. rescission
   d. release

127. In general, a valid written listing agreement between a seller and a real estate agent in which a buyer is not found is a(n):
   a. implied contract
   b. void contract
   c. unenforceable contract
   d. executory contract

128. If a sales contract states that "time is of the essence," this means that the contract must be performed:
   a. within a reasonable time period
   b. within one year
   c. on or before the date stipulated on the contract
   d. within three months

129. Which of the following is FALSE regarding an earnest money deposit? It:
   a. shows the sincerity of buyer
   b. legally must accompany an offer to purchase
   c. demonstrates financial capability to raise the money called for in the purchase offer
   d. may serve as possible liquidated damages to the seller if the buyer defaults

130. A contract with a minor is:
   a. automatically void
   b. illegal
   c. unenforceable
   d. voidable by the minor

The Contract of Sale and Leases

Part III Contract Preparation

131. A form of seller financing is a(n):
   a. assumable mortgage
   b. home equity loan
   c. FHA loan
   d. purchase money mortgage

132. A portion of the property's purchase price that is paid in cash and NOT part of the mortgage is the:
   a. binder
   b. down payment
   c. assumable mortgage
   d. mortgage commitment

133. Which of the following is generally the first to sign the contract of sale?
   a. Purchaser
   b. Seller
   c. Seller's attorney
   d. Real estate broker or salesperson

134. Rafael, a real estate salesperson, advises his buyer clients not to sign a contract of sale prepared by their attorney because he believes that the "as is" clause in the contract will cause them trouble later. Which of the following is TRUE? Raphael:
   a. can advise his clients as to legal matters as long as they don't have an attorney
   b. can advise his clients about any matters as long as they have signed the agency disclosure form
   c. can advise his clients on all contract matters
   d. is engaging in the illegal practice of law

135. An IOLA account is one held by:
  a. real estate brokers
  b. attorneys
  c. apartment sharing agents
  d. mortgage brokers

136. The Lawyer's Fund for Client Protection has to do with attorney:
  a. escrow accounts
  b. licensure
  c. relationships with real estate brokers
  d. court appearances

137. In certain upstate areas, should a real estate salesperson take a deposit, which of the following is TRUE? He:
  a. must keep it in his checking account
  b. must lock it in a safe place until the closing
  c. must turn it over to his broker
  d. can keep it as his commission

138. Keri is buying a residential single-family property for $450,000. Generally, what would be the customary deposit?
  a. $15,000
  b. $30,000
  c. $45,000
  d. $75,000

139. At what point is a real estate contract of sale binding?
  a. When it is signed by buyer and seller
  b. When it is signed by buyer and seller and agents for each
  c. When it is reviewed and approved by the attorneys for buyer and seller
  d. At closing

140. Which of the following documents are NOT required for closing?
  a. Survey
  b. Certificate of occupancy
  c. Prior deed
  d. Census statement

Real Estate Finance/ Real Estate Finance II

141. The mortgagor is the:
  a. lender
  b. broker
  c. borrower
  d. trustee

142. The mortgagee is the:
  a. lender
  b. broker
  c. borrower
  d. trustee

143. A mortgage is a(n):
  a. unilateral implied contract for repayment of a loan
  b. written document pledging a property as security for the repayment of a loan
  c. insurance policy to protect against a variety of hazards
  d. conveyance used to transfer title to real property

144. Which of the following best describes down payments for VA loans? They:
  a. are always 5% of the appraised value
  b. are typically $5,000
  c. are always 10% of the sales price
  d. do not always require a minimum down payment

145. A balloon mortgage is best described as:
  a. based on the borrower's ability to pay
  b. having a larger payment due at the end of its term
  c. covering more than one parcel of real property
  d. an amortized loan

146. When a lender is willing to lower the interest rate at the time the loan is made in return for extra payments of points up front, this is called:
  a. buydown
  b. usury
  c. apportionment
  d. satisfaction of mortgage

147. An amortized mortgage loan is one that is paid in monthly payments:
   a. with a balloon payment at the end
   b. of interest only
   c. of principal only
   d. of principal and interest

148. A wraparound mortgage:
   a. covers both the mortgaged property and mortgage insurance
   b. covers more than one parcel of real estate
   c. is a subordinate mortgage which includes the same principal obligation secured by a first mortgage against the same property
   d. is not a type of seller financing

149. A document for recording and acknowledging that a mortgage is paid in full is called a(n):
   a. payoff statement
   b. satisfaction
   c. HUD Form No. 1
   d. certificate of title

150. The New York agency that raises money from tax-free bonds and applies the money to mortgage loans is called:
   a. Fannie Mae
   b. SONYMA
   c. FDIC
   d. RHA

151. A conventional loan:
   a. involves participation by an agency of the federal government
   b. is always an amortized loan
   c. involves no participation by any agency of the federal government
   d. is an FHA loan

152. A blanket mortgage is one:
   a. that has matured and is open to foreclosure
   b. on personal property as opposed to real property
   c. in which two or more parcels are pledged as security for the mortgage debt
   d. that is junior in lien priority to a previous mortgage

153. One of the most difficult loans for a lender to underwrite because it asks for funds to create a project that does not exist is a:
   a. commercial loan of any type
   b. construction loan
   c. home equity loan
   d. purchase money mortgage

154. A type of amortized mortgage that calls for a large payment at the end of the term is a:
   a. amortized mortgage
   b. balloon mortgage
   c. an installment land contract arrangement
   d. a mortgage that is available only through government backed loans

155. A purchase money mortgage is:
   a. given by a purchaser to the seller to cover part of the purchase price
   b. given by the seller to the purchaser to cover part of the purchase price
   c. a type of swing loan
   d. the same as an installment land contract

156. The clause in a mortgage entitling the lender to declare the principal balance due and payable if the borrower sells the property during the mortgage term is the:
   a. defeasance clause
   b. alienation clause
   c. prepayment penalty clause
   d. granting clause

157. The process by which loan documentation is reviewed and the borrower's ability and willingness to repay the loan is evaluated is:
   a. investment analysis
   b. loan underwriting
   c. loan to value ratio analysis
   d. income qualification

158. A short-term loan that may provide funds over and above an already existing loan until permanent financing is in place is known as:
   a. convertible financing
   b. blanket financing
   c. gap financing
   d. flexible payment financing

159. A type of mortgage that gives the lender the option to convert the outstanding balance into an agreed upon percentage of ownership in the property is known as a:
   a. subordinate mortgage
   b. convertible mortgage
   c. flexible payment plan
   d. bridge loan

160. A transaction in which a property owner sells a property to an investor who immediately leases back the property to the seller is known as:
   a. release land subdivision financing
   b. ground lease
   c. conversion mortgaging
   d. sale-leaseback

Land Use Regulations/Development

161. Which of the following is generally TRUE?
   a. Escheat is the power of government to take private property for public purposes
   b. Zoning ordinances are private land use controls
   c. Deed restrictions are examples of the government's right to control land use
   d. Eminent domain allows government to take property for public use only if it is for the use and benefit of the public

162. The doctrine of laches refers to:
   a. loss of legal rights because of failure to assert them
   b. a special real estate lockbox
   c. government restrictions on land use
   d. a lessor's interest in leased property

163. The New York law that protects residents in the purchase of vacant subdivided land sold on the installment plan is:
   a. Article 12-A of the Real Property Law
   b. Article 9-A of the Real Property Law
   c. the General Business Law
   d. the Statute of Frauds

164. When property reverts to the state due to the lack of heirs, it is called:
   a. eminent domain
   b. equity
   c. escheat
   d. reversion

165. The agency that coordinates information relevant to an environmental impact statement is called the:
   a. office of the county clerk
   b. zoning board of appeals
   c. lead agency
   d. coordinating agency

166. Zoning ordinances are an example of the use of a government's:
   a. police power
   b. health regulatory power
   c. right of eminent domain
   d. private restrictions

167. The government agency that sends inspectors on-site to insure construction code compliance is the:
   a. zoning board of appeals
   b. U.S. Department of HUD
   c. Department of Environmental Conservation
   d. building department

168. An in-law apartment that is connected to a residential home is called a(n):
a. annexation
b. accessory use
c. home occupation
d. group home

169. Hospitals, schools, and courthouses are examples of which type of zoning?
a. Institutional
b. Industrial
c. Public open space
d. Commercial

170. A municipality that imposes a delay in developing property in a given area has issued a(n):
a. transfer of development rights
b. moratorium
c. demographic evaluation
d. infrastructure assessment

171. A subdivision plat is generally recorded with the:
a. Department of State
b. local zoning board
c. county clerk
d. assessor's office

172. The study of the physical features and contours of land is known as:
a. topography
b. infrastructure
c. demography
d. geology

173. The purpose of planning is to:
a. provide for the orderly growth of a community
b. create the greatest allowable density patterns
c. create a larger tax base
d. protect developers from excessive building code requirements

174. The agency that has the statutory authority to review and approve plans for subdivision development is the:
a. local building department
b. local planning board or commission
c. Department of Environmental Conservation
d. county assessor's office

175. The New York law that requires local government to assess the environmental significance of actions that it must approve is the:
a. Superfund Amendment
b. State Environmental Quality Review Act
c. Clean Air Act
d. EPA

176. If a property owner is denied a request for a variance, he:
a. must accept the decision
b. may petition the county assessor's office for a new ruling
c. may petition the New York Supreme Court through an Article 78 Proceeding
d. may request a new hearing before the planning board within 30 days

177. Vincent wants to use part of his house as a doctor's office. This use is not allowed in his neighborhood. Vincent must:
a. apply for use variance
b. apply for an area variance
c. forget about the idea, as New York residents cannot change the use of their homes for any reason
d. apply for a special zone

178. One of the differences between a request for a variance and a special use permit is that special use permits:
a. do not require that the applicant demonstrate undue hardship
b. are illegal in New York
c. are only allowed for large commercial projects
d. require an Article 78 proceeding

179. The New York agency that oversees wetland protection is the:
   a. Department of Health
   b. Department of Agriculture
   c. Department of State
   d. Department of Environmental Conservation

180. The federal organization that oversees wetland protection is the:
   a. U.S.D.A.
   b. Army Corps of Engineers
   c. U.S. Coast Guard
   d. Environmental Protection Agency Construction

Construction

181. Guidelines for minimum separation distances between a well and a septic system are furnished by the:
   a. Environmental Protection Agency
   b. NYS Department of Environmental Conservation
   c. U.S. Department of HUD
   d. NYS Department of Health

182. Which of the following is NOT a consideration in the design and development of a construction site?
   a. Drainage
   b. Appurtenances
   c. Insulation requirements
   d. Zoning

183. The concrete base below the frost line that supports the foundation of a structure is called the:
   a. foundation wall
   b. footing
   c. slab
   d. girder

184. The wooden skeleton of a residential property is called the:
   a. frame
   b. walls
   c. sheetrock
   d. foundation

185. Openings for doors and windows in a residential property are supported by:
   a. lally columns
   b. rafters
   c. headers
   d. the sill plate

186. Which of the following is TRUE?
   a. The lesser the degree of insulation, the greater the R-factor
   b. The greater the degree of insulation, the greater the R-factor
   c. R-factor ratings apply only to blanket insulation
   d. The R-factor has nothing to do with insulation

187. A type of heating system that heats water in a boiler and then uses circulator pumps to propel the heated water to convectors is called a(n):
   a. forced warm air system
   b. electric heating system
   c. heat pump
   d. hot water system

188. Which of the following is FALSE regarding the plumbing system?
   a. The systems for water supply and wastewater are combined
   b. It must follow local code guidelines as to materials used
   c. Private systems must adhere to minimum separation distances for wells and septic systems
   d. If no local code guidelines are available, systems must comply with the New York Fire Prevention and Building Code

189. The minimum electrical service installed in a residential home must be:
   a. 50 amps
   b. 100 amps
   c. 150 amps
   d. 200 amps

190. A device that melts and opens a circuit to stop electrical power when overheating occurs is called a:
  a. fuse
  b. distribution panel
  c. service drop
  d. voltameter

191. The first wooden member of the house which is used as the nailing surface for the floor system is the:
  a. foundation wall
  b. sill plate
  c. fascia
  d. ridge beam

192. The Act, administered by HUD that regulates the sale of unimproved lots across state lines is known as the:
  a. Superfund Amendment and Reauthorization Act
  b. Interstate Land Sales Full Disclosure Act
  c. Uniform Building Code
  d. Residential Warranty Corporation Act

193. The National Electric Code:
  a. only applies to commercial structures
  b. is not valid in New York
  c. offers minimum guidelines and standards for electrical installations
  d. is written by the New York Board of Fire Underwriters

194. The law that is the guideline for New York's drinking water regulations is the:
  a. Superfund Amendments and Reauthorizations Act
  b. Residential Lead-Based Paint Hazard Reduction Act
  c. Safe Drinking Water Act
  d. Department of Environmental Conservation regulations

195. The New York law that provides minimum standards for construction materials and safety is:
  a. the General Business Law
  b. not state law since only local statutes are used
  c. Article 9-A of the Real Property Law
  d. the NYS Fire Prevention and Building Code

196. According to the New York General Business Law, how many years must a builder warrant new construction against defects in construction?
  a. one
  b. two
  c. three
  d. five

197. After signing a home improvement contract, an owner has up to how many days to cancel it?
  a. One business day after the contract was signed
  b. Three business days after the contract was signed
  c. One week after the contract was signed
  d. One month after the contract was signed

198. The water supply system in New York is regulated by the:
  a. Army Corp of Engineers
  b. Department of Agriculture
  c. State Department of Public Works
  d. Department of Health

199. The New York law that sets minimum energy efficiency requirements for the design of new buildings and renovations and additions to existing buildings is:
  a. Article 9-A - of the Real Property Law
  b. the Energy Conservation Construction Code
  c. the General Business Law
  d. the Human Rights Law

200. A seller must sign an affidavit indicating the presence of a smoke alarm and carbon monoxide detector in the sale of:
   a. commercial properties
   b. one- and two-family residential properties and residential condominium sand cooperatives
   c. apartment units only
   d. only properties used by the public Environmental Issues

Environmental Issues

201. Which of the following imposed stringent clean up standards and expanded the definition of those responsible for clean up?
   a. The National Environmental Policy Act
   b. State Environmental Quality Review Act
   c. the Clean Air Act
   d. Superfund Amendments and Reauthorization Act

202. Local drinking water problems are remediated by the:
   a. Department of Environmental Conservation
   b. local Departments of Health
   c. Department of Agriculture
   d. Department of State

203. One of the biggest dangers in highly corrosive water is that it may contain large amounts of:
   a. radon
   b. PCBs
   c. lead
   d. CFCs

204. The regulatory agency that licenses individuals to apply termiticide in New York is the:
   a. Department of Environmental Conservation
   b. Department of Health
   c. Department of Parks
   d. Department of State

205. A fibrous mineral used in many construction applications such as ceiling tiles and roof shingles is called:
   a. lead
   b. asbestos
   c. radon
   d. UFFI

206. The Residential Lead-based Hazard Reduction Act calls for:
   a. a ban on the sale of all homes that contain lead paint
   b. homeowners to remove all lead paint before the property is put up for sale
   c. funding for homeowners to remove all lead paint from their home
   d. a mutually agreeable 10-day period for a lead paint assessment before a purchaser becomes obligated under a contract

207. Radon most generally enters the home:
   a. through openings in the attic or roof area
   b. when people leave their windows open for long periods of time
   c. when there is a heavy rainstorm
   d. through small cracks in the foundation wall

208. According to the EPA, which level of radon concentration is considered safe?
   a. no level
   b. more than one picocurie
   c. more than two picocuries
   d. more than four picocuries

209. If the indoor air quality of a commercial building causes large numbers of people to fall ill, this is called:
   a. an unhappy event
   b. sick building syndrome
   c. radon toxicity
   d. commercial building syndrome

210. A toxic liquid organic compound that was used as an insulating medium for electrical transformers and which has polluted both the soil and waterways in New York is/are called:
a. radon
b. UFFI
c. chlorofluorocarbons
d. PCBs

Valuation Process and Pricing Properties

211. An analysis of the competition in the market place that a property will face upon sale attempts is called a(n):
a. appraisal
b. evaluation
c. comparative market analysis
d. cost approach to value

212. Which of the following methods are NOT used for appraisal purposes?
a. income approach
b. sales comparison approach
c. cost approach
d. comparative market analysis

213. An owner who uses a residential property for vacation purposes only may attribute which type of value to this property?
a. assessed value
b. insurance value
c. value in use
d. investment value

214. Which of the following is a market value estimate of real property?
a. Appraisal of a single-family home
b. Feasibility studies
c. Highest and best use studies
d. Land utilization studies

215. A property will probably NOT sell for market value under which of the following conditions?
a. Buyer and seller are equally motivated
b. A reasonable time is allowed for exposure in the market place
c. The buyer and seller are related to each other
d. It is an arms-length transaction

216. Which of the following regarding the price of a property is TRUE? Price:
a. always equals cost
b. is always more than the cost
c. is always equivalent to the market value of a property
d. is not always equivalent to the market value of a property

217. In the construction of a property, if time schedules are not met or other construction problems occur, which of the following would most likely apply? The:
a. market value will equal the cost
b. cost may exceed the market value
c. cost will be below the market value
d. price will definitely have to equal the cost

218. In the construction of a property, the costs of architectural and engineering fees are called:
a. direct costs
b. hard costs
c. payment schedule
d. indirect costs

219. Comparables used in the creation of a comparative market analysis should be:
a. as similar as possible to the subject property
b. exactly the same as the subject property
c. as different as possible from the subject property
d. located in a different neighborhood from the subject property

220. Which of the following is NOT an appropriate comparable for a comparative market analysis?
 a. Expired listings
 b. Current competing properties
 c. Properties yet to be built
 d. Sold properties

Human Rights and Fair Housing

221. Redlining is:
 a. steering home seekers to a particular neighborhood
 b. drawing red circles on a zoning map indicating what areas are prime housing markets
 c. denying or restricting loans in a certain area by a lending institution
 d. a zoning procedure

222. The Civil Rights Act of 1866:
 a. prohibits all discrimination based on race
 b. prohibits discrimination in federally funded housing only
 c. allows an exception to racial discrimination for an owner occupied two-family dwelling
 d. does not apply to nonlicensed persons

223. Under the Federal Fair Housing Act, an administrative law judge may impose which of the following penalties for a "pattern of discrimination"?
 a. Up to $10,000
 b. Up to $50,000
 c. Not more than $1 million
 d. The penalty is not limited by statute and may be determined by the court

224. Illegal blockbusting is described as:
 a. purchase of a home in a neighborhood by a member of a minority group
 b. directing home seekers into an area to change its character
 c. directing certain home seekers away from an area in order to maintain its character
 d. homeowners being told by real estate salespeople that a member of a protected class is moving into their neighborhood, causing them to panic and place their homes for sale

225. What is illegal steering?
 a. Leading prospective homeowners toward or away from certain areas
 b. Refusing to make loans to persons in certain areas
 c. A requirement to join MLS
 d. A practice of fixing commission rates by an MLS steering committee

226. One of the differences between the federal Fair Housing Law and the New York Human Rights Law is that the:
 a. federal law does not cover rental housing
 b. New York law does not have exemptions as in the federal law
 c. New York law covers commercial property as well as residential
 d. federal law lacks monetary penalties for violation

227. The Americans with Disabilities Act covers:
 a. single-family homes
 b. vacant land
 c. places of amusement only
 d. buildings open to the public as well as multi-family dwellings

228. In addition to federal law, protected classes under the New York Human Rights Law include:
 a. familial status and race
 b. age and marital status
 c. race and religion
 d. disability and familial status

229. Nancy owns and lives in a duplex in Rochester, New York. She wishes to rent the other apartment. Nancy:
a. must rent her home to any person who is financially qualified
b. may not discriminate against individuals because they are a certain race
c. must rent her home to families with children, if approached
d. must place her property for rent in a local newspaper if she does not use the services of a salesperson

230. An area designated by the NYS Department of State where salesperson and brokers may not solicit listings is called a(n):
a. cease and desist zone
b. area under moratorium
c. quarantined zone
d. market allocation area

Real Estate Mathematics

231. A real estate broker earns a $12,500 commission in the sale of a condominium. His commission rate is 7%. What is the asking price of the condo? (Round off to the nearest dollar).
a. $158,600
b. $178,571
c. $357,269
d. $458,213

232. A broker earns a commission of $8,250. His commission rate is 7.5%. What is the selling price of the property?
a. $80,000
b. $90,000
c. $100,000
d. $110,000

233. A property valued at $475,000 appreciates 2% per year. How much is the property worth after two years?
a. $484,500
b. $493,175
c. $494,190
d. $501,160

234. An office space is 52 feet wide x 162 feet long and leases for $75,000 per year. What is the price per square foot?
a. $8.90
b. $15
c. $20
d. $25

235. An acre of land has a width of 425 feet. If this acre of land is rectangular in shape, what is its length?
a. 85.5 feet
b. 93 feet
c. 102.5 feet
d. 120 feet

236. The purchase price of a property is $175,000. The bank authorizes a loan-to-value ratio of 90%. What is the amount of the loan authorized?
a. $90,000
b. $100,000
c. $125,000
d. $157,500

237. A property closes on November 15. The yearly property taxes are $2,500. What is the credit to the seller on the closing statement?
a. $256
b. $312.50
c. $375
d. $476.89

238. A property sells for $120,000. The buyer obtains an 80% loan. If the bank charges 3 points at closing, how much in points must the buyer pay?
a. $1,589
b. $2,245
c. $2,880
d. $3,496

239. A loan of $50,000 is repaid in full one year after the loan is made. If the interest rate on the loan is 9.5%, what amount of interest is owned?
a. $4,750
b. $5,000
c. $5,765
d. $6,987

240. A property sells at the assessed value. The annual real property tax is $2,304 at a tax rate of $24 per thousand of tax value. The property is taxed at 80% of assessed value. What is the selling price?
a. $110,000
b. $120,000
c. $130,000
d. $140,000

Municipal Agencies

241. The legislative power of a city is vested in:
a. the mayor
b. its city council
c. the state legislature
d. zoning board of appeals

242. The main function of a city or town planning board is to advise on:
a. environmental issues
b. wetland regulation
c. school policy
d. land use matters

243. Which of the following government agencies may grant a variance?
a. Citizen's advisory council
b. Town board
c. Zoning board of appeals
d. Planning board

244. Xavier is seeking information about constructing a property near a wetland. He can find information and guidance from the:
a. conservation advisory council
b. architectural review board
c. zoning board of appeals
d. county legislature

245. Building departments CANNOT:
a. issue building permits
b. issue certificates of occupancies
c. inspect ongoing construction
d. rule on variance applications

246. The document containing each property's assessment in a municipality is the:
a. title register
b. city or town budget
c. assessment roll
d. tax map

247. In some cities and towns, the official or agency that collects fees for water usage and other permits is the:
a. tax assessor
b. receiver of taxes
c. engineer
d. building department

248. The NYS agency that oversees the placement of a property in or near a wetland is the:
a. Department of Environmental Conservation
b. Department of Health
c. Department of Public Works
d. Department of State

249. A town or village planning board consists of how many members?
a. two to four
b. five to seven
c. seven to nine
d. any numbers as decided by the town board or village board of trustees

250. Meri wants more information about renovating a historic property. Which agency would be LEAST likely to be involved in this process?
a. Historic preservation commission
b. Zoning board of appeals
c. Building department
d. Conservation advisory council

Property Insurance

251. A clause in an insurance policy that modifies or changes the insurance policy in some way is known as a (n):
a. endorsement
b. peril
c. deductible
d. umbrella

252. Insurance obtained through the New York Property Insurance Underwriting Association can be undesirable because:
    a. it is unreliable
    b. the premiums are higher than those obtained through the voluntary market
    c. only certain areas of New York are insured
    d. there is a long waiting list

253. The National Flood Insurance Program is administered by:
    a. the NYS Insurance Department
    b. FEMA
    c. HUD
    d. the Army Corps of Engineers

254. According to New York law, which of the following deductibles must be disclosed to the insured?
    a. Personal property
    b. Fire
    c. Flood
    d. Windstorm

255. As long as the insurance company states the reason for the cancellation, an insurance policy may be cancelled within how many days?
    a. 25
    b. 30
    c. 60
    d. 90

256. The cost of a homeowner's policy is directly related to:
    a. the policy holder only
    b. the property only
    c. a statewide fee schedule
    d. both a and b

257. The amount the insured must pay towards a claim before receiving any policy benefits is called the:
    a. premium
    b. peril
    c. deductible
    d. endorsement

258. An excess liability policy, providing additional coverage above that offered by primary policies is called a(n):
    a. replacement cost premium
    b. umbrella policy
    c. luxury coverage
    d. homeowner's special form policy

259. In the insurance policy contract, the basic coverage is outlined in which part of the policy?
    a. Declarations page
    b. Actual cost section
    c. Contingency plan endorsement section
    d. Statement of liability

260. Which of the following is NOT a type of coverage in an insurance policy?
    a. Dwelling
    b. Personal property
    c. Loss of use
    d. Functional obsolescence

Taxes and Assessments

261. Which of the following is an example of a property that is NOT tax exempt?
    a. VA hospital
    b. Synagogue
    c. Gas station
    d. State office building

262. The tax rate is determined by the:
    a. city or town council
    b. assessor
    c. amount of the tax levy
    d. the census

263. The percentage at which properties are assessed in a locality is called the:
    a. tax levy
    b. level of assessment
    c. residential assessment ratio
    d. tax rate

264. Reassessments can be performed on properties:
a. when improvements are made only
b. on a regular prescribed basis only
c. as a random spot check on any property in the locality
d. both a and b

265. Which of the following CANNOT collect real property taxes in New York?
a. Cities
b. Towns
c. Villages
d. The state

266. Which of the following CANNOT receive an exemption from paying real property taxes?
a. Those with disabilities
b. Property owners under 25 years old
c. Seniors
d. Veterans

267. The purpose of the board of assessment review is to:
a. levy taxes
b. set uniform percentages
c. develop the equalization rate
d. hear grievances

268. If a property owner believes that his property's assessed value is greater than the property's full value, he may claim that he has been subject to:
a. unequal assessment
b. excessive assessment
c. unlawful assessment
d. misclassification

269. A judicial review of a tax protest in the New York Supreme Court is called a (n):
a. tax certiorari proceeding
b. grievance
c. Article 78 proceeding
d. tax hearing

270. The first task in determining the assessment for tax purposes is to:
a. hold a referendum to decide who is exempt
b. evaluate the zoning regulations for the community
c. establish the market value of each parcel of land within the taxing unit
d. file a petition of appeal

271. Which of the following is generally completely exempt from property taxes?
a. all private hospitals
b. all industrial properties
c. government-owned properties
d. factories

272. Local governments in New York have the option of offering a reduction of property taxes to:
a. senior citizens
b. state employees
c. condominium and cooperative owners
d. minors who own real property

273. An in rem legal proceeding takes place:
a. only in assessing units of more than 1million people
b. against the real property directly and not the individual
c. only if the assessing unit has full value assessment
d. if the mortgage payment is overdue for more than three months

274. Tax maps for a tax unit are maintained by the:
a. local planning board
b. zoning board of appeals
c. tax assessor
d. mayor or town supervisor's office

275. The residential assessment ratio (RAR) is NOT used for which of the following purposes?
a. The grievance process
b. A small claims assessment review hearings
c. Municipalities conducting revaluation projects
d. A general measure of assessment equity

276. An appraisal for tax purposes and an appraisal for mortgage purposes are:
   a. exactly the same
   b. different in that a tax assessment takes the market value from the appraisal and applies a uniform percentage
   c. different only in that one is completed by an assessor and the other is completed by an appraiser
   d. different because an appraisal for mortgage purposes endeavors to find market value and a tax appraisal endeavors to find value in use

277. The New York agency that certifies the residential assessment ratios is the:
   a. Department of State
   b. Department of Taxation and Finance
   c. Office of Accounting
   d. Office of Real Property Tax Services

278. Which of the following is classified as non-homestead property?
   a. farm dwelling
   b. factory
   c. condominium
   d. duplex

279. A written complaint filed with the board of assessment review to protest an assessment is known as a(n):
   a. in rem legal proceeding
   b. summons and affidavit of complaint
   c. grievance
   d. legal protest

280. The NYS agency that oversees property taxes in New York is the:
   a. Office of Real Property Tax Services
   b. Department of State
   c. Department of Financial Services
   d. Department of Law

Condominiums and Cooperatives

281. Ownership in a cooperative is evidenced by:
   a. shares of stock
   b. a deed
   c. a recognition agreement
   d. an alteration agreement

282. The type of ownership interest that a cooperative owner has in his real property is:
   a. freehold
   b. leasehold
   c. fee simple absolute
   d. tenant at will

283. Which of the following is NOT included in a condominium offering plan?
   a. Initial declaration
   b. Prospectus
   c. Initial price of the units
   d. Proprietary lease

284. With regard to a condominium or cooperative, whether or not a tenant can advertise from their apartment window, is included in the:
   a. alteration agreement
   b. house rules
   c. recognition agreement
   d. letter of intent

285. A board package, submitted to the cooperative board of directors, consists mainly of:
   a. societal status information
   b. family history
   c. financial data
   d. reasons for purchase

286. An agreement that outlines the responsibilities between the cooperative corporation and the lender is called a (n):
   a. CSP1 statement
   b. subordination agreement
   c. alteration agreement
   d. recognition agreement

287. Which of the following characterizes a condop? A(n):
   a. cooperative that does not have board interviews
   b. building that has both condominium and cooperative ownership
   c. condominium that has no board of directors
   d. condominium or cooperative that does not have an offering plan adopted by the attorney general

288. Pet restrictions, repair obligations, and use of the common elements are disclosed in a condominium's:
 a. bylaws
 b. letter of intent
 c. CPS1 statement
 d. tenant declaration

289. During the CPS1 period or phase, which of the following is TRUE in the marketing of condominiums or cooperatives?
 a. The developer need not following any attorney general rules governing advertising
 b. Only the attorney general can set the price for the units
 c. The developer may set the market price for the units
 d. No firm price can be declared by the developer for individual units

290. Which of the following is TRUE regarding the mansion tax? The tax:
 a. applies to all residential properties sold for $1 million or more
 b. applies only to condominiums and cooperatives when the units are over 5000 square feet
 c. applies to one-, two-, and three-unit residential properties as well as condominiums and cooperatives sold for $1 million or more
 d. only applies in New York City

Commercial and Investment Real Estate/Real Estate Investments

291. Which of the following is a benefit that depreciation provides? Tax:
 a. credit
 b. deduction
 c. evasion
 d. basis

292. Which of the following is NOT a tax deductible expense for a business property?
 a. Advertising
 b. Utilities
 c. Mortgage principal
 d. Insurance

293. An investor purchases a $2,000,000 multi-family apartment complex with a $500,000 down payment. Each month, the cash flow from rentals, less expenses, is $15,000. What is the cash-on-cash return?
 a. 28 percent
 b. 31 percent
 c. 36 percent
 d. 42 percent

294. The value of an income property is $850,000 and the capitalization rate is 12%. What is the projected annual net income?
 a. $82,500
 b. $87,000
 c. $98,000
 d. $102,000

295. When offering available square footage to tenants, property owners generally charge for:
 a. usable square footage
 b. rentable square footage
 c. carpetable area
 d. effective square footage

296. Which of the following defines when an investment will generate a positive return?
 a. Attornment
 b. Expense stop
 c. Point of no return
 d. Natural breakeven point

297. A lease clause that states that the landlord's lender and future owners of the building cannot terminate the lease as long as the tenant fulfills lease obligations is called a (n):
 a. escalation clause
 b. estoppel
 c. subordination clause
 d. nondisturbance clause

298. Which of the following is a type of lease escalation clause?
 a. Porter's wage formula
 b. Estoppel
 c. Use clause
 d. Subordination

299. Generally, with a real estate investment, the greater the risk of loss means which of the following is TRUE?
   a. The greater the return on investment
   b. The less the return on investment
   c. Risk has nothing to do with return
   d. Risk and return are always equal

300. The use of OPM, or other people's money, describes:
   a. risk
   b. return
   c. leverage
   d. debt service

301. Which of the following is NOT a good reason to consider investment in property?
   a. As a hedge against an inflationary economic trend
   b. For tax savings generated by passive losses
   c. As a means of providing cash flow
   d. As a means of providing liquidity to one's investment portfolio

302. A real estate investor may defer capital gains taxes by:
   a. investing in income shelters
   b. dealing in cash transactions only
   c. exchanging like-kind properties
   d. selling high-end properties over $500,000 because capital gains may be deferred

303. An economic analysis of all data related to a project including its costs, rates of return, and benefit to the community is known as a(n):
   a. operating statement
   b. feasibility study
   c. potential gross income
   d. pro forma schedule

304. A short sale is a transaction in which:
   a. closing includes "time is of the essence"
   b. there is seller financing
   c. the sale proceeds fall short of the balance owed on the property
   d. there is always lender financing

305. Foreclosed properties are generally sold at:
   a. a short sale
   b. an auction
   c. the time of listing
   d. the request of the owner

306. A short sale is a:
   a. debt service
   b. financial loss for the lender
   c. financial loss for the purchaser
   d. credit loss

307. An operating statement adjusted to reflect a potential change in income and expenses based on the investor's assessment of the real estate market is known as:
   a. feasibility studying
   b. investment strategy
   c. timing planning
   d. a proforma schedule

308. Foreclosed properties are usually offered:
   a. "as is"
   b. by a lender
   c. when the borrower is in default on the mortgage
   d. all of the above

309. The percentage of income that the investor realizes on an investment is known as:
   a. loan-to-value ratio
   b. the rate of return
   c. leverage
   d. the time value of money

310. The study of how a change in one factor affecting a real estate investment can affect the income to the property is known as:
   a. a feasibility study
   b. risk analysis
   c. sensitivity analysis
   d. securitization

Income Tax Issues in Real Estate

311. According to IRS rules, real property taxes are deductible for:
   a. a personal residence
   b. a second home
   c. an inherited property
   d. all of the above

312. If a taxpayer's tax rate is above the 15% income bracket and he has held a property for longer than 12 months, when he sells the property, he will be taxed at a rate of:
a. 5 percent
b. 10 percent
c. 15 percent
d. 20 percent

313. Petros lost $15,000 of his personal funds in the stock market in the taxable year 20xx. Under what circumstances can he deduct this amount from his yearly income taxes?
a. Only if he earned under $25,000 for 2008
b. Only if he is in the 15 percent tax bracket
c. Only if he is unemployed
d. Under no circumstances

314. Property eligible for a tax-deferred exchange does NOT include:
a. industrial property
b. commercial property
c. a personal residence
d. a hotel or motel

315. Which of the following may be deducted on a real property purchaser's income tax return under certain conditions?
a. Appraisal fees
b. Points
c. Notary fees
d. Preparation fee for the mortgage

316. The main housing credit agency in New York is the:
a. NYS Division of Housing and Community Renewal
b. HUD
c. FEMA
d. NYS Division of Human Rights

317. In reference to the straight-line method for depreciating nonresidential property, it may be depreciated over how many years?
a. 15 years
b. 27.5 years
c. 35.5 years
d. 39 years

318. Which IRS rule allows first-time homebuyers to use IRA distributions to fund up to $10,000 of their new home cost without paying an early distribution penalty?
a. Rule of four
b. Age 59 1/2 rule
c. Safe harbor law
d. IRA exemption clause

319. How many days from the day of closing does a real estate exchangor have to contract for another (replacement) property?
a. 15 days
b. 30 days
c. 45 days
d. 60 days

320. In a tax-deferred exchange, any cash in the exchange is called the:
a. equity
b. collateral
c. cache
d. boot

Mortgage Brokerage

321. The New York agency that registers mortgage brokers is the:
a. Department of Financial Services
b. Insurance Department
c. Department of State
d. Attorney General's Office

322. Which of the following describes the experience requirement for a NYS licensed real estate broker to obtain a mortgage broker registration?
a. One year in the mortgage business
b. Two years in the mortgage business
c. A current real estate broker's license
d. A real estate salesperson who has been licensed for at least one year

323. A mortgage broker who represents a purchaser in negotiating a mortgage loan is a(n):
a. agent
b. intermediary
c. facilitator
d. none of the above

324. A mortgage broker who represents the purchasers in negotiating a mortgage while also representing the sellers as a real estate broker in the same transaction is acting as a(n):
a. general agent
b. facilitator
c. dual agent
d. single agent

325. The minimum line of credit required to be licensed in New York as a mortgage banker is:
a. $250,000
b. $500,000
c. $1 million
d. $2 million

326. Which of the following involve verifying a purchaser's credit and employment history?
a. Appraisal
b. Validation
c. Pre approval
d. Statement of net worth

327. A request by a purchaser to reserve a certain loan interest rate for a specified time is called a (n):
a. rate lock
b. commitment
c. rate cap
d. interest reserve

328. The process in which the lender evaluates all of the borrower's financial data and determines if the borrower will obtain the loan is called:
a. alienation
b. pre approval
c. clarification
d. loan underwriting

329. A lender's rebate is payment to the:
a. loan underwriter
b. seller
c. purchaser
d. mortgage broker

330. A loan that does NOT meet the Federal Reserve Bank loan criteria for funding is known as:
a. illegal
b. secondary
c. nonconforming
d. straight term

Property Management

331. If a property manager works for one owner, which of the following is TRUE? He:
a. must have a broker license
b. must have a minimum of a salesperson license
c. does not need a real estate license
d. is always an independent contractor

332. Which of the following creates an agency relationship between the property manager and the owner?
a. Management agreement
b. Management proposal
c. Listing agreement
d. Letter of intent

333. In managing a property, risk management has to do with:
a. financial risk
b. liability when the public enters the property
c. managing the activities of employees
d. tenant behavior

334. If a building is 98 percent occupied, the property manager may feel justified in:
a. believing that the laws of supply and demand are not in favor of the property
b. rewriting the leases during the lease term
c. lowering the rents
d. raising the rents

335. Property income and expenses for week-to-week operations are computed in which type of budget?
a. Cash flow
b. Capital reserve
c. Stabilized
d. Operating

336. Randy rents six apartments in his building for $750 per month and seven apartments for $1,050 per month. Figuring in a 5% vacancy rate, what is the annual projected rent roll?
a. $135,090
b. $139,500
c. $142,200
d. $185,300

337. Which document prepared by a property manager relates expense items to the operating budget for the period?
a. Property management agreement
b. Property management report
c. Rent roll
d. Stabilized budget

338. Lydia, a property manager, enlisted her maintenance team to go through the building and assess and repair all items that may need repair or replacement for the calendar year. This is an example of:
a. excessive oversight
b. due diligence
c. preventative maintenance
d. corrective maintenance

339. In New York if a property manager works for more than one owner, which of the following is required? A(n):
a. real estate broker license
b. BOMI affiliation
c. IREM designation
d. none of the above

340. In her position as managing agent for a small apartment complex, Alexa, a real estate broker, accepts a small bonus from the landscapers since she hired them to maintain the complex. Alexa does not tell the owners about the bonus. Which of the following is TRUE? Alexa:
a. is violating her fiduciary duty to the owners
b. may accept the bonus
c. may be illegally accepting payment
d. both a and c

341. A resident manager who is a salaried employee of the owner and only manages the property where she lives needs:
a. a salesperson license
b. an associate broker license
c. a broker license
d. no license

342. A management agreement most often creates which type of agency relationship?
a. Special agency
b. Agency by proxy
c. General agency
d. No agency relationship

343. The primary goal of a property manager should be:
a. to produce the highest possible net operating income from the property
b. collecting rents
c. residing on the property
d. screening tenants

344. To save on payroll and employee costs, some property managers are:
a. performing maintenance functions themselves
b. cutting costs by not allowing preventative maintenance activities
c. subcontracting individuals to perform maintenance tasks
d. attempting to allow items to break in hopes of collecting insurance cover age

345. A forecast of expected income and expenses projected over, for example, a five-year term is known as a(n):
a. operating budget
b. capital reserve budget
c. stabilized budget
d. variable expense budget predictable but subject to the needs of the property at any time

346. Which of the following should NOT influence a manager's strategy for marketing available rental space?
a. Present demand for space
b. Racial composition of the neighborhood
c. Tenant selection process
d. Newness of the project

347. The type of property where a manager may be more involved with the physical management of the property than with other types of management responsibilities is:
a. storefronts
b. office buildings
c. industrial property
d. condominiums and cooperatives

348. Which of the following designations is given by the Institute of Real Estate Management?
a. NYARM
b. BOMI
c. CPM
d. ABO

349. Which of the following is NOT a consideration for the property manager in setting rental rates?
a. Setting higher rates for families with children
b. The owner's goals
c. Supply and demand
d. Present vacancy rental rates

350. Adequate insurance coverage has to do with:
a. selecting tenants who will pay the rent on time and not need to be evicted
b. controlling and limiting financial risk by purchasing adequate insurance coverage
c. preventative maintenance
d. corrective maintenance

General Business Law (Broker course only)

351. Negotiable instruments are a substitute for:
a. contracts
b. money
c. deferred credit
d. mortgages

352. In New York, a corporation is formed by:
a. a contract between the parties
b. filing a certificate of incorporation
c. filing of a lis pendens
d. filing an agreement with the county clerk

353. The signor of a check is known as the:
a. drawer
b. drawee
c. payee
d. borrower

354. Which of the following applies to partnerships?
a. It may hold title to real estate
b. Partners have to have the same degree of interest in the partnership
c. Partners have to have the same degree of management authority
d. It is limited to two partners

355. An exemption to the Chapter 7 bankruptcy filing is a(n):
a. in rem
b. homestead
c. unified credit
d. tuition

356. The public official who oversees the registration of condominiums and cooperatives in New York is the:
a. State Comptroller
b. State Treasurer
c. Attorney General
d. local county clerk

357. The U.S. Supreme Court:
a. hears appeals from the highest state courts
b. holds trials with juries and witnesses
c. makes no final decisions
d. hears cases from lower state courts

358. The theory that all persons involved in legal matters have a legal proceeding according to established rules is called:
a. *caveat emptor*
b. justice for all
c. *ad valorem*
d. due process

359. Which of the following is NOT a way that legal disputes can be resolved?
a. Litigation
b. Mediation
c. Arbitration
d. Stagnation

360. The type of bankruptcy in which the debtor's nonexempt property is sold for cash, the proceeds distributed to creditors, and unpaid debts discharged is called:
a. Chapter 13
b. Chapter 11
c. Chapter 7
d. Chapter 10

Sample Licensing Exams

The following four practice exams, two for the salesperson and two for the broker are formatted to match the New York State licensing exam. That is, the topics, and the number of questions for each topic are similar to that of the actual test. The total number of exam questions, 75 for the salesperson, and 100 for the broker, are the same number as the state licensing exam. Because the practice exams are weighted to match the actual test, your performance on these should be a good indicator of your performance on the state exam.

Tear out the Answer Sheet on the next pages, and use it to record your responses. You may want to copy the blank answer sheet so that you can use it a second time.

Complete the practice exams under exam conditions-find a quiet place and allow 1.5 for each salesperson exam and 2.5 uninterrupted hours for each broker exam. This is the same amount of time allotted to the state exams. After completing the exam, check your answers with the "Answer Key for Practice Exams" at the back of this guide. Review all incorrect answers. The rationale for the correct answer appears in the Answer Key. For a complete study experience, use the references in the Answer Key to review the related content in the textbooks, *New York Real Estate for Salespersons, 5th e* or *New York Real Estate for Brokers, 5th e*.

Salesperson Practice Exam I

1. ______________
2. ______________
3. ______________
4. ______________
5. ______________
6. ______________
7. ______________
8. ______________
9. ______________
10. ______________
11. ______________
12. ______________
13. ______________
14. ______________
15. ______________
16. ______________
17. ______________
18. ______________
19. ______________
20. ______________
21. ______________
22. ______________
23. ______________
24. ______________
25. ______________
26. ______________
27. ______________
28. ______________
29. ______________
30. ______________
31. ______________
32. ______________
33. ______________
34. ______________
35. ______________
36. ______________
37. ______________
38. ______________
39. ______________
40. ______________
41. ______________
42. ______________
43. ______________
44. ______________
45. ______________
46. ______________
47. ______________
48. ______________
49. ______________
50. ______________
51. ______________
52. ______________
53. ______________
54. ______________
55. ______________
56. ______________
57. ______________
58. ______________
59. ______________
60. ______________
61. ______________
62. ______________
63. ______________
64. ______________
65. ______________
66. ______________
67. ______________
68. ______________
69. ______________
70. ______________
71. ______________
72. ______________
73. ______________
74. ______________
75. ______________

Salesperson Practice Exam 2

1. ______________
2. ______________
3. ______________
4. ______________
5. ______________
6. ______________
7. ______________
8. ______________
9. ______________
10. ______________
11. ______________
12. ______________
13. ______________
14. ______________
15. ______________
16. ______________
17. ______________
18. ______________
19. ______________
20. ______________
21. ______________
22. ______________
23. ______________
24. ______________
25. ______________
26. ______________
27. ______________
28. ______________
29. ______________
30. ______________
31. ______________
32. ______________
33. ______________
34. ______________
35. ______________
36. ______________
37. ______________
38. ______________
39. ______________
40. ______________
41. ______________
42. ______________
43. ______________
44. ______________
45. ______________
46. ______________
47. ______________
48. ______________
49. ______________
50. ______________
51. ______________
52. ______________
53. ______________
54. ______________
55. ______________
56. ______________
57. ______________
58. ______________
59. ______________
60. ______________
61. ______________
62. ______________
63. ______________
64. ______________
65. ______________
66. ______________
67. ______________
68. ______________
69. ______________
70. ______________
71. ______________
72. ______________
73. ______________
74. ______________
75. ______________

Broker Practice Exam 1

1. ______________
2. ______________
3. ______________
4. ______________
5. ______________
6. ______________
7. ______________
8. ______________
9. ______________
10. ______________
11. ______________
12. ______________
13. ______________
14. ______________
15. ______________
16. ______________
17. ______________
18. ______________
19. ______________
20. ______________
21. ______________
22. ______________
23. ______________
24. ______________
25. ______________
26. ______________
27. ______________
28. ______________
29. ______________
30. ______________
31. ______________
32. ______________
33. ______________
34. ______________
35. ______________
36. ______________
37. ______________
38. ______________
39. ______________
40. ______________
41. ______________
42. ______________
43. ______________
44. ______________
45. ______________
46. ______________
47. ______________
48. ______________
49. ______________
50. ______________
51. ______________
52. ______________
53. ______________
54. ______________
55. ______________
56. ______________
57. ______________
58. ______________
59. ______________
60. ______________
61. ______________
62. ______________
63. ______________
64. ______________
65. ______________
66. ______________
67. ______________
68. ______________
69. ______________
70. ______________
71. ______________
72. ______________
73. ______________
74. ______________
75. ______________
76. ______________
77. ______________
78. ______________
79. ______________
80. ______________
81. ______________
82. ______________
83. ______________
84. ______________
85. ______________
86. ______________
87. ______________
88. ______________
89. ______________
90. ______________
91. ______________
92. ______________
93. ______________
94. ______________
95. ______________
96. ______________
97. ______________
98. ______________
99. ______________
100. ______________

Broker Practice Exam 2

1. ______
2. ______
3. ______
4. ______
5. ______
6. ______
7. ______
8. ______
9. ______
10. ______
11. ______
12. ______
13. ______
14. ______
15. ______
16. ______
17. ______
18. ______
19. ______
20. ______
21. ______
22. ______
23. ______
24. ______
25. ______
26. ______
27. ______
28. ______
29. ______
30. ______
31. ______
32. ______
33. ______
34. ______
35. ______
36. ______
37. ______
38. ______
39. ______
40. ______
41. ______
42. ______
43. ______
44. ______
45. ______
46. ______
47. ______
48. ______
49. ______
50. ______
51. ______
52. ______
53. ______
54. ______
55. ______
56. ______
57. ______
58. ______
59. ______
60. ______
61. ______
62. ______
63. ______
64. ______
65. ______
66. ______
67. ______
68. ______
69. ______
70. ______
71. ______
72. ______
73. ______
74. ______
75. ______
76. ______
77. ______
78. ______
79. ______
80. ______
81. ______
82. ______
83. ______
84. ______
85. ______
86. ______
87. ______
88. ______
89. ______
90. ______
91. ______
92. ______
93. ______
94. ______
95. ______
96. ______
97. ______
98. ______
99. ______
100. ______

Salesperson Practice Exam 1

License Law and Regulations (3 hours) (3 questions)

1 The licensure term for real estate salespersons and brokers is:
a. one year
b. two years
c. three years
d. four years

2. A salesperson may receive compensation from:
a. his client
b. his principal
c. his sponsoring broker
d. any licensed broker

3. A salesperson may draw legal documents:
a. with permission of her sponsoring broker only
b. under no circumstances
c. with permission of the principal
d. if the salesperson has a notary public license

Law of Agency including Independent Contractor (11 hours) (11 questions)

4. If the parties to a residential real estate transaction agree to dual agency representation:
a. all confidential information given to the agent by the seller or buyer must be disclosed to both parties
b. both seller and buyer must pay a full commission to the agent
c. both seller and purchaser forfeit the right to undivided loyalty by the agent
d. DOS must be informed of the agreement

5. Which of the following is an illegal type of payment arrangement for brokers?
a. Percentage of final sales price
b. Flat fee
c. Commission schedule set forth by the local board of REALTORS®
d. Referral fee

6. Belinda, a salesperson, works for Broker Barry and in that capacity has received informed consent from a seller to represent him in the sale of his home. What is Belinda's relationship to this seller/principal?
a. Broker's agent
b. Dual agent
c. Subagent
d. Buyer agent

7. In a buyer agency relationship, the buyer is the:
a. customer
b. principal
c. subagent
d. third party

8. The agency disclosure form is required in which of the following circumstances?
a. At the time that a seller enters into a listing agreement with a broker
b. When prospects enter an open house
c. When prospects call to inquire about a property
d. At the closing

9. Belle Properties Brokerage and Ruby Real Estate decided that, since they were the only two companies that offered residential property for sale in a small town, they would both charge the same commission rate. These two firms are guilty of:
a. nothing at all
b. an illegal group boycott
c. illegal price fixing
d. an illegal market allocation agreement

10. In a dual agency situation within a brokerage firm, with disclosure and informed consent, one agent can represent the buyer and one the seller. Both of these agents are called:
    a. designated agents
    b. listing agents
    c. mandatory agents
    d. broker's agents

11. The sellers tell Carlos, a real estate agent, that the basement of their house floods every spring. The sellers do not wish to disclose this information. What should Carlos do?
    a. Agree with his sellers
    b. Inform his sellers that this information must be disclosed
    c. Obtain a signed release from the sellers so that Agent Carlos is not liable should there be a lawsuit
    d. Refuse to take a listing since the property has a material defect

12. What do subagents, listing agents, seller agents, and single agents have in common? They:
    a. are all dual agents
    b. all represent the seller
    c. all must belong to the multiple listing service
    d. are all cooperating agents

13. If a salesperson is NOT paid according to hours worked, the salesperson is most likely classified by IRS as a(n):
    a. common law employee
    b. statutory employee
    c. independent contractor
    d. sales associate

14. Regulations governing the status of employees or independent contractors are determined by:
    a. the broker
    b. New York State Association of REALTORS®
    c. federal and state statutes
    d. Department of State

Legal Issues Estates and Interests (3 hours) (3 questions)

15. Mike and Mindy held title to a property together with no right of survivorship. They most likely held the property:
    a. as joint tenants
    b. as tenants in common
    c. in severalty
    d. as joint tenants by the entirety

16. Which of the following water rights belong to an owner of property bordering a flowing body of water?
    a. Subsurface rights
    b. Riparian rights
    c. Chattel rights
    d. Bundle of rights

17. Juan plans to sell some household furnishings when he sells his house. He will most likely use a document called a (n):
    a. sales contract
    b. bill of sale
    c. transfer affidavit
    d. purchase offer

Legal Issues Liens and Easements (2.5 hours) (3 questions)

18. Real property taxes are examples of:
    a. voluntary specific liens
    b. involuntary specific liens
    c. voluntary general liens
    d. involuntary general liens

19. A lien filed by an individual who provides labor to a property and is NOT paid is called a:
    a. *lis pendens*
    b. subordination lien
    c. mechanic's lien
    d. real property judgment

20. Goldie allows her neighbor, Mattie, to use a path on her property to access the lakefront. Which of the following is TRUE?
    a. Goldie's property is the servient tenement
    b. This is an encroachment
    c. This is a type of lien
    d. This is type of grant

Legal Issues
Deeds (2.5 hours) (3 questions)

21. For a deed to be eligible for recording, it must have which of the following? A(n):
    a. metes and bounds description
    b. *habendum* clause
    c. acknowledgment
    d. covenant of warranty

22. Which of the following is NOT a judicial deed?
    a. Executor's deed
    b. Guardian's deed
    c. Sheriff's deed
    d. Installment land contract

Legal Issues
Title Closing and Costs (2 hours) (2 questions)

23. The seller will accept a purchase money mortgage from the buyer. On the closing statement, this amount appears as a:
    a. seller debit
    b. seller credit
    c. buyer debit
    d. balancing disbursement

24. Which of the following is NOT generally a purchaser closing cost?
    a. Title insurance policy
    b. Mortgage recording tax
    c. Discount points
    d. Delinquent real property taxes

The Contract of Sale and Leases
Leases (1 hour) (1 question)

25. Amy transferred her lease contract to her friend, Jamie. Jamie will now have to make the lease payments to the landlord. Which of the following has taken place? A(n):
    a. assignment
    b. sublease
    c. constructive eviction
    d. holdover tenancy

The Contract of Sale and Leases
Contracts (1 hour) (2 questions)

26. A court ordered Nancy to pay Tessie $10,000 because she did not purchase Tessie's property even though they had a valid contract. This monetary payment is called:
    a. specific performance
    b. rescission
    c. liquidated damages
    d. novation

The Contract of Sale and Leases
Contract Preparation (1 hour) (1 question)

27. In order for a real estate salesperson to prepare a fill-in-the-blanks contract of sale approved by the Board of REALTORS®, the contract must:
    a. be less than three pages
    b. be clearly captioned and easy to understand
    c. have an attorney review clause
    d. notarized

Real Estate Finance (5 hours) (5 questions)

28. Which type of mortgage loan requires, for example, monthly payments of $1,200 for 15 years and a final payment of $10,000?
    a. Graduated payment mortgage
    b. Flexible payment mortgage
    c. Wraparound mortgage
    d. Balloon mortgage

29. Up to the time a foreclosure sale is held, a borrower who has defaulted on his loan may be able to regain his property by paying the outstanding debt. This is a (n):
    a. deed in lieu of foreclosure
    b. equity of redemption
    c. deficiency judgment
    d. recovery grace period

30. The clause in a mortgage stating that a lender may declare the entire balance due if the borrower is in default is called the:
    a. prepayment penalty clause
    b. granting clause
    c. acceleration clause
    d. defeasance clause

31. In which type of mortgage are two or more parcels of real estate pledged as security for a mortgage debt?
    a. Package mortgage
    b. Blanket mortgage
    c. Bridge loan
    d. Installment land contract

32. An agency of HUD that insures loans to protect lenders against financial loss is:
    a. Fannie Mae
    b. Sonny Mae
    c. FHA
    d. Freddie Mac

Land Use Regulations (3 hours) (3 questions)

33. The New York law regulating the sale of unimproved lots across state lines is called:
    a. the Interstate Land Sales Full Disclosure Act
    b. Article 9-A of the Real Property Law
    c. the State Environmental Quality Review Act
    d. the Uniform Fire Prevention and Building Code

34. The taking of property under the government's right of eminent domain is called:
    a. escheat
    b. estoppel
    c. *in rem*
    d. condemnation

35. Emma wishes to add another story to her home; however, the new height would not comply with the current zoning ordinance. She would need to apply for a(n):
    a. nonconforming use
    b. use variance
    c. area variance
    d. spot zone

Construction and Environmental Issues (5 hours) (5 questions)

36. The foundation walls of a property are usually composed of:
    a. concrete
    b. wood
    c. steel
    d. iron

37. The area under the roof extension is called the:
    a. frieze board
    b. fascia
    c. soffit
    d. sheathing

38. For residential one- and two-family properties in New York, and condominiums and cooperatives, which of the following is required at closing?
    a. Smoke alarm and carbon monoxide detector affidavit
    b. Carbon monoxide detector affidavit only
    c. Agency disclosure
    d. Minimum compliance affidavit

39. The New York law that requires preparation of an environmental impact statement on a property that a government body has the jurisdiction to review is the:
    a. Superfund Amendment
    b. State Environmental Quality Review Act
    c. Real Estate Settlement Procedures Act
    d. Comprehensive Environmental Response, Compensation and Liability Act (CERCLA)

40. Sales contracts used for target properties under the Residential Lead-Based Hazard Reduction Act must include:
    a. nothing different than before the law was enacted
    b. specific disclosure and acknowledgment language
    c. approval by an agent of HUD
    d. an attachment indicating the exact age of the property

Valuation Process and Pricing Properties (3 hours) (3 questions)

41. The appraisal approach most similar to a comparative market analysis is the:
    a. income approach
    b. cost approach
    c. capitalization approach
    d. sales comparison approach

42. A land utilization study that does not necessarily produce an estimate of value can be best defined as a(n):
    a. evaluation
    b. appraisal
    c. comparative market analysis
    d. value in use

43. One of the most important aspects of marketing a property is:
    a. pricing the property at the lowest possible price to make sure of a timely sale
    b. knowing the competition and adjusting pricing and marketing strategies accordingly
    c. ignoring the competition and allowing the property to sell based on its own merits
    d. effecting a sale within 18 months of the listing date

Human Rights and Fair Housing (4 hours) (4 questions)

44. Individuals who visit real estate offices posing as prospective home seekers to see if race influences the buying process are called:
    a. civil rights inspectors
    b. real estate licensees
    c. testers
    d. inspectors

45. The owner of a single-family property in Syosset, Long Island asks a salesperson to find a "nice couple without children" to purchase their home. The broker:
    a. may take this listing because the property owner has the right to specify who purchases his property
    b. may take the listing but must ask for a written statement from the owner to cover any liability problems
    c. may take the listing only with permission of her supervising broker
    d. must refuse this listing

46. The term blockbusting refers to:
    a. phone calls soliciting prospective buyers or sellers in a cease and desist zone
    b. offering property for sale only to persons of a certain race
    c. prompting homeowners to sell their properties due to the entry of certain persons of a particular race or religion into the neighborhood
    d. the government's right of eminent domain to condemn and destroy older vacant buildings in a neighborhood

47. The lending department of Money Bank decided not to make home improvement loans to residents of Lonely Heights because a survey completed by the bank showed a higher number of single-parent families living in that neighborhood. Money Bank is guilty of:
    a. redlining
    b. steering
    c. nothing at all
    d. blockbusting

Real Estate Mathematics (1 hour) (2 questions)

48. A real estate salesperson sells a property for $90,000. The commission on this sale to the real estate firm with whom the salesperson is associated is 6%. The salesperson receives 60% of the total commission paid to the real estate firm. What is the firm's share of the commission in dollars?
    a. $2,450
    b. $3,240
    c. $4,500
    d. $4,750

49. If the assessed value of a property is $217,500 and the tax value is 100% of the assessed value, what is the annual tax if the rate is $2.00 per $100?
    a. $2,450
    b. $3,500
    c. $3,475
    d. $4,350

Municipal Agencies (2 hours) (2 questions)

50. A municipal agency is given the job of mapping a large parcel of land that was granted to the city. Which state agency would most probably be the lead agency for this project?
    a. Assessor's office
    b. Zoning board of appeals
    c. Planning board
    d. Architectural review board

51. A town on Long Island does not allow any buildings higher than four stories. Francesca wants to add two more floors to her two-story building. Which agencies might be involved in reviewing her construction application?
    a. Zoning board of appeals
    b. Architectural review board
    c. Conservation advisory council
    d. Both a and b

Property Insurance (2 hours) (2 questions)

52. The Kelly's had $2,500 worth of damage to their house when a tree fell through the front window during a storm. They received a payment of $1,500 from the insurance company. Which term explains the missing $1,000?
    a. Peril
    b. Deductible
    c. Umbrella
    d. Endorsement

53. The Lee's damaged their oven in a small kitchen fire and were reimbursed for the actual cost of replacing the oven. This means that their coverage was:
    a. for actual cash value
    b. for replacement cost
    c. for personal liability
    d. an umbrella policy

Taxes and Assessments (3 hours) (3 questions)

54. A type of map, drawn to scale, showing all of the property parcels with a city, town, or village, and their size shape and dimensions is called a (n):
    a. plat
    b. blueprint
    c. survey
    d. tax map

55. A property assessing unit may be a (n):
    a. city
    b. town
    c. county
    d. all of the above

56. Municipalities use residential assessment ratios:
    a. for revaluation projects
    b. if there are less than five residential sales that year
    c. for board of assessment review grievances
    d. to determine tax exemptions

Condominiums and Cooperatives (4 hours) (3 questions)

57. Which of the following is FALSE regarding a cooperative?
    a. It is a non for profit corporation
    b. It is formed for the benefit of its members
    c. It is owned by the cooperative cooperation
    d. A unit owner receives a deed to his individual unit

58. The owner or developer of a condominium or cooperative is called the:
    a. director
    b. sponsor
    c. trustor
    d. originator

59. The New York Attorney General's rules for testing the market for new condominium or cooperative developments are contained in:
    a. the UCC-1 statement
    b. the CPS1 statement
    c. Civil Practice Rules and Procedure
    d. Section 443 of the Real Property Law

Commercial and Investment Properties (10 hours) (9 questions)

60. An operating statement adjusted to reflect a potential change in income and expenses based upon the investor's knowledge of the real estate market is called a(n):
    a. cash flow statement
    b. operating statement
    c. statement of net worth
    d. pro forma statement

61. The net monthly income of a seven-unit apartment building is $2,250. The capitalization rate the lender uses is 7%. What is the value of the building?
    a. $299,010
    b. $385,714
    c. $410,926
    d. $450,509

62. A process that calculates the value of an asset in the past, present, and future is called:
    a. leverage
    b. the time value of money
    c. debt service
    d. net operating income

63. If a business property has an asset value of $1,000,000 with a debt of $750,000, what is the debt ratio?
    a. 50 percent
    b. 60 percent
    c. 75 percent
    d. 90 percent

64. Land is a more risky type of real estate investment for all of the following reasons EXCEPT:
    a. it may be more difficult to obtain financing
    b. there are no improvements on it
    c. it cannot be depreciated for tax purposes
    d. it always has less resale value

65. Income received on a property without deducting expenses is called:
    a. NOI
    b. gross income
    c. net income
    d. debt service

66. The net proceeds or cash remaining after all expenses and debt services are paid is called:
    a. tax shelter
    b. gross income
    c. cash flow
    d. cash-on-cash return

67. The ratio of annual before-tax cash flow to the total amount of cash invested, expressed as a percentage is called the:
    a. capitalization rate
    b. rate of return
    c. income expense ratio
    d. cash-on-cash return

68. Investment in commercial real estate does NOT provide:
    a. deductible expenses
    b. income shelters
    c. depreciation allowances
    d. guaranteed profit over time

Income Tax Issues in Real Estate Transactions (3 hours) (3 questions)

69. Which of the following is NOT a tax bracket for federal income tax purposes?
    a. 15 percent
    b. 25 percent
    c. 28 percent
    d. 39 percent

70. Which of the following items are allowed federal tax deductions on home ownership?
    a. Interest
    b. Principal
    c. Property taxes
    d. Both a and c

71. Annie and Xavier, a married couple, bought their house five years ago for $350,000.They are in the 35 percent tax bracket. They recently sold it for $400,000. What is the amount of capital gains tax they must pay when they file their tax return?
    a. $2500
    b. $7,500
    c. $50,000
    d. no capital gains tax

Mortgage Brokerage (1 hour) (2 questions)

72. If an individual holds a real estate broker's license and wants to apply for a mortgage broker registration, which of the following documents must be submitted to the NYS Department of Financial Services with his mortgage broker application?
    a. Dual agency affidavit
    b. Estoppel certificate
    c. Fee application
    d. Lender certification

73. Should a real estate salesperson want a mortgage broker registration, what is the experience required?
    a. Real estate salespersons do not need other experience to become a mortgage broker
    b. One year experience in the mortgage business
    c. Two years experience in the mortgage business
    d. One year experience managing a real estate brokerage office

Property Management (2 hours) (2 questions)

74. Advisors to property managers who focus on long-term financial planning rather than day-to-day operations of the property are:
    a. real estate gurus
    b. resident managers
    c. financial advisors
    d. asset managers

75. A document submitted to the property owner outlining the commitment of the manager if employed is the:
    a. management agreement
    b. management proposal
    c. property projection
    d. operating expense analysis

Salesperson Practice Exam 2

License Law and Regulations (3 hours) (3 questions)

1. To be licensed as a real estate broker, an individual must be at least how old?
    a. 16
    b. 18
    c. 20
    d. 21

2. Which of the following individuals is exempt from licensure?
    a. Attorneys admitted to practice in the New York courts
    b. Property managers who manage property for more than one individual or company
    c. Individuals who only list property for sale
    d. Auctioneers who only auction commercial real estate

3. To save on paperwork, Broker Bright decides to combine her office operating account with the deposits obtained from contracts of sale. Broker Bright is guilty of:
    a. nothing at all
    b. illegal commingling of funds
    c. an unauthorized practice of law
    d. accepting money without authorization

Law of Agency including Independent Contractor (11 hours) (11 questions)

4. A net listing is one:
    a. that requires the broker to have a fixed price for the property
    b. that is legal in New York
    c. that most brokers would prefer
    d. in which the seller specifies a certain amount of money to be received upon sale of the property and all monies above that amount are the broker's commission

5. A broker's agent is hired by the:
    a. principal
    b. seller
    c. customer
    d. broker

6. Which of the following is TRUE regarding dual agency relationships in New York?
    a. They are permissible with timely disclosure and informed consent
    b. They are illegal under all circumstances
    c. They are allowed only in commercial transactions
    d. They are allowed only in the sale of condominium or cooperative properties

7. A listing agreement in which the property is listed with only one broker who is entitled to a commission if he sells the property but not if the owner sells the property is called a(n):
    a. exclusive-right-to-sell agreement
    b. open listing agreement
    c. net listing agreement
    d. exclusive agency agreement

8. The first law to address antitrust violations was the:
    a. Clayton Antitrust Act
    b. Real Estate Settlement Procedures Act
    c. Sherman Antitrust Act
    d. New York Real Property Law

9. Sell-It-Today Brokerage requires that purchasers of its listed property apply for a mortgage with EZ Money Mortgage Company. This practice is:
   a. perfectly acceptable
   b. an example of an illegal tie-in arrangement
   c. an example of an illegal group boycott
   d. an example of an illegal market allocation agreement

10. An agency relationship created by an oral or written agreement between principal and agent is a (n):
    a. implied agency
    b. express agency
    c. dual agency
    d. power of attorney

11. Martin signs an exclusive right to sell listing agreement for six months with Broker Gerald. Within one month, Martin sells his house himself and refuses to pay a commission to Gerald. Martin's behavior is a possible:
    a. reformation
    b. breach of contract
    c. injunction
    d. assignment

12. Advance informed consent to dual agency is:
    a. illegal in New York
    b. only can occur in commercial transactions
    c. is used only in the marketing of condominiums and cooperatives
    d. is allowable in New York with disclosure and informed consent

13. Which of the following activities is NOT an element of an independent contractor relationship?
    a. No compensation for specific number of hours worked
    b. Salespersons can work any hours they choose
    c. Commissions are paid with deductions for income taxes
    d. Either the salesperson or broker may terminate the relationship at any time

14. Real estate licensees are classified as independent contractors under:
    a. Section 3508 (a) (b) of the IRS Code
    b. common law
    c. Article 12-A of the Real Property Law
    d. Section 443 of the Real Property Law

Legal Issues Estates and Interests (3 hours) (3 questions)

15. Which of the following is NOT one of the four unities required for joint tenancy?
    a. Time
    b. Interest
    c. Partition
    d. Possession

16. Francois and Helena purchase a property and their attorney tells them that their title offers the most complete form of ownership. Their ownership right is:
    a. fee simple on condition
    b. fee simple absolute
    c. fee simple defeasible
    d. a life estate

17. Kelly's mother deeds Kelly her beach house for Kelly's lifetime. Then the property goes to the A.S.P.C.A in memory of mother's favorite cat upon daughter Kelly's death. This is an example of a:
    a. fee simple absolute
    b. leasehold
    c. joint tenancy
    d. life estate

Legal Issues Liens and Easements (2.5 hours) (2 questions)

18. A judgment is an example of a(n):
    a. voluntary specific lien
    b. involuntary specific lien
    c. voluntary general lien
    d. involuntary general lien

19. A legal notice that a lawsuit is pending concerning title to a particular property is called a(n):
    a. injunction
    b. *lis pendens*
    c. judgment
    d. mechanic's lien

20. Lionel buys a cabin in a remote area and has no road access except through his neighbor's adjoining property. Lionel's property requires a(n):
    a. easement by condemnation
    b. negative easement
    c. easement by necessity
    d. encroachment

Legal Issues
Deeds (2.5 hours) (2 questions)

21. A type of deed used in bankruptcy proceedings and foreclosures is a(n):
    a. sheriff's deed
    b. executor's deed
    c. referee's deed
    d. guardian's deed

22. In order to claim title by adverse possession in New York, the use must be open and notorious for how many years?
    a. 5
    b. 10
    c. 15
    d. 20

Title Closing and Costs
(2 hours) (2 questions)

23. Which of the following would most likely prevent a closing from taking place?
    a. The imposition of discount points by the lender
    b. The hiring of an attorney by the purchaser
    c. The existence of outstanding unpaid liens against the property
    d. A purchase money mortgage given to the seller by the purchaser

24. On the closing statement, which of the following appears as a buyer credit?
    a. Earnest money deposit
    b. Prepaid real property taxes
    c. Prepaid insurance premium
    d. Sale of personal property

The Contract of Sale and Leases
Leases(1 hour) (1 question)

25. A lease that automatically renews itself for another time frame at the end of the lease term unless notice is given to terminate is a(n):
    a. illegal lease
    b. periodic lease
    c. standard lease
    d. proprietary lease

The Contract of Sale and Leases
Contracts (1 hour) (1 question)

26. An option is a contract that:
    a. specifies a time limit within which the optionee may choose to purchase or lease real property
    b. is a bilateral implied contract
    c. does not define a specific sales price
    d. conveys title when the optionee signs the contract

The Contract of Sale and Leases
Contract Preparation (1 hour) (1 question)

27. Which of the following is NOT a part of a real estate contract of sale?
    a. Contingency
    b. Addenda
    c. Rider
    d. Codicil

Real Estate Finance (5 hours) (5 questions)

28. A HUD agency that purchases VA and FHA mortgages on the secondary mortgage market is called:
    a. RHA
    b. SONYMA
    c. Ginnie Mae
    d. FDIC

29. A mortgage clause that allows a lender to declare the balance due if the borrower sells the property is the:
    a. prepayment penalty clause
    b. alienation clause
    c. granting clause
    d. defeasance clause

30. A mortgage that provides for paying the debt by monthly payment of principal and interest and in which the interest portion of the payments decreases as the principal portion increases is a(n):
    a. balloon mortgage
    b. installment land contract
    c. swing loan
    d. amortized mortgage

31. The federal law that provides for accurate advertising of financial credit terms is called:
    a. The Real Estate Settlement Procedures Act
    b. Regulation Z
    c. The Community Development Act
    d. Anti-Predatory Lending Law

32. A type of loan in which the mortgage rate floats based on the fluctuations of a standard index is called a(n):
    a. adjustable rate mortgage
    b. straight term mortgage
    c. fixed rate mortgage
    d. fluctuating mortgage specified time.

Land Use Regulations (3 hours) (3 questions)

33. Marcia has recently purchased an old barn in a rural community in upstate New York and wishes to turn it into an art studio. Which administrative body must she apply to for a variance? The:
    a. town planning board
    b. zoning board of appeals
    c. local building department
    d. county clerk

34. A document that shows the boundaries and physical dimensions of a property is called a(n):
    a. feasibility study
    b. plat
    c. survey
    d. architectural rending

35. Parks and forest land could be classified as being in which zone?
    a. Commercial
    b. Residential
    c. Public open space
    d. Institutional

Construction and Environment (5 hours) (5 questions)

36. A sprayed insulation that caused noxious fumes is called:
    a. loose fill insulation
    b. rigid insulation
    c. UFFI
    d. batt insulation

37. The amount of electrical current flowing through a wire is called:
    a. voltage
    b. amperage
    c. milligaus
    d. wattage

38. The New York statute that mandates minimum R-factors for insulation is the:
 a. Real Property Law
 b. Energy Conservation Construction Code
 c. Emergency Tenant Protection Act
 d. Sanitary Code

39. Which of the following is exempt from disclosure regulations of the Residential Lead-Based Hazard Reduction Act?
 a. A duplex built before 1978
 b. A single-family residence built before 1978
 c. Senior citizen housing
 d. A cooperative apartment built before 1978

40. One of the most prevalent concerns of underground storage tanks is:
 a. leakage
 b. combustion
 c. explosion
 d. fire

Valuation Process and Pricing Properties (3 hours) (3 questions)

41. One of the most important factors in selecting comparables for a comparative market analysis is to select properties:
 a. within a 50-mile radius of the subject property
 b. older than the subject property
 c. as close in location as possible to the comparable
 d. that have inferior curb appeal to the subject property

42. Surveyors' and appraisers' fees in relation to the development of a property are called:
 a. hard costs
 b. indirect costs
 c. direct costs
 d. impact fees

43. An arm's length transaction means that:
 a. the parties are not related either as relatives or business associates
 b. no salesperson or broker is involved in the transaction
 c. the transaction is a cash transaction and no financing is required
 d. the transaction takes place within six months of being placed on the market

Human Rights and Fair Housing (4 hours) (4 questions)

44. Hattie wants to sell her home in Kingston, New York. She decides not to use a broker so that she can sell her property to whomever she wants. Which of the following is TRUE? Hattie:
 a. is exempt from all fair housing laws as long as she does not use a broker
 b. is exempt from fair housing laws in the sale of a single-family home
 c. can only sell her property to whomever she want if she does not advertise
 d. and/or a broker are not entitled to any exemptions to fair housing laws in the sale of a single-family home in New York

45. The fine for a first offense in violation of the Federal Fair Housing Act can be up to:
 a. $1,000
 b. $5,000
 c. $10,000
 d. $20,000

46. Which of the following is required by law for real estate brokers?
 a. Memorizing the NYS Division of Human Rights poster
 b. Prominently displaying the HUD fair housing poster
 c. Accepting all real estate listings
 d. Keeping a copy of the New York Human Rights Law in the office as a reference

47. One of the differences between federal human rights law and New York human rights law is that the:
    a. federal law does not address discrimination based on familial status and the New York law does
    b. federal law does not address discrimination based on disability and the New York law does
    c. federal law has fewer protected classes than the New York law
    d. federal law does not address discrimination based on sex and the New York law does

Real Estate Mathematics (1 hour) (2 questions)

48. If Calvin buys three parcels of land for $8,000 and sells them as four separate parcels for $9,000 each, what percent profit does he make?
    a. 33%
    b. 40 %
    c. 45%
    d. 50%

49. The owner of a rectangular parcel of land measuring 500 feet wide (front) by 150 feet long is offered $20 per front foot or $5,000 per acre. What is the amount of the higher offer?
    a. $3,469
    b. $6,400
    c. $10,000
    d. $12,500

Municipal Agencies (2 hours) (2 questions)

50. Which of the following is NOT a function of the building department?
    a. Code compliance
    b. Requiring landowners to restore or rehabilitate a historic structure
    c. Inspection during construction
    d. Issuing building permits

51. Evelyn wants to grant an area of undeveloped wetlands to her town. What agency would most likely accept this grant?
    a. Conservation advisory council
    b. Planning board
    c. Architectural review board
    d. Building department

Property Insurance (2 hours) (2 questions)

52. Which of the following is FALSE?
    a. Lenders require homeowner's insurance to obtain a mortgage
    b. Perils are events that are always excluded from payment on the insurance policy
    c. An endorsement is an attachment to the insurance policy
    d. An insurance policy is a legal contract

53. Sam has an HO-3 homeowner's policy. When his storage shed was damaged in a fire, he received $20,000 on his insurance claim. Based on this information, what amount of insurance did he have on the residence?
    a. $100,000
    b. $120,000
    c. $150,000
    d. $200,000

Taxes and Assessments (3 hours) (3 questions)

54. If the assessor determines that the market value of a property is $300,000, and the level of assessment (LOA) in the taxing unit is 75 percent, what is the assessment for that property?
    a. $200,000
    b. $225,000
    c. $250,000
    d. $275,000

55. Property owners are charged an extra amount on their property tax bill for the addition of three new fire trucks in the taxing unit. This charge is known as a (n):
a. tax certiorari
b. reassessment
c. special assessment
d. tax levy

56. A legal action brought by the taxing authority when real property taxes are not paid when due is a(n):
a. *in rem* legal proceeding
b. injunction
c. Article 78 proceeding
d. reformation

Condominiums and Cooperatives (4 hours) (3 questions)

57. In a cooperative, who is generally in charge of the approval of the prospective buyer of a cooperative unit? The:
a. lender
b. board of directors
c. vote of the majority of the shareholders
d. the management company

58. In a cooperative, who owns the common areas? The:
a. the management company
b. the unit owner
c. cooperative corporation
d. all of the above

59. The terms under which a cooperative gives permission to a shareholder to make a structural change to the individual unit is called:
a. a letter of intent
b. house rules
c. a subscription agreement
d. an alteration agreement

Commercial and Investment Properties (10 hours) (9 questions)

60. An investor purchases a $2,300,000 apartment complex with a $600,000 down payment. Each month the cash flow from rentals, less expenses, is $20,000. Over a year's time, the cash-on-cash return would be:
a. 25 percent
b. 28 percent
c. 32 percent
d. 40 percent

61. The profit from income producing property, less income tax, is known as:
a. after tax cash flow
b. before tax cash flow
c. debt service
d. the debt-to- equity ratio

62. If a property generates a $10,000 cash flow and a $2,000 tax loss that is used to offset other income, the after-tax cash flow for an investor in the 35 percent tax bracket is:
a. $3,560
b. $4,200
c. $4,320
d. $5,490

63. A paper income loss on investment property that is sometimes desirable to property owners is known as:
a. gross income
b. debt service
c. leverage
d. a tax shelter

64. What is the value estimate of a property (rounded) if the net operating income is $650,000 and the capitalization rate is 12 percent?
a. $678,000
b. $4,678,000
c. $5,216,000
d. $5,416,667

65. Generally, property owners lease commercial space according to the:
a. rentable square footage
b. usable square footage
c. effective square footage
d. carpetable area

66. Commercial lessees may view the difference between the rentable and usable area in a commercial space as the:
a. vacancy factor
b. loss factor
c. unused perimeter
d. common areas

67. One of the main differences between a loft and other types of commercial space for a lease is that a loft:
a. is not usually divided into rooms
b. is always more expensive per square foot than other types of space
c. always has a private elevator
d. is generally under rent control

68. A lease agreement for commercial property is generally:
a. standard throughout the state
b. customized to the particular space and tenant
c. for ten years or more
d. a periodic lease

Income Tax Issues in Real Estate Transactions (3 hours) (3 questions)

69. JayCee paid $400,000 for an investment property. She also has a loss of $50,000 due to a fire. She values her property at $350,000. This value is the:
a. appraised value
b. adjusted basis
c. basis
d. market value

70. Harry has an ownership interest in a 60-unit apartment building as a limited partner. According to IRS rules, this kind of ownership is:
a. active income
b. passive income
c. portfolio income
d. deductible income

71. In a tax-deferred exchange, the individual who accepts the funds from the sale and handles the contracts is called the:
a. arbitrator
b. mediator
c. qualified intermediary
d. coordinator

Mortgage Brokerage (1 hour) (2 questions)

72. Which of the following documents do mortgage brokers use to make certain disclosures to potential borrowers?
a. Agency disclosure form
b. Pre-approval letter
c. Letter of intent
d. Pre-application disclosure and fee agreement

73. Which of the following is FALSE? A mortgage banker:
a. may lend money
b. may collect the loan payments
c. closes the loan in its own name
d. is licensed by the Federal Deposit Insurance Corporation

Property Management (2 hours) (2 questions)

74. The property manager's fee is generally:
a. a percentage of all rental income when the rent roll exceeds a certain pre agreed upon amount
b. a lump sum paid in advance on a yearly basis
c. 25 percent of the rental income
d. a base fee and a percentage of the rents collected

75. Laurel, a real estate broker, is also a property manager for an eight-unit residential property. In her role as property manager, Laurel is a (n):
a. general agent
b. fiduciary
c. special agent
d. both a and b

Broker Practice Exam 1

The Broker's Office: Operation, Management, and Supervision (10 hours) (17questions)

1. If a broker accepts deposit money, it may be kept:
   a. with the office operating account
   b. in a separate escrow account in an insured bank
   c. in a safety deposit box
   d. in an interest-bearing stock portfolio account

2. When a listing agent discloses a material defect that he has knowledge of to a prospective buyer, the agent:
   a. has breached the fiduciary duty to the seller
   b. has done the right thing under his/her duty to disclose
   c. may only disclose this defect with permission of the sellers
   d. should report the information to MLS for publication so that prospective buyers will see it there

3. A broker may receive compensation from more than one party in a real estate transaction:
   a. automatically, as long as the other party is an unlicensed individual
   b. automatically, as long as the other party is a licensed individual
   c. with the knowledge and consent of all parties to the transaction
   d. only if the compensation arrangement is approved by MLS

4. According to DOS regulations, which of the following is TRUE?
   a. a broker may not list his home phone number on business cards
   b. a broker may not advertise on television
   c. all ads must indicate that the advertiser is a real estate broker
   d. all ads must include the type of structure, such as Cape Cod, ranch, raised ranch

5. Property condition disclosure forms are completed by the:
   a. seller
   b. buyer
   c. listing broker
   d. cooperating broker

6. When a seller authorizes a broker to procure a specified amount for the property and then allows the broker to keep as a commission any money above this specified amount, this is known as a (n):
   a. illegal open listing
   b. illegal net listing
   c. exclusive agency agreement
   d. exclusive right to sell agreement

7. Ron, a sales agent, has just obtained a listing and has forgotten to ask his sellers if he can put a for sale sign on the property. Since the sellers are out of town, he asks his broker what to do. He may:
   a. put the sign on the property since he has obtained the listing
   b. not put any sign on the property without the permission of the sellers
   c. put the sign on the lawn as long as he has the permission of his broker
   d. put a sign on the lawn without permission as long as it includes the words "licensed real estate broker"

8. Broker Lately had several salespeople under her supervision, all of whom had not renewed their licenses, which had come due last month. Broker Lately:
   a. should not allow these salespeople to transact real estate
   b. may allow the salespeople to transact as it is not the broker's responsibility to make sure salespeople renew their licenses
   c. may allow the salespeople to service existing listings but not obtain new listings
   d. may allow the salespeople to discuss listings and negotiate real estate transactions in the office only but not drive buyers around or visit sellers

9. Under IRS rules, a salesperson violates his independent contractor status if he:
a. becomes an associate broker
b. has specific work hours
c. works under a written contract specifying independent contractor status
d. has no specific work hours

10. The administrative federal agency that has the broad power to declare trade practices unfair is known as the:
a. Attorney General's Office
b. Department of State
c. Federal Trade Commission
d. Department of HUD

11. ABC Realty and Bluebird Realty agreed not to compete in their neighboring towns. ABC Realty would handle all business in the town where it was located, and Bluebird would handle all business in the town where it was located. This is an example of an illegal:
a. market allocation agreement
b. tie-in arrangement
c. price-fixing arrangement
d. group boycott

12. Redding Realty told their buyer customers that as a condition of purchasing one of the firm's listed properties they would have to obtain financing from Quick Mortgage Associates. This is an example of an illegal:
a. group boycott
b. price-fixing arrangement
c. market allocation agreement
d. tie-in arrangement

13. Broker Bleary placed a newspaper ad that did not indicate that he was a broker. This is an example of a(n):
a. lawful advertisement
b. acceptable ad if it is used to advertise listings only
c. blind ad
d. ad that is only permissible in the advertisement of commercial property

14. The fee for an appraisal license in New York is:
a. $150 payable to the NYS Department of State
b. $325 payable to the NYS Department of State
c. $50 payable to the NYS Department of Financial Services
d. $200 payable to the NYS Department of Financial Services

15. When listing one-to-three unit properties, except for condominiums and cooperatives, the agent must provide a (n):
a. profile of the brokerage firm
b. definition of a net listing agreement
c. explanation as to why the use of a multiple listing service is a good idea
d. definition of the difference between exclusive right to sell and exclusive agency agreements

16. Tia works for commercial Broker Sadie in Queens, NY but decides that she also wants to work for a residential broker too. Which of the following applies? This:
a. is allowable under DOS regulations with the acknowledgement of both brokers
b. is not allowable under license law
c. arrangement is permissible only for brokers and not for salespersons
d. arrangement is permissible only if the salesperson holds the second license in a reciprocal state

17. When a salesperson or associate broker terminates their association with the broker, the broker must file a termination of association notice online to DOS with a fee in the amount of:
a. $10
b. $15
c. $25
d. $50

Real Estate Agency Disclosure (4 hours) (10 questions)

18. A seller's broker, in his fiduciary role, may NOT:
    a. advise a seller that a listing price is too high
    b. negotiate on behalf of the seller a price below that at which the property is listed
    c. advise a buyer that the seller is anxious to sell because of a job transfer
    d. represent both the buyer and seller with disclosure and informed consent from both parties

19. The fiduciary relationship between broker and principal allows a broker to:
    a. conceal any material defects to prospective buyers
    b. follow the seller's instructions as to what classes of protected groups under the Human Rights Law should be shown the property
    c. refuse any low offers that she feels will not interest the sellers
    d. obey reasonable and lawful instructions from the principal

20. As to material defects in a property, brokers may be NOT liable because of:
    a. disclosure by the principal
    b. their skill and training
    c. inspection of the property
    d. fraudulent concealment by the principal

21. In New York, franchise firms:
    a. may engage unlicensed individuals to sell real estate to others
    b. are illegal unless they obtain special franchisee permission from DOS
    c. may deduct a portion of the franchise fee from the final commission due to the sales associate
    d. may revoke a broker's license if the franchise fees are not paid

22. Which one of the following does NOT constitute an agent's responsibility to the principal?
    a. Loyalty
    b. Reasonable care
    c. Confidentiality
    d. Legal advice

23. Herman, a seller, lists with a brokerage firm but does not want to accept vicarious liability for any of the agents hired by his broker. Which type of agent can this broker hire to conform to the wishes of his principal?
    a. Broker's agent
    b. Subagent
    c. Dual agent
    d. Double agent

24. In New York, dual agency is:
    a. illegal under all circumstances
    b. legal with timely disclosure and informed consent
    c. legal only in firms that advertise themselves as doing business as dual agents
    d. legal only in buyer brokerage firms

25. A principal who lists a property:
    a. automatically permits subagency
    b. has the option of accepting or rejecting subagency when signing the listing agreement
    c. automatically allows subagency by permitting the property to be placed in the MLS
    d. is not liable, under any circumstances, for the acts of subagents

26. Subagents of the seller:
    a. have no duty to the buyer
    b. only have the duty to disclose whom they represent to the buyer and no other obligation
    c. must deal fairly and ethically with the buyer
    d. owe the same loyalties to the seller as the buyer

27. An undisclosed dual agency is a violation of the Real Property Law and is legally classified as a:
   a. felony
   b. perjury
   c. criminal act
   d. misdemeanor

Real Estate Finance II (5 hours) (12 questions)

28. A clause in the note accompanying a mortgage that states that a borrower may incur a penalty if the mortgage is paid before expiration is known as:
   a. the defeasance clause
   b. novation
   c. the alienation clause
   d. the prepayment penalty clause

29. The importance of the prevailing loan- to-value ratio is in determining:
   a. the down payment amount
   b. whether the mortgage will be sold on the secondary market
   c. the investment quality of the property
   d. the borrower's ability to repay the loan

30. A secondary mortgage institution is known as:
   a. VA
   b. SONYMA
   c. Fannie Mae
   d. FHA

31. A type of gap financing, generally not secured by a mortgage in which the borrower uses the equity that he has in one property to obtain the funds to buy another property, is known as a:
   a. purchase money mortgage
   b. swing loan
   c. package mortgage
   d. convertible mortgage

32. Usually, priority of mortgage liens is established by the date:
   a. the mortgage is drawn
   b. of the closing
   c. the mortgage is recorded
   d. the mortgage is due

33. Melissa arranges to pay the seller of her property a certain sum of money each month. However, the sellers have also transferred title to Melissa in exchange for her promise to pay secured by a lien on the property. The sellers have taken back from Melissa which type of mortgage?
   a. Bridge loan
   b. Installment land contract
   c. Wraparound mortgage
   d. Purchase money mortgage

34. A developer finances his subdivision through a lender who releases a portion of the mortgage lien on each lot as the developer completes the property and pays for each lot. This method of finance is known as:
   a. gap financing
   b. wraparound mortgage financing
   c. release land subdivision financing
   d. sale leaseback

35. A type of transaction in which an owner can free up capital invested in a property and still retain possession and control of the property under a lease is known as a:
   a. sale leaseback
   b. ground lease
   c. wraparound mortgage
   d. purchase money mortgage

36. A long-term lease for unimproved land to be used for construction purposes is known as a:
   a. sale leaseback
   b. periodic lease
   c. gap lease
   d. ground lease

37. At what point is legal title to real property generally transferred to the purchaser under an installment land contract?
    a. Upon execution of the contract
    b. Within 30 days after the contract is signed
    c. Upon the purchaser's full payment of the purchase price
    d. Upon the issuance of a satisfaction of mortgage by the lender

38. A type of mortgage in which the lender makes payments to the borrower for a contracted period and then recaptures the equity upon the death of the homeowner or sale of the property is called a:
    a. balloon mortgage
    b. straight term mortgage
    c. shared appreciation mortgage
    d. reverse annuity mortgage

39. A type of mortgage in which personal property in addition to real property is pledged to secure payment of the loan is known as a:
    a. purchase money mortgage
    b. convertible mortgage
    c. package mortgage
    d. home equity loan

Real Estate Investments (5 hours) (12 questions)

40. The greatest amount of leverage can be obtained if an investor:
    a. uses only personal funds
    b. uses an equal amount of personal funds together with borrowed funds
    c. uses solely borrowed funds
    d. invests in a property for a minimum of one year

41. Preston purchased a four-family apartment house for $300,000. He made a $100,000 down payment and financed the balance. Five years later he sold the property for $550,000. Preston has realized a:
    a. portfolio income
    b. capital gain
    c. debt service
    d. tax loss

42. The tax deductible expenses, including depreciation of a property, are greater than the income. For tax purposes, which of the following is a result?
    a. Negative amortization
    b. Capital gain
    c. Tax shelter
    d. Boot

43. A property's cash flow refers to:
    a. the amount of activity of a certain investment account
    b. the sum total of income for any given day's activity
    c. debt service
    d. the net proceeds after all expenses and debt services are met

44. A provision of the tax law that permits a property owner to take a deductible allowance from the net income of property is known as:
    a. economic depreciation
    b. tax depreciation
    c. adjusted basis
    d. capital loss

45. A type of organizational trust that can earn income from real estate investments avoiding a double tax on trust income is known as a:
    a. real estate investment trust
    b. cooperative venture trust
    c. real estate exchangor's trust
    d. portfolio development company

46. A mortgage in which the borrower allows the lender to share in the net income generated by the commercial property as inducement for the lender to make the loan is called a:
    a. leasehold mortgage
    b. participation mortgage
    c. gap financing
    d. blanket mortgage

47. Which of the following is NOT a classification for income according to the tax law?
  a. Active income
  b. Portfolio income
  c. Projected income
  d. Passive activity income

48. Hope wants to exchange her office building for a luxurious single-family home in Florida that she would use as her primary residence. This exchange:
  a. qualifies unequivocally as a tax-deferred exchange
  b. does not qualify as a tax-deferred exchange as only investment or business property qualifies as a tax-deferred exchange
  c. only qualifies as a tax-deferred exchange if both the office building and house are the same price
  d. only qualifies as a tax-deferred change if the properties exchanged are in the same state

49. To effectively use the buying power of leverage, investors will NOT want to:
  a. put the least possible money down
  b. obtain the lowest available interest rate over the longest period of time
  c. make a major down payment so as to minimize monthly payments
  d. accumulate a maximum of real estate with a minimal amount of personal funds

50. An owner's office building is producing a net annual operating income of $140,000. If the owner paid $1,166,666 for the property, what rate of return is the owner receiving on the investment?
  a. 8.3%
  b. 14%
  c. 12%
  d. 16.3%

51. For income tax purposes, property taxes may be deducted for which types of real property?
  a. All types of real property
  b. Income-producing property only
  c. The personal residence only
  d. inherited property and vacant land only

General Business Law (5 hours) (12 questions)

52. A corporation may be set up for:
  a. profit only
  b. nonprofit only
  c. profit or nonprofit
  d. only businesses related to commerce

53. Which of the following is FALSE regarding securities?
  a. All securities, public or private, must register with the SEC
  b. The Securities Act of 1933 was the first securities law
  c. The SEC may issue a cease and desist order to stop a certain violation
  d. The prospectus is a disclosure statement

54. State laws formulated to protect securities investors are known as:
  a. red herring laws
  b. black book laws
  c. private placement exemption laws
  d. blue sky laws

55. Which of the following is NOT a negotiable instrument?
  a. Check
  b. Promissory note
  c. CD
  d. Cash

56. Which of the following is NOT a requirement for negotiability? The instrument must:
  a. be in writing
  b. be signed
  c. be worth less than $25,000
  d. contain a promise or order to pay

57. Frederick owns his own brokerage firm and has no partners. He does business under the name of FRD Realty. This form of business organization is called a:
a. limited liability company
b. general proprietorship
c. sole proprietorship
d. private venture

58. Which of the following is NOT taxed by the IRS as a partnership?
a. Limited liability company
b. S corporation
c. Limited liability partnership
d. C corporation

59. Which of the following is a federal district court?
a. U.S. Bankruptcy Court
b. County Court
c. New York State Court of Appeals
d. New York State Supreme Court

60. The law that addresses promises made by different parties to one another is known as:
a. torts
b. contract law
c. real property law
d. due process of law

61. Which of the following is NOT a cause of action for divorce in New York?
a. Cruel and inhuman treatment
b. Abandonment
c. Adultery
d. Severance

62. A reorganization form of bankruptcy is known as which chapter of the Bankruptcy Code?
a. Chapter 7
b. Chapter 11
c. Chapter 13
d. Chapter 15

63. The law that imposes time limits within which litigation may be commenced is known as the:
a. Statute of Limitations
b. Statute of Frauds
c. Doctrine of Laches
d. notice of pendency

Construction and Development (4 hours) (10 questions)

Construction

64. Which law requires the filing of an environmental impact statement with government agencies that must approve land use projects?
a. Article 9-A of the Real Property Law
b. Comprehensive Environmental Response, Compensation and Liability Act
c. Interstate Land Sales Full Disclosure Act
d. State Environmental Quality Review Act

65. According to New York law, all contracts of sale for new construction carry how long a warranty for material defects in workmanship?
a. one year
b. two years
c. five years
d. six years

66. Betty Broker was told by her sellers that the basement of their house flooded every spring. The sellers said that since it was winter and the cellar was dry, they did not want to inform any prospective purchasers. Betty should:
a. agree with her sellers
b. inform her sellers that this information must be disclosed to all interested parties
c. obtain a signed release from her sellers so that Betty is not liable should a purchaser eventually sue
d. refuse to take a listing under any circumstances since the property has a material defect

67. New York State requires a minimum electric service with:
 a. 50 amps
 b. 100 amps
 c. 110 amps
 d. 220 amps

68. The first phase in a due diligence review is generally the:
 a. management phase
 b. investigative phase
 c. testing phase
 d. clean-up phase

Development

69. One of the main purposes of subdivision regulations is to:
 a. control property development within the subdivision
 b. keep out undesirable individuals
 c. raise the tax base of the community
 d. limit the developer to a certain amount of profit on the project

70. The actual taking of property under the government's right of eminent domain is known as:
 a. escheat
 b. estoppel
 c. condemnation
 d. *in rem*

71. Before any type of construction can take place, which of the following documents must be obtained?
 a. Certificate of occupancy
 b. FHA certification
 c. Building permit
 d. State builder's certificate of approval

72. Tall Building Builders has purchased development rights from a small building nearby that had not fully utilized its development rights. This practice is:
 a. illegal in New York
 b. only legal in New York City
 c. only allowable if money does not change hands
 d. known as transfer of development rights

73. Restrictions in a deed that provide for a reversions of title if they are violated are called:
 a. conditions
 b. laches
 c. variables
 d. regulations

Conveyance of Real Property and Title Closing (3 hours) (8 questions)

Conveyance of Real Property

74. A practice in which landowners set aside a certain portion of land in a development for public use is known as:
 a. forfeiture
 b. dedication
 c. involuntary alienation
 d. accession

75. The term intestate refers to:
 a. persons who die without leaving a valid will
 b. roadways that cross over two or more states
 c. the transfer of possession of property from one person to another after death
 d. a person who carries out the provisions of a will

76. Alienation is:
 a. land held through adverse possession
 b. a tenant at sufferance
 c. the transfer of title to property
 d. the same as alluvion

77. Title may be acquired to real estate through voluntary alienation by:
 a. dedication
 b. bankruptcy
 c. eminent domain
 d. adverse possession

Title Closing

78. One of the main purposes of a survey before closing is to:
    a. ensure that no encroachments exist
    b. ensure that a deed exists
    c. verify the chain of title
    d. prepare an abstract of title

79. Gale holds the deed to an investment property where she does not reside. The deed was recorded July 28, 20xx. The recordation of the deed protects her title to the property under the theory of:
    a. actual notice
    b. caveat emptor
    c. lis pendens
    d. constructive notice

80. A tax imposed on the seller of a cooperative is known as a:
    a. capital gains tax affidavit
    b. flip tax
    c. real property transfer tax
    d. sales tax

81. At closing, a cooperative purchaser obtains a (n):
    a. deed
    b. proprietary lease
    c. option
    d. installment land contract

Real Estate Property Management (5 hours) (12 questions)

82. A property manager's fee is:
    a. always a flat fee
    b. always a percentage of the gross rental income
    c. always requires a down payment together with a percentage of the rents actually collected
    d. negotiable between the property owner and the manager

83. Which of the following is NOT generally a duty of a property manager?
    a. Prudently investing the owner's profits
    b. Maintaining the property
    c. Collecting rents
    d. Establishing a budget for property operation

84. Which of the following is NOT an item that should be included in an annual property management maintenance schedule?
    a. window cleaning
    b. exterior painting
    c. legal fees
    d. parking lot repair

85. Which of the following should NOT be considered in selecting tenants?
    a. credit history of the tenant
    b. past landlord references
    c. marital status of the tenant
    d. employment status of the tenant

86. If a real estate broker enters into a property management agreement with an owner, the broker becomes a:
    a. trustee
    b. fiduciary
    c. facilitator
    d. lessor

87. Which of the following is NOT generally included in a typical property management agreement?
    a. Scope of agent's management authority
    b. Manager's fee
    c. Accounting responsibilities
    d. Portfolio of the owner's other investment holdings

88. If a property management office works for more than one property owner and collects rents for these owners, which of the following licenses is generally required?
    a. No license
    b. An apartment information vendor's license
    c. A broker license
    d. No license, but a designation from a professional property management organization

89. A skill NOT needed to manage office property includes:
a. analyzing demographics
b. knowledge of commodity prices
c. negotiating leases
d. developing a competitive rent schedule

90. Developing an appropriate tenant mix is probably most important in which type of nonresidential property?
a. shopping centers
b. industrial parks
c. apartment housing
d. residential planned unit developments

91. The Pains have not paid their rent in two months. One day they come home to find their possessions thrown out on the street and a "for rent" sign on their apartment. In this case, the landlord has performed a:
a. constructive eviction
b. lawful eviction
c. illegal actual eviction
d. *lis pendens*

92. A type of estate that exists for a fixed period is called a(n):
a. tenancy for years
b. estate at will
c. freehold estate
d. homestead estate

93. A key feature of a periodic lease is it:
a. terminates automatically
b. is used only for commercial leases
c. can be terminated at will by the parties
d. renews itself automatically for another period unless notice is given by either party

Taxes and Assessments (2 hours) (7 questions)

94. *Ad valorem* refers to:
a. acquiring title
b. the verification
c. according to value
d. additional valuation

95. A special assessment is an example of a(n):
a. general lien
b. specific lien
c. illegal charge against real property
d. special charge levied against larger homes or buildings to increase the tax base

96. A legal action brought against the real property and not against the individual and his personal property is called a(n):
a. certiorari proceeding
b. Article 78 proceeding
c. grievance
d. *in rem* legal proceeding

97. The accepted fair type of value for setting assessments is:
a. market value
b. value in use
c. investment value
d. book value

98. Which of the following is classified as a homestead type of property for tax purposes?
a. commercial
b. industrial
c. mixed used parcel if primarily used for residential purposes
d. utility property

99. The government body that hears grievances is called the:
a. zoning board of appeals
b. board of assessment review
c. town planning board
d. citizens' tax advisory committee

100. A property with a market value of \$80,000 is assessed at 75%. What is the tax rate per \$100 if the tax bill is \$900?
a. \$1.125
b. \$1.50
c. \$15.00
d. \$11.25

Broker Practice Exam 2

The Broker's Office-Operation, Management, and Supervision (10 hours) (17 questions)

1. The continuing education requirement for brokers who have been licensed for 15 or more continuous years before July 1, 2008, is:
   a. 45 hours upon license renewal
   b. 22.5 hours upon license renewal
   c. 45 hours every four years
   d. exemption from any continuing education requirements

2. Broker Lawless advised some buyers that he was working with that a full covenant and warranty deed was preferable to a quitclaim deed. Broker Lawless:
   a. is allowed to give this advice as long as he discloses to the sellers that he is not an attorney
   b. can give this advice as long as there are witnesses present
   c. should not give out legal advice of any kind
   d. should consult guidelines furnished by the local Board of REALTORS® before giving legal advice

3. How many years of experience as a salesperson is required for a broker license?
   a. one
   b. two
   c. three
   d. five

4. The maximum fine that can be imposed by DOS for violation of the license law is:
   a. $500
   b. $1,000
   c. $2,500
   d. no specific penalty under the law

5. Applicants for whom English is a second language:
   a. may not obtain licensure in New York
   b. must demonstrate a fair knowledge of English by passing the state exam without assistance
   c. may qualify under the statute to use a dictionary while taking the state exam
   d. must complete an extra 15 hours of study in English before taking the state exam

6. Applicants for the broker license must be at least how old?
   a. 18
   b. 20
   c. 21
   d. 25

7. George owns more than 50 apartment buildings that he has managed over the past 25 years. Now George wishes to obtain a broker license. Which of the following is TRUE?
   a. George's experience as an apartment manager should give him the qualifying experience to obtain a broker license
   b. George must obtain a salesperson license before applying for broker licensure
   c. George's experience in managing apartments does not count toward the experience requirement for broker licensure
   d. George does not need to become a salesperson first, but he must pass the salesperson state exam before applying for broker licensure

8. A trade name broker is:
   a. a corporation
   b. a form of business organization that uses a name already used by another brokerage firm in New York
   c. generally a sole proprietorship using a name other than the personal name of the broker
   d. a brokerage firm which does not belong to the Board of REALTORS®

9. The IRS form that must be prepared yearly by the broker for salespersons who are independent contractors is:
   a. W-2
   b. 941
   c. FICA
   d. 1099 misc.

10. An allowable activity under the law for multiple listing services is:
   a. fixing commission rates
   b. adopting rules prohibiting a member from doing business with another
   c. admitting part-time brokers to MLS
   d. suggesting a commission rate in an educational course

11. According to antitrust law:
   a. boards of REALTORS® may fix commission rates
   b. boards of REALTORS® may suggest commission rates in education courses
   c. MLS services may refuse a listing if it does not find the commission rate acceptable
   d. commission rates are negotiable between agent and principal

12. A consent decree is:
   a. when a seller agrees in writing to accept the offer put forth by the buyer
   b. a compromise in which the accused party agrees to stop any alleged illegal activity without admitting wrongdoing
   c. an independent contractor agreement between broker and principal
   d. an admission of wrongdoing by a guilty party with heavy penalties for these acts

13. The regulatory agency that administers the license law is the:
   a. Department of Law
   b. the Attorney General's office
   c. Department of State, Division of Corporations
   d. Department of State, Division of Licensing Services

14. Which of the following is NOT a category of real estate agent licensure?
   a. salesperson
   b. broker
   c. associate broker
   d. mortgage loan originator

15. Property managers must be licensed if they:
   a. manage both residential and commercial property
   b. work for more than one owner or company
   c. have employees
   d. manage condominiums or cooperatives exclusively

16. A mortgage loan servicer is licensed by which of the following New York agencies?
   a. Department of Financial Services
   b. Department of State, Division of Licensing Services
   c. Department of State, Division of Corporations
   d. Department of Law

17. Which of the following are exempt from licensure as long as they have no sales agents working under them?
   a. Brokers who have 15 or more years experience
   b. Attorneys
   c. Brokers, associate brokers, or sales agents who have 15 or more years experience
   d. Personal investors who have 15 or more years experience

Real Estate Agency Disclosure (4 hours) (10 questions)

18. The required use of the agency disclosure form for property sales or a rental refers to:
   a. one- to four-unit residential properties only
   b. all properties for sale or rent in New York
   c. one- to four-unit residential properties together with land to be used for residential subdivisions
   d. one- to four-unit residential properties as well as condominiums and cooperatives in any size building

19. The overall purpose of the agency disclosure law is to:
   a. protect the commissions earned by real estate agents
   b. ensure that buyers realize that a seller's agent does not represent their best interests
   c. make consumers aware of the agency relationship of a real estate agent and the choices available to them
   d. protect the broker from being liable for the acts of principals who have listed with them

20. If a prospective purchaser refuses to sign the agency disclosure form:
   a. the agent cannot legally show the property
   b. the agent may show the property but must complete and keep on file a declaration form stating the facts of the refusal
   c. the broker may show the property only after obtaining special permission from DOS
   d. the agent may show the property if he has the buyers sign a statement saying they were shown the disclosure form

21. An exclusive single agency relationship:
   a. is not allowable under DOS regulations
   b. only occurs when there is a buyer agency relationship
   c. is not a fiduciary relationship
   d. occurs if a broker represents either the buyer or the seller but not both

22. In a brokerage firm, the listing contracts are typically owned by the:
   a. brokerage firm
   b. salesperson who listed the property
   c. multiple listing service together with the brokerage firm
   d. principals who engaged the firm to market their properties

23. Which of the following is TRUE?
   a. A buyer or seller can agree to dual agency in advance of it occurring
   b. Dual agency can only be agreed to when it occurs
   c. Dual agency is illegal in New York under all conditions
   d. All real estate agents are dual agents

24. Broker Beverly, an agent of the owner, is waiting for some prospective tenants to arrive to show them office space. She realizes that she forgot her disclosure forms. Beverly should:
   a. go back to her office and obtain the form
   b. forget about the disclosure form and simply use the declaration form stating why the prospects would not sign it
   c. nothing, since in this situation, she does not have a duty to disclose whom she represents
   d. she need not obtain the disclosure form as this form does not have to be used for the rental of commercial property

25. Who has vicarious liability for the acts of a broker's agent?
   a. Listing agent
   b. Buyer's agent
   c. Tenant's agent
   d. All of the above

26. The compensation paid to a broker is negotiable between the:
 a. broker and the multiple listing service
 b. broker and the principal
 c. broker and the real estate board
 d. office policy together with the decision of the listing agent

27. A payment arrangement that is illegal in New York is:
 a. a percentage of the selling price
 b. a flat fee agreed to between agent and principal
 c. any sum of money over and above a specified amount that the principal wishes to obtain for his property
 d. a combination of a flat fee arrangement and a percentage of the selling price

Real Estate Finance II (5 hours) (12 questions)

28. The function of the FHA is to:
 a. make mortgage loans
 b. buy mortgages on the secondary market
 c. insure loans to protect lenders against financial loss
 d. make loans for targeted low-income housing

29. The mortgagor is the individual who:
 a. receives the payments
 b. lends the mortgage funds
 c. holds the mortgage lien
 d. signs the note and gives the mortgage

30. A mortgage loan payable in monthly installments of principal and interest that will fully retire the debt is known as a(n):
 a. balloon mortgage
 b. amortized mortgage
 c. subordinate mortgage
 d. convertible mortgage

31. The loss of funds available to lending institutions for making mortgage loans caused by the withdrawal of funds by depositors is known as:
 a. disintegration
 b. stagflation
 c. disintermediation
 d. illiquidity

32. A capital short market occurs when:
 a. funds for underwriting are plentiful
 b. lenders do not have available funds for underwriting mortgages
 c. lenders are selling mortgages to the secondary mortgage market
 d. mortgages are assignable and are sold to the secondary mortgage market before the borrower repays the debt

33. When unemployment levels are high, which of the following happens?
 a. The demand for housing is less
 b. Economic instability
 c. The number of houses for sale increases
 d. All of the above

34. A value estimate used by banks to adjust the interest rate is called a(n):
 a. index
 b. multiplier
 c. ratio
 d. percentage

35. A moderate and temporary decline in economic activity that occurs during a period of otherwise increasing prosperity is known as:
 a. recession
 b. depression
 c. stagflation
 d. marginal regression

36. An economic condition in which economic growth is at a standstill but inflation still exists is known as:
 a. inflation
 b. depression
 c. recession
 d. stagflation

37. Creditor A, whose lien is secured by Mr. Jones' property, obtained a judgment against Mr. Jones on July 10; Banker B lent money to Mr. Jones and took back a mortgage on August 1; Mrs. Jones obtained a judgment for failure to pay child support on August 20. Which of the above-listed liens will be paid first at foreclosure?
a. Creditor A
b. Banker B
c. Mrs. Jones
d. They will be paid on a pro rata basis

38. The type of mortgage in which two or more parcels of real estate are pledged as security for repayment of the mortgage debt is known as a(n):
a. shared appreciation mortgage
b. bridge loan
c. installment land contract
d. blanket mortgage

39. A type of mortgage in which personal property is pledged to secure payment and is sometimes used in the sale of condominiums if the sale includes all furnishings is called a:
a. shared appreciation mortgage
b. purchase money mortgage
c. package mortgage
d. convertible mortgage

Real Estate Investments (5 hours) (12 questions)

40. In a leasehold mortgage, the type of leasehold acceptable to a lender is a(n):
a. long-term estate for years
b. estate at will
c. estate pur autre vie
d. short-term estate for years

41. A qualified intermediary plays a role in:
a. release land subdivision financing
b. a real estate investment trust
c. a tax-deferred exchange
d. C corporation filings

42. Ted owns several income-producing properties in a state other than where he resides. He employs a property management company to oversee them. Under the tax law, Ted's income could be classified as:
a. active income
b. passive activity income
c. portfolio income
d. absentee ownership income

43. A large retail store that has a well known name that a mall depends on to draw in business is known as a(n):
a. anchor store
b. regional center
c. multiplex
d. mixed retail center

44. One of the most popular forms of investment for the beginning investor because it can be carried out on a small scale is investment in:
a. regional malls
b. mixed developments
c. office buildings
d. apartments

45. A risk in real estate investment does NOT include:
a. a downturn in the real estate market
b. illiquidity of the investment
c. environmental problems associated with a proposed development
d. lender participation in the financing

46. Eugene is considering the purchase of a 10-year-old office building and is analyzing the project to determine the price he wants to pay. What factor is NOT important in determining the price?
a. The initial cost to construct the building
b. His desired rate of return
c. The vacancy level of the building
d. How long he wishes to hold the property

47. In which type of investment must investors also have a sophisticated knowledge of the industry?
a. Small office buildings
b. Hotels and motels
c. Duplexes
d. Four-family dwellings

48. If a real estate exchanger receives cash or some other type of nonqualifying property in addition to the like-kind property, this is known as:
a. an illegal payment
b. a bonus
c. boot
d. basis

49. In estimating the value of an office building containing 22,400 square feet, an appraiser established the annual rental income to be $400,000. The appraiser also learned that monthly expenses averaged $16,700. If an investor in this property was realizing a net return of 13.5%, what would be the appraiser's estimate of the property's value?
a. $2,962,962
b. $1,484,444
c. $1,478,518
d. $2,964,600

50. Which of the following will negatively affect the market value and probably the price a property will bring?
a. Buyer and seller are equally motivated
b. Payment is made in cash or its equivalent
c. A reasonable amount of time is allowed for exposure in the open market
d. Time constraints on market exposure

51. In the sale of a capital asset held for twelve months, the seller realizes a gain of $242,000. The amount of taxable gain is:
a. $193,600
b. $96,800
c. $145,200
d. $242,000

General Business Law (5 hours) (12 questions)

52. A notice that a lawsuit has been filed concerning a specific property is called a(n):
a. mechanic's lien
b. mediation
c. *lis pendens*
d. torts

53. What is one of the differences between a C and an S corporation? A(n):
a. S corporation is taxed as a partnership
b. S corporation can only do business in New York
c. brokerage firm cannot be set up as an S corporation
d. S corporation pays a greater franchise tax.

54. An example of laws enacted on local levels are:
a. banking laws
b. agency laws
c. torts
d. zoning laws

55. A signature on the back of a promissory note by someone other than a maker, drawer, or acceptor is known as a(n):
a. assignment
b. endorsement
c. bearer's signature
d. acknowledgement

56. The purpose of limited partners in a limited partnership organization includes:
a. management of the partnership
b. origination of the partnership
c. providing accounting services
d. providing the funds to purchase the investment

57. Which of the following is NOT a county level court in New York?
a. Supreme Court Appellate division
b. Family Court
c. County Court
d. Surrogate's Court

58. Which is New York's highest court?
a. Supreme Court Appellate Division
b. Supreme Court
c. Court of Appeals
d. Court of Claims

59. The law that addresses the acquisition, transfer, and possession of an interest in real property is known as:
a. Contract law
b. Torts
c. Agency Law
d. the Real Property Law

60. One of the advantages of a limited liability company is that it:
a. pays a lower corporation franchise tax
b. is taxed as a partnership
c. cannot be dissolved by judicial decree
d. is the only form of corporation allowed for real estate brokerage

61. Statutory laws are:
a. illegal in New York
b. not applicable to real estate practice
c. created by acts of the legislature
d. created by decisions of the U.S. Supreme Court

62. According to NYS and IRS regulations, which of the following is TRUE?
a. Most gifts of money are subject to the federal gift tax
b. Most estates are subject to estate tax
c. Gifts to spouses are taxable gifts
d. The gift tax does not apply to the first $13,000 given to another in each year

63. A mechanic's lien is:
a. the same as any other lien
b. specific only to personal property
c. filed by a person who provides labor to a property
d. allowed in New York only for work performed on commercial properties

Construction and Development (4 hours) (10 questions)

Construction

64. The Americans with Disabilities Act applies mainly to:
a. duplexes
b. residential single-family houses
c. commercial and public facilities
d. hospitals and housing for the physically challenged only

65. Under the Residential Lead-Based Hazard Reduction Act, what is the maximum timeframe for the seller and buyer to agree to a lead paint assessment?
a. Three days
b. Four days
c. One business week
d. Ten days

66. The water supply in New York is regulated by the:
a. Department of Agriculture
b. Department of Health
c. Department of State
d. Department of Law

67. In New York, which of the following bodies have the statutory authority to review site plans? The:
a. mayor's office
b. local court system
c. local building department
d. local planning board

68. Building specifications are:
a. the same as blueprints
b. similar to a survey of the property
c. written narratives that explain the building plan
d. explanations of the demographics of the property Development

69. The study of the social and economic statistics of a community is known as:
a. demographics
b. topography
c. infrastructure
d. sensitivity analysis

70. A developer may need to give a municipality assurance that offsite improvements to the subdivision will be made. This is known as a(n):
a. construction bond
b. completion bond
c. participation insurance
d. errors and omissions insurance

71. One of the first things a developer must do to determine if a subdivision project will work is to:
a. ask for a moratorium
b. conduct a feasibility study
c. create subdivision regulations
d. apply for a building permit

72. Under New York law, how many agencies may be involved in the environmental review process?
a. Only the planning board
b. A maximum of two agencies
c. A maximum of five agencies
d. As many agencies as necessary may be involved

73. Laura, a developer, would like to assure that homeowners in her subdivision do not park RVs on the front lawn. Laura can accomplish this through (a(n):
a. deed restrictions
b. special use permit
c. amendments to the building code
d. carefully screening purchasers who wish to buy a house in the subdivision

Conveyance of Real Property and Title Closing (3 hours) (8 questions)

Conveyance of Real Property

74. A testatrix is:
a. a witness who appears at a bankruptcy hearing
b. a woman who makes a valid will
c. a person who is unlawfully in possession of another's property
d. a man who has died and who has not left a valid will

75. The loss of land when a sudden or violent change in a watercourse washes it away is:
a. accretion
b. avulsion
c. erosion
d. annexation

76. In a mortgage foreclosure, the property owner may satisfy the lien up to the foreclosure sale through:
a. the law of eminent domain
b. a partition proceeding
c. the right of redemption
d. fulfilling the requirements of the adverse possession statute in New York

77. The importance of an acknowledgment on a deed is that:
a. it is required by New York state law
b. title cannot be transferred without it
c. it allows the deed to be recorded
d. it gives the attorneys for all parties an opportunity to review and validate the deed

Title Closing

78. One of the main differences between the purchase of a cooperative and a condominium is that a cooperative purchase:
a. does not generally require financing
b. involves the transfer of shares of stock in a corporation
c. involves the transfer of title by deed and a condominium purchase does not
d. is not legal in some upstate areas, whereas a condominium purchase is

79. To provide constructive notice, evidence of the document must be:
a. recorded
b. seen and read by all interested parties
c. validated by a court of competent jurisdiction
d. a real estate-related document only

80. Under the Real Estate Settlement Procedures Act, a good faith estimate provided to the buyer provides for:
a. selling price of the property only
b. costs likely to be incurred at settlement
c. appraised price of the property
d. lender attorney's fees only

81. A document required to be filed after closing with the NYS Department of Taxation and Finance is:
a. a real property transfer report
b. HUD form No. 1
c. a Combined Real Estate Transfer Tax Return
d. a satisfaction of mortgage

Real Estate Property Management (5 hours) (12 questions)

82. Which type of insurance covers the risks an owner assumes when the public enters a property?
a. Public liability insurance
b. Error and omissions insurance
c. Health insurance
d. Life insurance

83. The document that creates an agency relationship in which the owner is the principal and the property manager is the agent is the:
a. listing agreement
b. management agreement
c. risk management agreement
d. disclosure statement

84. A skill NOT required for a property manager is to:
a. understand building systems
b. supervise others
c. handle landlord-tenant relations
d. draw contracts

85. To minimize lawsuits for collection of rents, the property manager must:
a. charge the lowest rents allowable in the market area
b. threaten tenants who do not pay on time
c. exercise care in tenant selection
d. collect all rents in person

86. A property manager who must be familiar with commodity prices, soil types, and environmental controls would manage what type of property?
a. Industrial
b. Condominium
c. Retail
d. Agricultural

87. For the optimum functioning of a property management office, the company should:
a. effectively service existing clients
b. handle the legal affairs of its clients
c. have as few employees as possible to handle the workload
d. keep the focus on profit first, service second

88. James is employed by a property management company that works for multiple owners. His job is to collect rents and assist in other management functions. James needs a minimum of:
a. an apartment sharing agent's license
b. an apartment information vendor's license
c. a salesperson's license
d. a broker's license

89. Samantha, a property manager, felt that it was her duty to add up the yearly rent roll and report this information to the owner's accountant. The owner found out and told Samantha that this activity was not within the scope of her authority. Where would Samantha and the property owner look to find out who was right? The:
a. accountant's financial files for the company
b. bank account where the rents are deposited for the property
c. management agreement
d. listing agreement

90. Bradley wants to open a management company to manage several apartment buildings for different owners. He will negotiate leases and collect rents. In order to take on these responsibilities, Bradley must have:
a. a broker license
b. a salesperson license
c. a designation from a property management organization
d. neither a license nor a designation

91. Gene rents an apartment to Melissa under a one-year lease. However, after six months, the apartment building is sold. Which of the following applies?
a. Melissa's lease is not affected by the sale
b. The new owner may ask all tenants including Melissa to vacate the premises and break their leases as long as he gives 30 days notice
c. Melissa may break her lease because it is now void as it was not made with the new owner
d. The new owner can immediately raise Melissa's rent

92. The Innocents have not had adequate heat or water in their apartment for two weeks and are forced to leave the premises. This departure is an example of:
a. an illegal act to avoid rental payments
b. a constructive eviction which is necessary under the circumstances
c. a legal use of self help
d. tenants at sufferance

93. A property manager's fee usually consists of a base fee plus a percentage of the:
a. effective gross income
b. potential yearly income
c. value of the property
d. stabilized budget

Taxes and Assessments (2 hours) (7 questions)

94. The amount that a municipality must raise by taxes on real property is known as the:
a. stabilized budget
b. tax levy
c. special assessment
d. assessment roll

95. Which of the following is NOT an example of an assessing unit?
a. Village
b. City
c. District court
d. School district

96. The purpose of the tax rate is to:
a. make sure that property owners pay the highest taxes allowable within the municipality
b. equalize taxes throughout the state
c. force homeowners who cannot afford property taxes to sell their homes
d. provide the amount of revenue needed to meet the municipality's budgetary requirements

97. Most of the funds for a typical town budget are raised through:
a. property taxes
b. state aid
c. fees for water and other services
d. federal funding

98. The state's measure of a municipality's level of assessment at a given point in time is represented by:
a. the tax levy
b. the equalization rate
c. apportionment
d. assessed value

99. The Mores have been unable to pay their property taxes for the past two years. Recently, they discovered that their property was encumbered. Based on these facts only, which of the following has most likely encumbered the property?
a. Mechanic's lien
b. Grievance
c. Tax lien
d. Homestead misclassification

100. If the assessed value of a property is $200,000 and the tax value is 100% of the assessed value, what is the annual tax if the rate is $1.50 per $100?
a. $3,000
b. $3,500
c. $5,000
d. $7,500

Answer Key

All answers provided are referenced to *New York Real Estate for Salespersons, 5th e*, by Marcia Darvin Spada, Cengage Learning 2013 (indicated by the letter "S") and *New York Real Estate for Brokers, 5th e* by Marcia Darvin Spada, Cengage Learning, 2013 (indicated by the letter "B").

Answer Key For Review Questions

License Law and Regulations/The Broker's Office: Operation, Management and Supervision

1. D
A licensee must only accept a commission from his sponsoring broker so this is not a violation of the license law.
REF: S 27; B 61

2. D
Building superintendents working for one owner, public officers, and attorneys who do not employ salespersons do not require a license. Auctioneers who sell real property must have a real estate license.
REF: S 16; B 23

3. B
A licensee who deposits an earnest money check in his personal checking account instead of in the broker's trust account is guilty of commingling. Conversion is the illegal use of another's money. Escheat is the state's right to a decedent's property if no heirs are found.
REF: S 32; B 41

4.C
A major purpose of the license law is to protect the public.
REF: S 11; B 18

5. C
A broker must complete 120 hours of qualifying education.
REF: S 13; B 25

6. B
The regulatory agency that oversees the licensure process in New York is the NYS Department of State.
REF: S 11; B 18

7. B
The minimum age for salesperson licensure is 18.
REF: S 13; B 25

8.C
Individuals do not need U.S. citizenship to obtain a salesperson license in New York.
REF: S 12; B 25

9. C
When transacting real estate business, a licensee must carry his pocket card.
REF: S 21; B 37

10. A
Licensees must complete continuing education requirements every two years upon license renewal unless exempt.
REF: S 23; B 39

11. D
Jamie is an unlicensed assistant and does not require a real estate license.
REF: S 35; B 24

12. B
To open a real estate brokerage firm, Bill must decide the type of business organization for the brokerage. He must indicate this on the broker application with supporting documentation.
REF: B 29

13. C
A legal requirement for operation of a broker's office does NOT include submission of all contract forms for DOS approval.
REF: S31-33; B 40-45

14. B
The NYS Department of State's Occupational Licensing Management System is called *eAccessNY*. RESPA is short for the Real Estate Settlement Procedures Act. The Mortgage Nationwide Licensing System is used by the NYS Department of Financial Services to process mortgage broker and mortgage banker registrations and licenses in New York. TILA is short for the Truth in Lending Act.
REF: S 14; B 24

15. A
If a broker moves a principal or branch office, DOS must be notified online within five days. The broker may indicate a change of address to the DOS using his or her account online through *eAccessNY.*
REF: S 21; B 38

16. C
To obtain exam results from the either the salesperson or broker NYS licensure exam, applicants should view exam results through their accounts in *eAccessNY.*
REF: S 14; B 27

17. C
Andy, the broker, is entitled to the full commission as originally agreed upon as he has brought about a meeting of the minds. His commission is not legally dependent upon the closing going through; however, he may have to litigate to collect his commission.
REF: S 51; B 42

18. D
A seller broker or buyer broker cannot write or rewrite any form of contract. This act constitutes the illegal practice of law. In New York, only attorneys can draw real estate contracts.
REF: S 32; B 42

19. A
This ad violates DOS guidelines because it does not mention the name of the geographical area in which the property is located
REF: S 28; B 45

20. B
Much of the New York Real Property Law relating to real estate licenses is in Article 12-A. Article 9-A protects New York residents in the purchase of vacant subdivided land sold within and without New York on the installment plan.
REF: S 11; B 17

Law of Agency/ Real Estate Agency Disclosure

21. B
A broker's commission is determined by agreement between the broker and principal. There are no set fee schedules for broker commissions.
REF: S 55; B 78

22. D
In the sale of one- to four-unit residential real estate and residential condominiums and cooperatives in any size building, a listing agent must first disclose her status to a prospective buyer at the first substantive meeting such as when the listing contract is signed.
REF: S 78; B 99

23. B
A person empowered to act on behalf of another is called an agent. The principal is the party the agent represents. A party of the first part is the grantor on a deed.
REF: S 47; B 71

24. C
In this example, Danielle must have signed an exclusive right to sell agreement that states that she must pay Robert his commission no matter who sells the property.
REF: S 73; B 94

25. A
A buyer broker who represents the buyer as a client can never be a subagent of the seller which implies seller representation.
REF: S 58; B 80

26. D
An agency relationship is always consensual. There has to be an agreement between the parties.
REF: S 47; B 71

27. A
The most common agency relationship that brokers have with their principals is as a special agent. A general agent manages various affairs pertaining to the property. A power of attorney is permission to handle the limited affairs of another. A universal agency is an all-encompassing power of attorney.
REF: S 50; B 72

28. D
If there is no specific contact with an agent and no substantive contact, then the agency disclosure form is not required.
REF: S 78; B 99

29. B
Price fixing occurs when competitors in a certain group charge the same or similar price. A group boycott is a conspiracy in which a person or group is coerced into not doing business with another person or group. An illegal market allocation agreement occurs when competing companies agree to split a territory among them. A tie-in arrangement occurs when a party selling a service to a buyer, as a condition of sale, has the buyer purchase another product from the seller.
REF: S 57; B 51

30. D
A tie-in arrangement occurs when a party selling a service to a buyer, as a condition of sale, has the buyer purchase another product from the seller. A group boycott is a conspiracy in which a person or group is coerced into not doing business with another person or group. Price fixing occurs when competitors in a certain group charge the same or similar price. An illegal market allocation agreement occurs when competing companies agree to split a territory among them.
REF: S 57; B 52

31. A
In general, most real estate licensees, through an agreement with the broker, and allowable under IRS law, are independent contractors.
REF: S 94; B 55

32. D
An associate broker-independent contractor can be an office manager.
REF: S 21; B 38

33. D
There is no law that says a broker must accompany a sales agent/independent contractor when showing a property. However, the seller may request this.
REF: S 94; B 55

34. A
IRS regulations require that the sales agent enter into a written independent contractor agreement with the broker.
REF: S 95; B 56

35. B
In order to qualify under IRS regulations for independent contractor status, the sales agent must be licensed.
REF: S 95; B 56

36. C
The IRS requires the filing of Form 1099 misc. for all independent contractors who earn $600 or more in the calendar tax year.
REF: S 98; B 59

37. D
Independent contractors must file yearly federal and state tax returns just as employees do.
REF: S 98; B 59

38. C
In New York, brokers must keep records as to the sale or mortgage of one-to-four unit properties for at least three years.
REF: S 99; B 60

39. B
Under IRS regulations, although a salesperson is an independent contractor, the broker supervises the sales agent.
REF: S 94; B 59

40. D
The salesperson-independent contractor is responsible for all withholding and other tax obligations.
REF: S 98; B 56

41. C
A real estate agent is a special agent who has narrow authorization to act on behalf of the principal. A general agent has more authority to act on behalf of a principal, for example, as a property manager.
REF: S 50; B 72

42. D
An exclusive agency listing is only listed with one broker although other brokers can market the property as subagents.
REF: S 78; B 99

43. A
In the rental of one- to four-unit residential properties and condominium and cooperatives in any size building, at the first substantive contact, an agent must present the agency disclosure form.
REF: 78; B 99

44. A
By disclosing the divorce action to the buyer, Broker Beth has violated her fiduciary duty of loyalty to her client.
REF: S 62; B 73

45. B
A broker's agent works through another broker to assist in the marketing of a property. A principal is not vicariously liable for acts of the broker's agent.
REF: S 70; B 82

46. C
In New York, dual agency is legal with timely disclosure and informed consent.
REF: S 61; B 84

47. D
Subagents, listing agents, seller agents, and single agents are all cooperating agents.
REF: S 53; B 82

48. C
In an exclusive right to sell contract, the listing broker entitled to a commission when anyone including the broker, owner or other brokers sell the property.
REF: S 73; B 94

49. C
Vacant land is not covered under Section 443 of the Real Property Law that requires the use of the agency disclosure form.
REF: S 78; B 103

50. D
Sellers, buyers, landlords, and tenants may consent to dual agency in advance of it occurring and may indicate consent on the agency disclosure form. This consent applies to the sale or rental of one-to-four unit residential property and residential condos and coops in any size building. Dual agency is legal in New York with disclosure and informed consent.
REF: S 82-83; B 84

Legal Issues
Part I Estates and Interests

51. D
The term, *pur autre vie*, means for another life. Therefore, the term refers to a life estate measured by the life of someone other than the life tenant.
REF: S 121; B 447

52. C
Real property is in a fixed place and has the characteristic of immobility.
REF: S 117; B 440

53. B
Tenants by the entirety refer to husband and wife.
REF: S 125; B 452

54. D
Public parks and historical monuments are examples of special purpose real estate.
REF: S 116; B 450

55. A
A life estate is ownership or possession for someone's lifetime. A leasehold estate is a rental estate with possession, not ownership.
REF: S 120; B 442

56. B
Fee simple absolute, fee simple defeasible, and fee simple on condition all imply some form of ownership. A leasehold estate implies possession, not ownership.
REF: S 118; B 442

57. A
Because the condition states that the daughter cannot use the property for commercial purposes, the example is a fee simple on condition.
REF: S 120; B 438

58. A
Ownership in severalty refers to ownership by one owner. Think of the concept as the owner being "severed" from others.
REF: S 123; B 445

59. B
Chattel is another term for personal property.
REF: S 115; B 214

60. A
An estate for years can be for any fixed time as short as one day. Joint tenancy is a type of ownership. Usury is a practice that charges more interest than is lawfully allowed.
REF: S 194; B 335

Legal Issues
Part II Liens and Easements

61. C
A lien is a claim that one person has against the property of another for a debt.
REF: S 129;B 224-225

62. B
An easement is a nonpossessory use of land by another.
REF: S 133; B 435

63. A
The meaning of the term, *lis pendens*, is that a lawsuit is pending.
REF: S 130; B 225

64. C
Mortgages are voluntary specific liens because a mortgagor contracts for the mortgage and creates a specific lien against a specific real property.
REF: S 130; B 127

65. D
A mechanic's lien is involuntary because it is against an individual who owes a debt. A mechanic's lien creates a specific lien against the real property.
REF: S 130; B 224-225

66. B
Although certain types of liens have priority over other types, the factor that determines the priority is the time and date of filing.
REF: S 132; B 225

67. A
Utility companies obtain an easement in gross. Easement appurtenant describes all other types of easements. Easement by prescription and easement by grant are other types of easements.
REF: S 134; B 435

68. C
The dominant tenement is the property that benefits from the easements. The servient tenement is the property that allows the easement and where the easement is located.
REF: S 134; B 435

69. D
Items that extend into another's property are called encroachments. Easements are nonpossessory interests in another's property.
REF: S 137; B 436

70. C
A license is a temporary privilege.
REF: S 138; B 442

Legal Issues
Part III Deeds/Conveyances

71. C
The deed is the document that conveys title to real property.
REF: S 149; B 291

72. C
In Latin, *habendum* means to have, so the clause means "to have to and to hold." The defeasance clause appears in a mortgage.
REF: S 150; B 292

73. D
A quitclaim deed has no guarantee of title. A full covenant and warranty deed has the broadest guarantee of title. A deed of trust is a financing instrument.
REF: S 157; B 298

74. C
To execute a deed or any other legal document means to sign it.
REF: S 156; B 292

75. B
The party that conveys title to real property is the grantor. The grantee receives title and is the party of the second part on the deed.
REF: S 150; B 291

76. A
The legal term for the transfer of property is called alienation. *Lis pendens* is type of notice indicating that a legal action is pending.
REF: S 149; B 291

77. B
A correction deed may be ordered by the court to correct a typographical error. All of the other deeds in the question are judicial deeds.
REF: S 157; B 300

78. C
A type of property description used in a deed that starts with a point or place of beginning is called a metes and bounds description. Description by monument may refer to a large rock or other landmark and is not commonly used in New York. Description by lot and block, also found on a deed, refers to the location of the property. Description by reference links the description to another document such as a plat or tax map.
REF: S 153; B 293

79. A
When a landowner donates a parcel of land for public use, this is called dedication. Adverse possession is a method of acquiring title to real property by conforming to certain statutory requirements.
REF: S 161; B 298

80. D
The person appointed in a will to carry out its provisions is the executor. The legatee receives something from the will. A testator or devisor is one who makes a will. A woman is a testatrix.
REF: S 160; B 302

81. B
Alienation after death is through a will.
S 160; B 303

82. B
Dedication is a voluntary type of alienation. Adverse possession, a lien foreclosure sale, or a bankruptcy are all examples of involuntary alienation.
REF: S 161; B 298

83. A
The Statute of Frauds requires all documents that create an interest in real estate be in writing. The Statute of Limitations has to do with the statutory time limit to bring a legal action against a party. The Sullivan Law addresses clarity in written contracts.
REF: S 149; B 224

84. D
A person may receive title under adverse possession in New York if the possession been open and notorious for at least 10 years and a court has ruled in favor of the adverse possessor.
REF: S 190; B 301-302

85. C
If a person dies and leaves a valid will, he is said to die testate. A person who does not leave a valid will is said to die intestate. A devise is a gift of real property though a will. An estate, in New York, is processed through Surrogate's Court and this process is called probate.
REF: S 160; B 302

86. A
A gift of real property in a will is called a devise.
REF: S 161;B 303

87. C
The gradual buildup of land in a watercourse over time by deposits of silt, sand, and gravel is called accretion.
S 162; B 301

88. D
A quitclaim deed contains no warranties whatsoever. The grantor makes no statement or even implies ownership of the property being quitclaimed to the grantee.
REF: S 157; B 298

89. B
Tenancy in common, the correct answer, is an estate characterized by two or more people who hold title to a property at the same time with no rights of survivorship. A tenancy in common requires that each tenant holds an undivided interest in the entire property.
REF: S 124; B 452

90. B
Evidence that something of value is present in a deed is known as consideration. Earnest money is the deposit money in a real estate contract of sale. Chattel is another name for personal property. A devise is a gift of real property through a will.
S 150; B 292

Legal Issues
Part IV Title Closing and Costs

91. C
Title to real estate is transferred upon execution and delivery of a valid deed.
REF: S 149; B 291

92. A
Generally, in the closing process, attorneys for a lender represent the best interests of the lending institution. The purchasers' attorney, if the purchasers hire one, represents their best interests.
REF: S 163; B 309

93. D
A federal statute that regulates disclosure and closing requirements for mortgage loans on residential property is the Real Estate Settlement Procedures Act. The Truth-in-Lending Act promotes the informed use of consumer credit. The Interstate Land Sales is a federal law regulating the sale across state lines of subdivided land.
REF: S 169; B 316

94. C
The successive conveyances of title, starting with the current deed and going back an appropriate time (typically 40 to 60 years) is the chain of title; title must be unbroken to be good and, therefore, marketable.
REF: S 166; B 311

95. B
The document that illustrates the measurement, boundaries, and area of a property is called a survey. A feasibility study determines a project's usefulness and projected success in the community. A plat is subdivision map.
REF: S 164; B 310

96. A
A condensed history pertaining to the title of a property is called an abstract of title. A chain of title is the successive conveyances of title to a property. Title insurance insures the policy owner against loss if the title is not good.
REF: S 166; B 312

97. D
One of the most important roles of a licensee just before closing is to arrange and accompany a prospective purchaser through a final inspection of the property. Generally, attorneys examine the deed, prepare the abstract of title, and prepare the closing statement.
REF: S 169; B 314

98. B
A New York tax on the conveyance of title to real property is called the real estate transfer tax. The capital gains tax is a federal tax on profits from the sale of real estate. The mortgage recording fee is the charge for recording a mortgage.
REF: S 177; B 324

99. A
Unpaid utility bills are the responsibility of the seller at closing.
REF: S 177; B 325

100. C
The seller will not require mortgage insurance as his mortgage will generally be paid off at closing.
REF: S 177; B 325

101. B
When all interested parties to a title closing meet, their main purpose is to transfer title to real property from seller to buyer.
REF: S 163: B 309

102. B
The January 20xx takes priority over the June 20xx deed because the June 20xx deed is not recorded.
REF: 165; B 311

103. C
The Commission Escrow Act applies to one-to -four unit residential properties as well as individual condominiums and cooperatives sold by real estate brokers and sales agents. The law protects the broker's real estate commission when a seller does not pay the full commission upon closing.
REF: S 179; B 314

104. A
Although the property was granted to C, Grantor D then transferred the title to E. There was no transfer from Grantor C to Granter D. Therefore, there is a break in the chain of title.
REF: S 166; B 311

105. A
A title insurance policy is required by the lender and is not issued without an acceptable abstract or title opinion. An abstract of title is a history of the title showing the transfers of property over the years. State insurance departments have nothing to do with this process.
REF: S 166; B 312

106. B
The Real Estate Settlement Procedures Act (RESPA) regulates activities of lending institutions in making mortgage loans for housing. The Act applies only to residential federally financed or refinanced properties, not all properties.
REF: S 169; B 316

107. D
The earnest money deposit is a credit to the buyer on the closing statement. The purchase price, loan origination fee, and discount points are buyer debits on the closing statement.
REF: S 177; B 325

108. C
The purchase price is a seller credit on the closing statement. Delinquent property taxes, a purchase money mortgage, and the broker commission are all seller debits.
REF: S 177; B 325

109. A
FIRPTA stands for the Foreign Investment in Real Property Tax Act. The purpose of the federal law is to impose a tax on capital gains derived by foreign people from the sale of their U.S. property. A flip tax is sometimes imposed on the transfer of cooperatives.
REF: S 178; B 326

110. C
A cooperative is a type of property ownership in which the owner receives shares of stock in a cooperative corporation. All of the other choices in the question may be transferred with a deed.
REF: S 529; B 308

The Contract of Sale and Leases
Part I Leases

111. A
A periodic lease automatically renews itself at the end of the term unless notice is given.
REF: S 194; B 336

112. B
A leasehold estate implies possession, not ownership Therefore, it is never conveyed by a deed.
REF: S 193; B 336

113. C
An estate at will can be for any timeframe. A periodic estate automatically renews itself unless notice is given. A freehold estate is an ownership estate.
REF: S 194-195; B 337

114. B
A tenant who was originally in lawful possession of the premises but does not leave after the right to possession ends is a holdover tenant. A trespasser was never in lawful possession in the first place.
REF: S 195; B 338

115. C
A lease is a type of contract. A deed is not contract but an option and a promissory note are.
REF: S 193; B 335

116. D
There are no statutory requirements for the term of a lease in New York. It can be for one-day and for any specified duration.
REF: S 195

117. D
According to New York law, leases must be in clear language and appropriately captioned.
REF: S 199; B 224

118. C
Should there be an emergency; the landlord has a right to enter a premises without specific permission in the lease.
REF: S 202; B 349

119. A
If a tenant is forced to leave the premises because of lack of basic services, it may be a constructive eviction. Actual eviction occurs when a landlord physically forces tenants to leave the premises. A *lis pendens* is a pending lawsuit regarding a property.
REF: S 205; B 349

120. D
A new owner of a leased property must abide by all of the terms of the leases that are in place at the time and may not make changes until lease expiration.
REF: S 206; B 338

The Contract of Sale and Leases
Part II Contracts

121. B
Consideration is the giving of something of value as an inducement to contract. Quiet enjoyment has to do with possession of one's property. A power of attorney gives a person authority to act for another in legal matters.
REF: S 211; B 292

122. C
Many real estate contracts do not require financing so financing is not an essential element of a valid contract.
REF: S 210

123. A
The Statute of Limitations addresses time limits to sue. The Real Estate Settlement Procedures Act addresses lender disclosures for closings. The law that requires real estate contracts be in writing is called the Statute of Frauds. The Uniform Commercial Code regulates commercial paper (notes, drafts, checks).
REF: S 212; B 223

124. B
A contract between two parties who have definitely agreed to the contract terms is called an express bilateral contract.
REF: S 221

125. A
Under an installment land contract, the purchaser does not have legal title to the property. Legal title is conveyed when the contract terms have been fulfilled.
REF: S 221; B 136

126. B
Assignment is the giving over of the contract to another. The contract does not transfer to another with a sublet. Rescission means to annul the contract.
REF: S 203; B 201

127. D
The listing contract between the seller and agent is executory because a buyer has not been found and the contract is not complete. An implied contract arises through the actions of the parties. Void and unenforceable contracts are not valid.
REF: S 209; B 437

128. C
A contract stating, "time is of the essence," means that the contract must be performed on or before the date stipulated in the contract.
REF: S 221; B 453

129. B
An earnest money deposit is not legally necessary for an offer to purchase.
REF: S 214; B 41

130. D
A contract with a minor can generally go forward but is voidable by the minor.
REF: S 210

The Contract of Sale and Leases
Part III Contract Preparation

131. D
Assumable, home equity, and FHA are types of mortgages. A purchase money mortgage is a type of seller financing.
REF: S 267 B 138

132. B
A portion of a property purchase price that is paid in cash and not a part of the mortgage is the down payment. A binder is a type of agreement to purchase. An assumable mortgage is a type of mortgage. A mortgage commitment is a lender's promise to loan a certain amount of funds.
REF: S 230; B 132

133. A
The purchaser is generally the first to sign the contract of sale because he is making the contract offer to the seller.
REF: S 232

134. D
Raphael's advice regarding the "as is" clause in the contract constitutes the illegal practice of law.
REF: S 32; B 42

135. B
An IOLA account (Interest on Lawyer's Account) is held by an attorney.
REF: S 231

136. A
The Lawyer Fund for Client Protection has to do with the protection of escrow accounts that attorneys hold for client monies.
REF: S 230

137. C
The accepted practice in many upstate areas is for the broker to hold a purchaser's deposit in escrow until closing. Should a salesperson receive a deposit check, he must turn it over to his broker.
REF: S 230

138. C
A customary deposit is 10 percent of the purchase price, so Keri would put down a deposit of $45,000. This percentage can vary from deal to deal.
REF: S 230; B 144

139. C
A contract of sale is binding when the attorney for each party approves the contract.
REF: S 229

140. D
A survey, certificate of occupancy, and prior deed are all used by attorneys and others to prepare for a closing. A census statement is not necessary.
REF: S 164-165; B 310-311

Real Estate Finance/Real Estate Finance II

141. C
The mortgagor is the borrower. The mortgagee is the lender.
REF: S 255; B 127

142. A
The mortgagee is the lender. The mortgagor is the borrower.
REF: S 255; B 127

143. B
A mortgage is a written document pledging a property as security for the repayment of a loan.
REF: S 255; B 127

144. D
VA loans up to a certain amount do not require a down payment.
REF: S 273; B 134

145. B
A balloon mortgage is best described as having a larger payment due at the end of its term.
REF: S 287; B 135

146. A
When a lender is willing to lower the interest rate at the time the loan is made in return for extra payments of points up front, this is called a buydown. Usury is the charging of a higher interest rate than allowed by law. A satisfaction of mortgage is a document stating that the mortgage debt is fully paid.
REF: S 262; B 133

147. D
An amortized mortgage loan is one that is paid in monthly payments of principal and interest.
REF: S 265; B 136

148. C
A wraparound mortgage is a subordinate mortgage that includes the same principal obligation secured by a first mortgage against the same property. It is a type of seller financing.
REF: S 268; B 138

149. B
A satisfaction of mortgage is a document from the lender stating that the loan is paid in full. A certificate of tile sets forth the title examiner's opinion of the title. HUD Form No. 1 is used by lenders to itemize closing costs.
REF: S 264; B 327

150. B
The New York agency that raises money from tax free bonds and applies the money to mortgage loans is called SONYMA (State of New York Mortgage Association). Fannie Mae (short for Federal National

Mortgage Association) is part of the secondary mortgage market. FDIC is a federal agency that protects bank deposits. The RHA (Rural Housing Authority) is a federal agency that makes loans for rural housing.
REF: S 274; B 134

151. C
A conventional loan involves no participation of a federal government agency such as FHA and is not always amortized.
REF: S 264; B 134

152. C
A blanket mortgage is one in which two or more parcels are pledged as security for the mortgage debt.
REF: S 267; B 137

153. B
One of the most difficult loans for a lender to underwrite because it asks for funds to create a project that does not exist is a construction loan. A home equity loan uses a the residence as collateral for a loan. A purchase money mortgage is a form of seller financing.
REF: S 269; B 140

154. B
A balloon mortgage is an amortized mortgage that calls for a final large payment at the end of the term. An amortized mortgage is one in which uniform installment payments include payment of principal and interest. With an installment land contract, title is not transferred to the buyer until the mortgage is paid.
REF: S 287; B 135

155. A
A mortgage given by a purchaser to the seller to cover part of the purchase price is known as a purchase money mortgage. A swing loan is a type of interim loan in which a borrower uses the equity in one property to obtain the funds necessary to buy another property. With an installment land contract, title is not transferred to the buyer until the mortgage is paid.
REF: S 267; B 138

156. B
The mortgage alienation clause allows the lender to declare the balance due if the mortgagor sells the property during the mortgage term. The defeasance clause protects the borrower in having the lien released upon full payoff of the debt. Because the balance is being paid off early, the lender may be entitled to or is exercising its right to a prepayment penalty. Not all lenders charge this penalty should the loan be paid off early.
REF: S 257; B 129

157. B
Loan underwriting is the process in which the financial data and credit history of a prospective borrower are analyzed by the lender.
REF: S 181; B 133

158. C
A short-term loan that may provide funds over and above an already existing loan until permanent financing is in place is known as gap financing.
REF: S 268; B 138

159. B
A type of mortgage that gives the lender the option to convert the outstanding balance into an agreed upon percentage of ownership in the property is known as a convertible mortgage. A subordinate mortgage is one that is second in priority to another. A bridge loan is a short-term loan used to obtain interim financing
REF: B 140

160. D
A sale-leaseback is a transaction in which a property owner sells a property to an investor who immediately leases back the property to the seller as agreed to in the sales contract. Release land subdivision financing occurs when a lender releases a portion of the indebtedness on a mortgage when a certain portion of land is developed and paid for. A ground lease is a lease on unimproved land. There is no such thing as conversion mortgaging.
REF: S 271; B 141

Land Use Regulations/Development

161. D
Eminent domain allows government to take property for public use only if it is for the use and benefit of the public. Escheat allows property to revert to the state only if heirs cannot be found. Zoning ordinances are public land use controls and deed restrictions are private land use controls.
REF: S 336; B 255

162. A
The doctrine of laches refers to a loss of legal rights because of failure to assert them.
REF: S 333; B 224

163. B
The New York law that protects residents in the purchase of vacant subdivided land sold on the installment plan is Article 9-A of the Real Property Law. Article 12-A is a New York law pertaining to salespersons and brokers. The Statute of Frauds states that contracts that create an interest in real estate must be in writing.
REF: S 335; B 245

164. C
When property reverts to the state due to the lack of heirs, it is called escheat. Eminent domain is the governments right to take property for the use and benefit of the public with just compensation.
REF: S 339; B 303

165. C
The agency that coordinates information relevant to an environmental impact statement is called the lead agency. The zoning board of appeals oversees variance requests.
REF: S 334; B 274

166. A
Zoning ordinances are an example of a government's police power.
REF: S 334; B 255

167. D
Local building departments oversee building code compliance. The zoning board of appeals oversees variance requests. HUD is a federal agency that oversees housing issues. The Department of Environmental Conservation oversees water-related and other environmental issues.
REF: S 336; B 256

168. B
An in-law apartment that is connected to a residential home is called an accessory use.
REF: S339; B 280

169. A
Hospitals, schools, and courthouses are examples of institutional zoning. Public open space includes parks.
REF: S 340

170. B
The imposition of a delay in developing property in a given area is a moratorium. Transfer of development rights involve the exchange of zoning privileges from areas with low population needs, such as farmland, to areas of high population needs, such as downtown areas. Demographics are the study of the social and economic statistics of a community. Infrastructure refers to the support systems of a community.
REF: S 345; B 443

171. C
A subdivision plat in New York is generally recorded with the local county clerk's office.
REF: B 271

172. A
Topography is defined as the physical features and contours of land. The services of a community such as roads, hospitals, police, and fire departments are known as the infrastructure. The study of the social and economic statistics of a community is called demography. Geology is the study of the location of cities, countries, and waterways.
REF: S 347; B 272

173. A
The purpose of planning is to provide for the orderly growth of a community.
REF: S 344; B 269

174. B
The agency that has the statutory authority to review and approve plans for subdivision development is the local planning board or commission. Building permits allowing construction to occur and certificates of occupancy are given by the building department if the structure meets code requirements. The Department of Environmental Conservation is a New York agency. The county assessor's office oversees the real property tax assessment process.
REF: S 344; B 269

175. B
The New York law that requires local government to assess the environmental significance of actions that it must approve is the State Environmental Quality Review Act. Under the Superfund Amendment to CERCLA, innocent landowners who purchase property not knowing about contamination have a defense against liability for cleanup and fines. The Federal Clean Air Act regulates air quality standards. The Environmental Protection Agency (EPA) oversees a variety of environmental concerns.
REF: S 333; B 273

176. C
If a property owner is denied a request for a variance, he may petition the New York Supreme Court through an Article 78 Proceeding. An Article 78 proceeding is a lawsuit brought against an administrative agency.
REF: S 347; B 274

177. A
Vincent would need a use variance. A use variance allows an owner to use the property for a certain purpose.
RE: S 347; B 275

178. A
One of the differences between a request for a variance and a special use permit is that special use permits do not require that the applicant demonstrate undue hardship. A special use permit is not permitted in the zone except with the special permission of the planning board or other legislative body. An Article 78 proceeding is a lawsuit brought against an administrative agency.
REF: S 349; B 276

179. D
The New York agency that oversees wetland protection is the NYS Department of Environmental Conservation.
REF: S 405; B 271

180. B
The federal organization that oversees wetland protection navigation, flood control, and dredging projects is the Army Corps of Engineers. The U.S.D.A. stands for the U.S. Department of Agriculture. The Environmental Protection Agency is a federal agency that oversees many environmental issues.
REF: B 272

Construction

181. D
The NYS Department of Health furnishes guidelines for minimum separation distances between a well and a septic system and other sanitary guidelines.
REF: S 377; B 248

182. C
Insulation has to do with the interior of the structure, not the exterior or site.
REF: S 381-382

183. B
The concrete base below the frost line that supports the foundation of a structure is the footing. The foundation wall rests upon the footing. A slab on grade is a type of foundation. A girder is a support beam.
REF: S 382; B 234

184. A
The wooden skeleton of a residential structure of a residential property is called the frame. It is composed of wooden framing members.
REF: S 384; B 235-236

185. C
Openings for doors and windows in a residential property are supported by headers. Lally columns are support columns. Rafters are framing members for the roof. The sill plate is the base for the framing.
REF: S 386; B 237

186. B
The R- factor is a measure of heat transfer through the walls of a structure. The greater the degree of insulation, the greater the R-factor.
REF: S 390; B 247

187. D
A type of heating system that heats water in a boiler and then uses circulator pumps to propel the heated water to convectors is called a hot water system. Forced warm air systems include a duct system that blows warm air. A heat pump produces cool and warm air.
REF: S 392

188. A
The water supply and waste water systems are always separated with two different piping systems. The supply pipes bring clean water into the structure and the waste water systems carries used water from the structure.
REF: S 394-395

189. B
The minimum electrical service installed in a residential home must be 100 amps but new construction generally has 150 to 200 amp service.
REF: S 397; B 239

190. A
A device that melts and opens a circuit to stop electrical power when overheating occurs is called a fuse. The distribution panel is where the fuses or circuit breakers are located. The service drop is the electrical service coming into the property.
REF: S 397; B 241

191. B
The first wooden member of the house which is used as the nailing surface for the floor system is the sill plate. The foundation wall rests upon the footing. The fascia is a board that is perpendicular to the soffit. The ridge beam is part of the roof structure.
REF: S 384; B 236

192. B
The Act, administered by HUD, that regulates the sale of unimproved lots across state lines is known as the Interstate Land Sales Full Disclosure Act. The Superfund Amendment addresses environmental liability upon transfer of title.
REF: S 334; B 243

193. C
The National Electric Code offers minimum guidelines and standards for electrical installations. The Code is a national standard for electrical installation and service written to safeguard people and property from hazards arising from the use of electricity.
REF: S 399; B 243

194. C
The law that is the guideline for New York's drinking water regulations is the Safe Drinking Water Act. The Superfund Amendment addresses environmental liability upon transfer of title. The Residential Lead-Based Paint Hazard Reduction Act of 1992 sets forth the procedures in disclosing the presence of lead-based paint for sales of target properties built before 1978.
REF: S 402; B 244

195. D
The New York law that provides minimum standards for construction materials and safety is the NYS Fire Prevention and Building Code. The New York General Business Law provides for a one-year builder's warranty against construction defects and a six-year warranty against material defects. The New York law that protects residents in the purchase of vacant subdivided land sold on the installment plan is Article 9-A of the Real Property Law.
REF: S 364; B 245

196. A
According to New York General Business Law, a builder must warrant new construction against defects in construction for one year.
REF: S 400; B 247

197. B
According to New York law, after signing a home improvement contract, an owner has three business days after the contract was signed to cancel it.
REF: S 400; B 247

198. D
The water supply system in New York is regulated by the Department of Health. The federal organization that oversees navigation, flood control, and dredging projects is the Army Corps of Engineers.
REF: S 402; B 248

199. B
The New York law that sets minimum efficiency requirements for the design of new buildings and renovations and additions to existing buildings is the Energy Conservation Construction Code (ECCCNYS). Article 9-A protects New York residents in the purchase of vacant subdivided land sold within and without New York on the installment plan.
S 380; B 246

200. B
A seller must sign an affidavit indicating the presence of a smoke alarm and carbon monoxide detector in the sale of one- and two-family residential properties, residential condominiums and cooperatives, and residential dwellings that have appliances or systems that may emit carbon monoxide or that have an attached garage.
REF: S 401; B 246

Environmental Issues

201. D
The Superfund Amendments and Reauthorization Act imposed stringent cleanup standards and expanded the definition of those responsible for clean up. The National Environmental Policy Act and Clean Air Act are other federal environmental laws. The State Environmental Quality Review is a New York law.
REF: S 416; B 244

202. B
Local drinking water problems are remediated by local departments of health.
REF: S 367; B 250

203. C
One of the biggest dangers in highly corrosive water is that it may contain large amounts of lead. Although radon may enter a house through the water supply systems (i.e. a well), it is a gas and not corrosive. PCBs are a byproduct of electrical transformers. CFCs are a gas and are not corrosive.
REF: S 403

204. A
The NYS Department of Environmental Conservation licenses pest inspectors in New York.
REF: S 405

205. B
Asbestos is a fibrous mineral that was used in many construction applications in the past but is no longer used.
REF: S 406; B 429

206. D
The Residential Leadbased Hazard Reduction Act calls for a mutually agreeable 10-day period for a lead paint assessment before a purchaser becomes obligated under a contract. The Act applies to target properties built before 1978.
REF: S 408; B 259

207. D
Radon most generally enters the home through small cracks in the foundation wall. This is because radon comes from the ground.
REF: S 412

208. A
No level of radon is considered safe. If a property has more than four picocuries of radon, remediation is generally necessary.
REF: S 413

209. B
If the indoor air quality of a commercial building causes large numbers of people to fall ill, the building is said to have sick building syndrome.
REF: S 415; B 450

210. D
A toxic liquid organic compound used as an insulating medium for electrical transformers and has polluted the soil and waterways are called PCBs. Radon is a radioactive gas. UFFI is an insulation that contains formaldehyde. Chlorofluorocarbons are a chemical that is dangerous to our ozone layer.
REF: S 415; B 446

Valuation Process and Pricing Properties

211. C
An analysis of the competition in the market place that a property will face upon sale attempts is called a comparative market analysis. An appraisal employs at least one of the approaches to value such as the cost approach. An evaluation is not necessarily used to find market value.
REF: S 436; B 432

212. D
The income, sales, and cost approach are all appraisal approaches to value. The comparative market analysis is not.
REF: S 436-437

213. C
An owner who uses a residential property for vacation purposes only may attribute value in use to this property. Assessed value is applied by an assessor; insurance value is replacement value; and investment value is the return expected by an investor.
REF: S 434; B 169

214. A
Feasibility studies, highest and best use studies, and land utilization studies are all forms of evaluation studies. An appraisal of a single-family home is an estimate of market value.
REF: S 433

215. C
A property will probably not sell for market value if the buyer and seller are related to each other. An arm's length transaction means that buyer and seller do not know each other.
REF: S 435; B 169

216. D
Price is not always equivalent to the market value of the property. It may be either more or less.
REF: S 436

217. B
If there are construction problems and time constraints, the cost of the property may exceed the market value. One reason is that time is money.
REF: S 436

218. D
Indirect costs are the costs of architectural, engineering, licensing, permits and other expenses. Hard or direct costs are for labor and materials.
REF: S 436; B 440

219. A
Comparables used in the creation of a comparative market analysis should be as similar as possible to the subject property.
REF: S 447

220. C
Properties yet to be built are not an appropriate comparable for a comparative market analysis because market conditions may be different when these properties are placed on the market.
REF: S 438

Human Rights and Fair Housing

221. C
Redlining is an illegal practice by lenders that excludes people from culturally diverse neighborhoods from receiving housing loans. Steering is a violation of the Federal Fair Housing Act and is practice by real estate brokers that encourages culturally diverse people toward or away from certain areas.
REF: S 468; B 149

222. A
The Civil Rights Act of 1866 prohibits all discrimination based on race in the buying, selling, and leasing of property-no exceptions.
REF: S 459; B 346

223. B
Under the Federal Fair Housing Act, an administrative law judge may impose up to a 50,000 fine for a "pattern of discrimination."
REF: S 461

224. D
Blockbusting occurs when real estate salespeople tell homeowners that a member of a protected class is moving into their neighborhood causing them to panic and place their homes for sale.
REF: S 467-468; B 45

225. A
Steering occurs when real estate agents lead prospective homeowners toward or away from certain areas.
REF: S 453; B 451

226. C
One of the differences between the federal Fair Housing Law and the New York Human Rights Law is that the New York law covers commercial property as well as residential. There are other differences such as New York has more protected classes that the federal law does.
REF: S 463

227. D
The Americans with Disabilities Act covers buildings open to the public as well as multi-family dwellings.
REF: S 462; B 243

228. B
In addition to federal law, protected classes under the New York Human Rights Law include age and marital status. Other protected classes in New York, not covered by federal law, include sexual orientation and military status.
REF: S 463

229. B
Nancy cannot discriminate because of race in the rental of her apartment. The Civil Rights Act of 1866 prohibits all racial discrimination. There are no exemptions.
REF: S 459

230. A
An area designated by the NYS Department of State where salesperson and brokers may not solicit listings is in a cease and desist zone. Homeowners may request that the DOS place them on a cease and desist list.
REF: S 472; B 42

Real Estate Mathematics

231. B
$12,000 ÷ 0.07 = $78,571
REF: S 312; B 392

232. D
$8,250 ÷ 0.075 = $110,000
REF: S 312; B 392

233. C
$475,000 x .0.02 = $9,500
$475,000 + $9,500 = $484,500
$484,500 x 0.02 = $9,690
$484,500 + $9,690 = $494,190
REF: S 314

234. A
52 x 162 = 8,424 square feet
$75,000 ÷ 8,424 = $8.90
REF: S 317; B 397

235. C
43,560 ÷ 425 = 102.5 feet (rounded)
REF: S 319; B 396

236. D
$175,000 x 0.90 = $157,500
REF: S 322; B 400

237. B
\$2,500 ÷ 12 = \$208.33
\$208.33 ÷ 2 = \$104.17
\$208.33 + \$104.17 = \$312.50
REF: S 182; B 397

238. C
\$120,000 x 0.80 = \$96,000
\$96,000 x 0.03 = \$2,880
REF: S 315; B 399

239. A
\$50,000 x 0.095 = \$4,750
REF: S 313; B 398

240 B
\$2,304 ÷ 0.024 = \$96,000
\$96,000 ÷0.80 = \$120,000
REF: S 324; B 404

Municipal Agencies

241. B
The legislative power of a city is vested in its city council. The legislative power of towns is vested in the town council; and in villages, in the village board of trustees.
REF: S 357

242. D
The main function of a city or town planning board is to advise on land use matters.
REF: S 359; B 273

243. C
In most cities and towns, the zoning boards of appeals or other similar agencies hear variance requests. The town board deals with policy and laws and the planning board addresses land use issues.
REF: S 360; B 274

244. A
In many municipalities, the conservation advisory council advises on wetland regulations. The architectural review board oversees building design. The zoning board of appeals hears various requests.
REF: S 362

245. D
Building departments do not rule on variance applications. This is performed by another agency; usually the zoning board of appeals.
REF: S 364; B 251-252

246. C
The document containing each property's assessment in a municipality is the assessment roll. The tax map shows the boundaries and measurements of lots in the taxing jurisdiction.
REF: S 365; B 370

247. B
In some cities and towns, the official or agency that collects fees for water usage and other permits is the receiver of taxes. The tax assessor performs assessments.
REF: S 365

248. A
The New York agency that oversees wetland regulations is the Department of Environmental Conservation. The Department of Health oversees water related issues, disease control, and licensing of physicians, and other health professionals.
REF: S 362; B 245

249. B
A town or village planning board consists of five to seven members who are appointed.
REF: S 359-360

250. D
The historic preservation commission, zoning board of appeals, and building department would most likely deal with renovating historic property. The conservation advisory council usually addresses environmental issues.
REF: S 362

Property Insurance

251. A
A clause in an insurance policy that changes or modifies the policy is called an endorsement. A peril is a type of known hazard. A deductible is the amount the insured must pay towards a claim before receiving any policy benefits. An umbrella policy is an excess liability policy, providing additional coverage above that offered by primary policies.
REF: S 485

252. B
Insurance obtained through the New York Property Insurance Underwriting Association can be undesirable because the premiums are higher than those obtained through the voluntary market.
REF: S 490

253. B
FEMA (Federal Emergency Management Agency) administers the National Flood Insurance Program. Local programs work with FEMA.
REF: S 490

254. D
In New York, a windstorm deductible must be disclosed to the insured.
REF: S 491

255. C
As long as the insurance company states the reason for the cancellation, an insurance policy may be cancelled within 60 days. Other insurance department regulations apply to cancellations.
REF: S 491

256. D
The cost of a homeowner's policy is directly related to the policyholder and the property. There are no statewide fee schedules.
REF: S 492

257. C
The insured must pay a deductible before receiving policy benefits from a claim. A premium is the money the property owner must pay for insurance coverage. Perils are events that do damage. An endorsement is a document attached to the policy that modifies or changes the original policy in some way.
REF: S 492

258. B
An umbrella policy is an excess liability policy providing additional coverage above that offered by primary policies. A homeowner's special form policy is a type of homeowner's insurance.
REF: S 493

259. A
The declarations page of the policy outlines the basic coverage contained in the policy.
REF: S 485

260. D
Functional obsolescence is flawed or faulty property rendered inferior because of advances and change. This is not specifically covered in the insurance policy.
REF: S 485

Taxes and Assessments

261. C
Government buildings such as a VA hospital and state office building are property tax exempt as well as religious organizations such as a synagogue. Gas stations are private and not tax exempt.
REF: S 501; B 366

262. C
The tax rate is determined by the amount of the tax levy. The assessor values property for tax purposes.
REF: S 502; B 365

263. B
The percentage at which properties are assessed in a locality is called the level of assessment. The tax levy is the amount that a municipality must raise to meet budgetary requirements. The residential assessment ratio (RAR) is the assessed value divided by the sales price of the property. The tax rate is the amount of money needed by a municipality to meet budgetary requirements divided by the taxable assessed and nonexempt value of all the real property within that jurisdiction.
REF: S 505; B 383

264. D
Reassessments can be performed on properties when improvements are made, and on a regular prescribed basis.
REF: S 507; B 375

265. D
Cities, towns, and villages may be taxing jurisdictions. The state does not collect property taxes.
REF: S 510; B 369

266. B
People with disabilities, seniors, and veterans can be partially exempt from paying real property taxes. Property owners under 25 are not exempt from paying property taxes if the only reason is their age.
REF: S 512-513; B 366-369

267. D
The purpose of the board of assessment review is to hear grievances. Taxes are levied by the taxing jurisdiction, and uniform percentages are determined by the taxing jurisdiction. The equalization rate is developed by the NYS Office of Real Property Tax Services.
REF: S 514; B 378

268. B
If a property owner believes that his property's assessed value is greater than the property's full value, he may claim that he has been subject to excessive assessment. Unequal assessment occurs when a property is assessed at a higher percentage of value than the average of all other properties on the same assessment roll. Unlawful assessment includes properties that under law are fully exempt from real property taxation. Misclassification occurs when a property is wrongfully classified on the assessment roll such as if a property is classified as a homestead property when it is a nonhomestead property.
REF: S 518; B 380

269. A
A judicial review of a tax protest in the New York Supreme Court is called a tax certiorari proceeding. A grievance is a property tax complaint brought before the board of assessment review. An Article 78 proceeding is a lawsuit brought against an administrative agency.
REF: S 520; B 381

270. C
The first task in determining the assessment for tax purposes is to establish the market value of each parcel of land within the taxing unit.
REF: S 505; B 370

271. C
Government owned property is generally completely exempt from the payment of property taxes.
REF: S 501; B 366

272. A
Local governments in New York have the option of offering a reduction of property taxes to senior citizens. The other choices in the question do not have property tax exempt status.
REF: S 512-513; B 366-369

273. B
An in rem legal proceeding takes place against the real property directly and not the individual.
REF: S 521; B 384

274. C
Tax maps for the assessing are maintained the local assessor.
REF: S 365; B 366

275. C
The RAR is an indication of the level of assessment for residential real property in a municipality. The residential assessment ratio (RAR) is not used by municipalities conducting revaluation review projects.
REF: S 506; B 374

276. B
An appraisal for tax purposes and an appraisal for mortgage purposes are different in that a tax assessment takes the market value from the appraisal and applies a uniform percentage.
REF: S 365; B 370

277. D
The New York agency that certifies residential assessment ratios is the Office of Real Tax Property Services.
REF: S 506; B 374

278. B
A farm dwelling, condominium, or duplex would be classified as a type of residential or homestead property. A factory is not a homestead property.
REF: S 504; B 377

279. C
A written complaint filed with the board of assessment review to protest an assessment is known as a grievance. An *in rem* legal proceeding occurs when an action is brought against the real property directly and not against an individual and his personal property.
REF: S 514; B 378

280. A
The NYS Office of Real Property Tax Services oversees property tax laws and regulations. It is within the NYS Department of Taxation and Finance. The NYS Department of State oversees the licensure process for salespersons and brokers, among other duties. The NYS Department of Financial Services oversees insurance and banking laws and regulations. The Department of Law includes the NYS Attorney General's office.
REF: S 506; B 374

Condominiums and Cooperatives

281. A
Ownership in a cooperative is evidenced by shares of stock, not a deed. A recognition agreement is an agreement between the cooperative and other entities. An alteration agreement is an agreement for improvements to the unit between the cooperative corporation and the unit owner.
REF: S 529; B 309

282. B
A cooperative owner has a leasehold interest in the unit that is evidenced by a proprietary lease. Freehold and fee simple absolute indicate ownership in real property.
REF: S 532; B 309

283. D
The proprietary lease is given to a cooperative shareholder upon purchase of the unit. The declaration, prospectus, and initial price of the units are included in the condominium offering plan.
REF: S 533; B 309

284. B
House rules govern daily behavior in the cooperative. The alteration agreement is an agreement between a shareholder and the cooperative corporation to make improvements to the unit. A recognition agreement is an agreement between the cooperative and other entities. A letter of intent is agreement to purchase a condominium that may or may not be binding.
REF: S 533

285. C
Although a board package addresses a number of issues, some of them personal, it mainly consists of financial data.
REF: S 534

286. D
An agreement that outlines the responsibilities between the cooperative corporation and the lender is called a recognition agreement. The CPS1 statement defines how a condominium or cooperative must be advertised and rules for testing the market before the offering plan is approved by the Attorney General. The alteration agreement is an agreement between a cooperative owner and the cooperative corporation regarding an owner's improvements to the unit.
REF: S 536

287. B
A condop is a building that has both condominium and cooperative ownership.
REF: S 540

288. A
Pet restrictions and repair obligations are disclosed in the condominium's bylaws. A letter of intent is an agreement to purchase a condominium. A CPS1 statement contains the Attorney General's regulations to advertise and market the condominium before the offering plan is approved.
REF: S 542; B 281

289. D
During the CPS1 phase, the Attorney General will not allow the condominium or cooperative developer to set a definite price for the units.
REF: S 545

290. C
The mansion tax is statewide and applies to one-, two- and three-unit properties as well as condominiums and cooperatives that sell for $1 million or more.
REF: S 550; B 328

Commercial and Investment Real Estate/Real Estate Investments

291. B
Depreciation is a tax-deductible paper loss that allows investors to show less income or a deduction for tax purposes.
REF: S 607; B 182-183

292. C
The mortgage principal is not tax deductible.
REF: S 259; B 131

293. C
$15,000 x 12 = $180,000 ; $180,000 ÷ $500,000 = 36 percent
REF: S 568

294. D
$850,000 x .012 = $102,000
S 571; B 405

295. B
Property owners generally charge for the rentable square footage that includes elevators, hallways, and other common areas, not the usable square footage which is the specific office space.
REF: S 573

296. D
The natural breakeven point describes when an investor will generate a positive return. Attornment refers to a transfer of a right usually in a lease. Expense stop is a type of lease payment arrangement.
REF: S 576

297. D
A lease clause that states that future owners cannot terminate a lease if the owner fulfills his obligations is a nondisturbance clause. An escalation clause allows for increments in the lease payment. An estoppel clause confirms the lease terms. A subordination clause subordinates a lease to any mortgages on the property.
REF: S 577

298. A
A type of lease escalation clause is the Porter's wage formula that allows lease increments according to the Porter's hourly wage. Estoppel, use, and subordination clauses are other types of lease clauses.
REF: S 579

299. A
Generally, the more dollars the investor risks or puts up for an investment, the greater his return.
REF: S 559; B 176

300. C
Leverage, or borrowed funds, describes the use of other people's money. The more leverage an investor has, the less of his own funds he needs to put into the investment.
REF: S 561; B 172

301. D
Real estate investment is not a liquid investment as are investments in the stock or bond market. Real estate investment is not characterized by instant or short term turnover.
REF: S 590; B 171

302. C
A real estate investor may defer capital gains taxes by exchanging like kind properties. This type of investment is made according to a 1031 exchange allowable under IRS regulations.
REF: S 598; B 186

303. B
A feasibility study is a detailed economic analysis that considers the cost of site development, construction, financing, tax considerations, rates of return on similar investments, and the benefit to the community. An operating statement is a report of rental property receipts and disbursements, resulting in net income. The potential gross income is a projection of the gross income for a property. The proforma statement reflects a potential change in income and expenses.
REF: S 435; B 278

304. C
A short sale is a transaction in which the sale proceeds fall short of the balance owed on the property.
REF: S 581; B 175

305. B
Foreclosed properties are generally sold at an auction. A short sale is a transaction in which the sale proceeds fall short of the balance owed on the property. A lender forecloses on a property.
REF: S 581; B 175

306. B
In a short sale, the borrower sells the mortgaged property for less than the outstanding balance on the loan, and turns over the proceeds of the sale to the lender. The lender incurs the financial loss but avoids the cost and uncertainty of a foreclosure or continued nonpayment of the mortgage.
REF: S 581; B 175

307. D
The proforma schedule reflects a potential change in income and expenses. A feasibility study is a detailed economic analysis that considers the cost of site development, construction, financing, tax considerations, rates of return on similar investments, and the benefit to the community.
REF: S 568; B 168

308. D
Foreclosed properties are usually offered "as is," by a lender, and when the borrower is in default on the mortgage.
REF: S 581; B 175

309. B
The rate of return is the percentage of income that the investor receives back on an investment. The loan-to-value ratio compares a lender's loan amount to the property value. Leverage, or borrowed funds, describes the use of other people's money The time value of money calculates the value of an asset in the past, present, or future.
REF: S 560; B 176

310. C
The study of how a change in one factor affecting a real estate investment can affect the income to the property is known as sensitivity analysis. A feasibility study is a detailed economic analysis that considers the cost of site development, construction, financing, tax considerations, rates of return on similar investments, and the benefit to the community.
REF: B 177

Income Tax Issues in Real Estate

311. D
According to IRS rules, property taxes are deductible for a personal residence, a second home, and an inherited property. Real property taxes are deductible for commercial real estate as well.
REF: S 594; B 180

312. C
By law, the long-term (12 or more months) capital gains tax is 15 percent for property owners in the 15 percent tax bracket and above.
REF: S 595; B 181

313. D
Petro's misfortune is not tax deductible.
REF: S 597; B 180

314. C
According to regulations for a 1031 exchange, a personal residence is not eligible for a tax-deferred exchange.
REF: S 599; B 186

315. B
Appraisal fees, notary fees, and a mortgage preparation fee do not qualify for a tax deduction. Points, under certain conditions, are tax deductible.
REF: S 601-604

316. A
The main housing credit agency in New York is the NYS Division of Housing and Community Renewal. HUD is a federal housing agency. FEMA is a federal agency that addresses various disasters. The NYS Division of Human Rights addresses civil rights issues.
REF: S 606

317. D
According to IRS regulations, nonresidential property may be depreciated over 39 years.
REF: S 607; B 183

318. B
The 59 1/2 rule allows first-time homebuyers to use IRA distributions to fund up to $10,000 of their new home cost without paying an early distribution penalty. Safe harbor laws apply to independent contractor status.
REF: S 593

319. C
According IRS regulations for a tax-deferred exchange, a real estate exchangor has 45 days from the closing to contract for another (replacement) property.
REF: S 601; B 188

320. D
In a tax-deferred exchange, any cash in the exchange is called the boot.
S 601; B 188

Mortgage Brokerage

321. A
The New York agency that registers mortgage brokers and licenses mortgage bankers is the NYS Department of Financial Services.
REF: S 294; B 20

322. C
A NYS licensed real estate broker can use that experience to obtain a mortgage broker's registration. A salesperson needs two years experience in the mortgage business.
REF: S 296; B 21

323. A
A mortgage broker who represents a purchase in negotiating a mortgage loan has a fiduciary relationship with the client and is the client's agent.
REF: S 47; B 71

324. C
A mortgage broker who represents the purchasers in negotiating a mortgage while also representing the sellers as a real estate broker in the same transaction is acting as a dual agent.
S 298

325. C
According to the banking law, a minimum line of credit to be licensed in New York as a mortgage banker is $1 million
REF: S 300; B 21

326.C
A lender's pre approval letter verifies the applicant's credit and employment history. This letter shows the capability of the purchaser to obtain a mortgage commitment although the letter is not a commitment. An appraisal is an estimate of value.
S 301

327. A
A request by a purchaser to reserve a certain loan interest rate for a specified time is called a rate lock. A commitment is a promise by a lender to make a mortgage loan. A rate cap is a limit on an interest rate.
S 302

328. D
Loan underwriting is the process in which the financial data and credit history for a prospective borrower is analyzed by the lender. Pre approval requires that a lender validate a borrower's credit and employment history. This evaluation precedes the underwriting process and is not as involved.
REF: S 303; B 133

329. D
A lender's rebate is a form of payment to a mortgage broker for negotiating a loan from the lender.
REF: S 304

330. C
A loan that does not meet the Federal Bank loan criteria for funding is called a nonconforming loan. A straight term loan is one that may have interest only payments in the early stages of the loan.
REF: S 303

Property Management

331. C
According to New York law, if a property manager works for one owner, he does not need a license.
REF: S 615; B 338

332. A
The management agreement, which is a contract between the owner and the manager, creates an agency relationship between the two. The management proposal outlines what the property manager will do for the owner. A listing agreement is an agreement to market a property. A letter of intent is an agreement to purchase a property.
REF: S 617; B 340

333. B
In managing a property, risk management has to do with the liability of the owner when the public enters a property. This risk is covered by property insurance.
REF: S 618; B 341

334. D
If a building is 98 percent occupied, the property manager may feel justified in raising the rents. This is because the building is already generating a positive cash flow and there is less risk due to competition.
REF: S 620; B 343

335. D
Property income and expenses for week-to-week operations are computed in an operating budget. Cash flow is the profit after income and expenses are deducted. Capital reserve is a budget for repairs and improvements to the property. The stabilized budget is an income and expense projection over a number of years.
REF: S 623; B 343

336. A
$750 x 6 = $4,500 x 12 = $54,000; 7 x $1,050 = $7,350 x 12 = $88,200; $88,200 + $54,000 = $142,200 x 0.05 = $7,110; $142,200 - $7,110 = $135,090.
REF: S 621; B 393

337. B
The property management report relates expense items to the operating budget for a certain period. The property management agreement is the terms for management of the property agreed to between the manager and the owner. The rent roll is the total annual rents for the property. The stabilized budget is a projection of income and expenses over time.
REF: S 628; B 346

338. C
Lydia's assessment of items that may need repair is an example of preventative maintenance. Actually repairing an item when needed is corrective maintenance.
REF: S 625; B 342

339. A
If a property manager works for more than owner, a broker or salesperson license is required. BOMI and IREM designations are obtained from professional property management organizations if certain requirements are met.
S 615; B 338

340. D
Alexa, as fiduciary, must disclose to the owner, all monies received, and place these monies into the property management account.
REF: S 617; B 340

341. D
A resident manager who is a salaried employee of the owner and only manages the property where she lives does not need a real estate license.
S 615; B 338

342. C
The management agreement automatically creates a general agency relationship between the owner and the manager. The property manager becomes a fiduciary; a position of trust. A special agency covers one specific transaction.
REF: S 618; 341

343. A
Providing the greatest net return possible for the owner is the primary function of the property manager. Most other functions serve to produce this net maximum return. Collecting rents, residing on the property, and screening and locating tenants are possible functions of a property manager, but not required.
REF: S 615; B 341

344. C
With regard to maintenance, a property manager must supervise physical property maintenance and routinely inspect the building. To save payroll and other employee costs, the property manager may subcontract individuals and companies.
REF: S 625; B 342

345. C
The stabilized budget is a forecast of income and expenses as may be reasonably projected over a short term, typically five years. The operating budget is an annual budget and includes income and expenses for week-to-week operation. The capital reserve budget, also called a replacement reserve, is a projected budget over the economic life of the property. It includes variable expenses such as repairs, decorating, remodeling, and capital improvements.
REF: S 623; B 344

346. B
A property manager's function is to solicit tenants, hire, train, and supervise employees, and maintain adequate insurance for the owner. It is a violation of federal and state fair housing laws for a property manager to maintain records on the racial composition of the neighborhood.
REF: S 459; B 346

347. D
Although not always involved with leasing or renting, a manager for a condominium, cooperative, or PUD homeowners' association is very involved in the physical management of the property. Tasks may include coordinating common facility maintenance, landscaping, security, and enforcement of the association's or board of directors' regulations.
REF: S 622; B 355

348. C
The Certified Property Manager (CPM) designation is a National Association of REALTORS® designation given through the Institute of Real Estate Management (IREM), an NAR affiliate.
REF: S 628; B 357

349. A
Setting higher rates for families with children violates fair housing laws. However, the property manager must consider supply and demand and present vacancy rates.
REF: S 459; B 346

350. B
In managing a property, risk management has to do with the liability of the owner when the public enters a property. This risk is covered by property insurance. Corrective and preventative maintenance are other functions overseen by the property manager.
REF: S 459; B 346

General Business Law

351. B
Negotiable instruments are a substitute for money.
REF: B 197

352. B
The formation of a corporation is subject to New York statutes governing its creation. It is formed by filing articles of incorporation.
REF: S 128; B 203

353. A
The signor of a check is known as the drawor. A drawee is a person ordered in a draft to make payment. The payee is the recipient of money.
REF: B 197

354. A
Partners may hold title to real estate. Partners do not have to have the same degree of interest in the partners or the same degree of management authority. There may be two or more partners in a partnership.
REF: S 128; B 202

355. B
A homestead exemption refers to an exemption, up to a certain amount, from the bankruptcy, of the primary residence of the person filing bankruptcy. An *in rem* legal proceeding occurs when an action is brought against the real property directly and not against an individual and his personal property.
REF: B 218-219

356. C
The public official who oversees the registration of condominiums and cooperatives in New York is the NYS Attorney General.
REF: S 533; B 208

357. A
The U.S. Supreme Court hears appeals from the highest state courts. The U.S. Supreme Court does not hold trials with juries and witnesses as do lower courts.
REF: B 208

358. D
Due process mandates that anyone involved in a legal matter is entitled to have a legal proceeding according to established rules and regulations. *Caveat emptor* is Latin for 'let the buyer beware'. *Ad valorem* is Latin for 'according to value'.
REF: B 214

359. D
Stagnation is an economic cycle and is not a way a lawsuit can be resolved. Legal disputes may be resolved through one of three ways: litigation, mediation, or arbitration.
REF: B 215

360. C
The type of bankruptcy in which the debtor's nonexempt property is sold for cash, the proceeds distributed to creditors, and unpaid debts discharged is called a Chapter 7 bankruptcy. Chapter 13, consumer debt adjustment, is a rehabilitation form of bankruptcy for individuals. Chapter 11, reorganization bankruptcy, provides a method for reorganizing the debtor's financial affairs under the supervision of the bankruptcy court.
REF: B 217

Answer Key for Practice Exams

Salesperson Practice Exam 1

License Law and Regulations

1. B
The salesperson and broker licensure terms are for two years.
REF: S 23

2. C
A salesperson may receive compensation only from his sponsoring broker.
REF: S 27

3. B
It is unlawful for a salesperson or broker to draw legal documents.
REF: S 32

Law of Agency

4. C
A dual agent cannot give the fiduciary duty of undivided loyalty.
REF: S 61

5. C
A local board of REALTORS® cannot set a commission schedule. The commission is negotiated between the broker and the principal.
REF: S 55

6. C
Belinda, because of her relationship with her broker, is a subagent of the principal. The broker is the agent of the principal.
REF: S 58

7. B
In buyer agency, the buyer is the principal.
REF: S 67

8. A
From the choices in the question, the only circumstance where the disclosure form is required is when the listing agreement is signed.
REF: S 88

9. C
When two real estate firms conspire to charge the same commission rate, they are guilty of illegal price fixing. An illegal group boycott occurs when one group or person is persuaded or coerced to not do business with another group or person. An illegal market allocation agreement occurs when competing companies agree to split a territory among them.
REF: S 57

10. A
Designated agents are agents in the same brokerage firm where one agent represents the buyer and the other represents the seller. Designated agency is used when a dual agency situation arises. A broker's agent is hired by another agent to work for the client.
REF: S 65

11. B
Although many properties listed for sale have material defects, the agent has a duty to disclose the defects to all interested parties.
REF: S 52

12. D
There is no requirement that all agents be dual agents, represent the seller, or belong to the multiple listing service. However, all types of agents that work together to bring about the real estate transaction are cooperating agents.
REF: S 53

13. C
A real estate salesperson who is an independent contractor, under IRS rules, is one who is not paid according to hours worked but according to an independent contractor agreement between the agent and the broker.
REF: S 94

14. C
Independent contractors are governed by the Federal IRS code and conforming New York statutes.
REF: S 94

Legal Issues
Estates and Interests

15. B
Tenancy in common occurs when two or more people hold title to a property at the same time. Joint tenancy and tenants by the entirety (husband and wife) are ownerships attained with the unities of time, title, interest, and possession. Ownership in severalty implies sole ownership.
REF: S 124

16. B
Riparian rights belong to an owner of property bordering a flowing body of water. Chattel refers to personal property. Subsurface rights are rights to property below the surface of the earth. The bundle of rights is all of the rights inherent in real property ownership.
REF: S 115

17. B
Juan will most likely use a bill of sale. Sales contracts and purchase offers are used in the sale of real property.
REF: S 115

Legal Issues
Liens and Easements

18. B
Real property taxes are involuntary because they are imposed by the taxing jurisdiction. They are specific to the real property.
REF: S 129

19. C
A mechanic's lien is a claim by someone who has performed work on a property and has not been paid. A *lis pendens* is a notice that a lawsuit is pending.
REF: S 132

20. A
Goldie's property allows the easement so it is the servient tenement. An encroachment is the intrusion of an object on another's property. A lien is a change against another's property.
REF: S 134

Legal Issues
Deeds

21. C
A deed must have an acknowledgment to be recorded. Not all deeds have a metes and bounds description, a *hadendum* clause, or a covenant of warranty.
REF: S 153

22. D
An executor's deed, guardian's deed, and sheriff's deed are all forms of judicial deeds. An installment land contract is not a deed but rather a contract for a deed.
REF: S 157

Legal Issues
Title Closing and Costs

23. A
The purchase money mortgage is a form of seller financing. The seller is giving a mortgage rather than receiving money so it is a debit to the seller.
REF: S 177

24. D
Delinquent real property taxes generally must be paid before a closing can take place. Most often, the seller pays his back taxes before closing.
REF: S 177

The Contract of Sale and Leases
Leases

25. A
Because the lease contract has been transferred to Jamie, an assignment has taken place. Under a sublease, the original tenant, Amy, would be responsible for the lease payments. Constructive eviction occurs when the tenant is forced to move out of a leased premise because of unlivable conditions. A holdover tenancy occurs when a tenant remains in a leased premise after lease expiration.
REF: S 203

The Contract of Sale and Leases
Contracts

26. C
Nancy had to pay Tessie liquidated damages. Had there been specific performance, Nancy may have had to pay the purchase price of the property. Rescission is a withdrawal of the contract. Novation is the substitution of new contract for an old contract.
REF: S 213

The Contract of Sale and Leases
Contract Preparation

27. C
In order for a real estate salesperson to prepare a fill-in-the-blanks contract of sale approved by the Board of REALTORS®, it must contain an attorney review clause.
REF: S 234

Real Estate Finance

28. D
A balloon mortgage is a type of mortgage that is not fully amortized. A larger payment, called a balloon, is due at the end of the mortgage term. A graduated payment is a type of mortgage in which payment is lower in the early years and increase on a scheduled basis. A wraparound mortgage is a subordinate mortgage that includes the same principal obligation secured by a first mortgage against the same property. It is a type of seller financing.
REF: S 287

29. B
Equity of redemption occurs when a borrower who has defaulted on his loan may be able to regain his property by paying the outstanding debt. A deficiency judgment is a charge by a lender to parties who default on their loan and when a foreclosure proceeding does not cover the full debt on the property. A deed in lieu of foreclosure is a document transferring a property to the lender to avoid foreclosure proceedings.
REF: S 262

30. C
The acceleration clause allows the lender to declare the entire balance due if the borrower defaults. The prepayment penalty clause is a fine imposed by the lender if the mortgage is paid off before it is due. The granting clause is part of a deed. The defeasance clause gives the borrower the right to pay off the loan.
REF: S 255

31. B
A blanket mortgage allows two or more parcels to be pledged as security for the loan. A package mortgage allows personal property, in addition to real property, to be pledged to secure payment of the mortgage loan. A bridge loan is a short-term loan. An installment contract allows title to pass to the borrower once the mortgage obligations are fulfilled.
REF: S 267

32. C
FHA, the Federal Housing Authority, is an agency of HUD. Fannie Mae, Sonny Mae, and Freddie Mac are not affiliated with HUD.
REF: S 271

Land Use Regulations

33. B
Article 9-A is the New York law that regulates the sale of unimproved lots across state lines. The Interstate Land Sales Full Disclosure Act is a similar federal law. The State Environmental Quality Review Act is a New York law regulating environmental issues when land is improved. The Uniform Fire Prevention and Building Code is a New York construction code.
REF: S 335

34. D
Condemnation is the act of taking a property because of an eminent domain action. Escheat occurs when the government takes property of the deceased if no heirs are found. Estoppel is generally a court order to stop an act. *In rem* is a type of legal proceeding against real property and not the individual's personal property.
REF: S 336

35. C
Emma would need an area variance. A use variance allows a property to be used for a certain purpose. A nonconforming use is one that already existed before the zoning was changed. Illegal spot zoning occurs when property does not conform to the surroundings.
REF: S 348

Construction and Environmental Issues

36. A
Foundations are poured concrete or concrete block.
REF: S 383

37. C
The soffit is the area under the roof extension. The fascia is a board that is perpendicular to the soffit. The third component of the roof overhang is the frieze board. This is a wooden framing member fastened directly under the soffit, against the top of the wall. Sheathing is a plywood material that covers the roof rafters.
REF: S 387

38 . A
In the sale of one- and two-family residential properties as well as condominiums and cooperatives in New York, the seller must present a signed smoke alarm and carbon monoxide detector affidavit at closing.
REF: S 401

39. B
The New York law that requires preparation of an environmental impact statement on properties that a government body has the jurisdiction to review is the State Environmental Quality Review Act. The Superfund Amendment and CERCLA address liability upon transfer of title. The Real Estate Settlement Procedures Act is a federal law applying to real estate closings.
REF: S 416

40. B
Disclosure of knowledge of the existence of leadbased paint must be made in the sale or lease of pre-1978 target residential properties.
REF: S 408

Valuation Process and Pricing Properties

41. D
Because both the comparative market analysis and the sales comparison approach compare properties that are similar to the subject, the CMA is most similar to the sales comparison approach. The income (capitalization) approach and cost approach are other appraisal approaches to value.
REF: S 436-437

42. A
Evaluations do not necessarily produce an estimate of value, as does an appraisal or CMA. Value in use is not a land utilization study but defines the usefulness of a property to the owner.
REF: S 434-435

43. B
A real estate agent must be able to adjust the listing price according to the market.
REF: S 447

Human Rights and Fair Housing

44. C
Testers are volunteers who visit real estate firms and other businesses to assess equal treatment for all.
REF: S 453

45. D
Real estate agents cannot violate human rights laws in taking listings or any other real estate activity.
REF: S 461

46. C
Illegal blockbusting includes prompting homeowners to sell their properties due to the entry of certain persons of a particular race or religion into the neighborhood.
REF: S 467

47. A
The lender is guilty of illegal redlining; that is, denying or restricting loans in a certain area by a lending institution. Steering is a practice by real estate brokers that encourages culturally diverse people toward or away from certain areas. Blockbusting occurs when real estate salespeople tell homeowners that a member of a protected class is moving into their neighborhood causing them to panic and place their homes for sale. These activities are all violations of the Federal Fair Housing Act and New York laws.
REF: S 468

Real Estate Mathematics

48. B
$90,000 x .06 = $5,400
$5,400 x .60 = $3,240
REF: S 312

49. D
$217,500 ×.02 = $4,350
REF: S 323-324

Municipal Agencies

50. C
The planning board would most likely have the task of mapping a large parcel of land that was granted to the city. The assessor's office values property for tax purposes. The zoning board of appeals hears variance requests. The architectural review board oversees building design.
REF: S 344-345

51. D
Francesca will have to apply for a variance so she will need to go before the zoning board of appeals. But she probably also has to gain approval for the project from the architectural review board. It is possible that the board will not allow the project and then she will not need to apply for the variance. The conservation advisory council oversees environmental issues including wetlands.
REF: S 361-362

Property Insurance

52. B
The missing $1,000 is the deductible that is paid by the insured toward the claim before he receives any policy benefits. Perils are events that cause damage. An umbrella policy is an excess liability policy, providing additional coverage above that offered by primary policies. An endorsement is a document attached to the policy that modifies or changes the original policy in some way.
REF: S 492

53. B
The coverage that the Lee's have is for replacement cost. Replacement cost means that the insured is covered and reimbursed for the actual cost of replacing the damaged property. Actual cash value means that the insured is reimbursed for the replacement cost minus the physical depreciation of the lost or damaged property. An umbrella policy is an excess liability policy providing additional coverage above that offered by primary policies.
REF: S 488

Taxes and Assessments

54. D
The map referred to in the question is a tax map. A plat is a property map such as a subdivision map. A blueprint is an architect's rendering of a structure. A survey is a detailed rendering of the physical boundaries, elevations, and other details of a property.
REF: S 502

55. D
An assessing unit that levies real property taxes can be a city, town, or county.
REF: S 501

56. C
Residential assessment ratios (RAR) are used for board of assessments review grievances and small claims hearings. RARs are not used if there are less than five residential sales that year in the taxing unit, for revaluation projects, or determining tax exemptions.
REF: S 506

Condominiums and Cooperatives

57. D
A cooperative shareholder receives a proprietary lease to the cooperative unit, not a deed.
REF: S 529

58. B
The owner or developer of a condominium or cooperative is called the sponsor. A trustor transfers a trust fund or other account to a trustee.
REF: S 543

59. B
The CPS1 statement contains the Attorney General rules for testing the market for a new condominium or cooperative development. The UCC-1 statement is filed with the county clerk when a condominium is transferred. The Civil Practice Rules and Procedure (CPLR) addresses legal procedures in New York. Section 443 of the Real Property law addresses agency disclosure.
REF: S 545

Commercial and Investment Properties

60. D
The pro forma statement reflects a potential change in income and expenses. The cash flow statement, operating statement, and statement of net worth are other types of financial statements.
REF: S 568

61.B
$2,250 x 12 = $27,000; $27,000 ÷ 0.07 = $385,714 (rounded)
REF: S 572

62. B
A process that calculates the value of an asset in the past, present and future is called the time value of money. Leverage is the use of other people's money. Debt service is the payment of principal and interest. Net operating income is property expenses deducted from gross income.
REF: S 560

63. C
$750,000 ÷$1,000,000 = 75 percent
REF: S 561

64. D
Land does not necessarily have less resale value than other types of investment property.
REF: S 563

65. B
Income received on a property without deducting expenses is gross income. Once expenses are deducted, the remaining monies are net income. NOI stands for net operating income. The net operating income is the operating income minus operating expenses and debt service or the cash flow. Debt service is the annual amount to be paid to pay off or reduce a loan.
REF: S 566

66. C
Once all expenses and debt service are paid, the monies remaining are called cash flow. A tax shelter is method of protecting income from taxation. Gross income is income received without subtracting expenses. The cash-on-cash return is a value measurement for a property that considers the equity in the property measured against the cash flow.
REF: S 568

67. D
The cash-on-cash return considers the equity in the property against the cash flow. The capitalization rate is the annual return that an investor expects to receive. The rate of return is the percentage amount that an investor receives back on the investment.
REF: S 568

68. D
Just as other types of investments, like the stock market, for example, profit is never guaranteed for any type of investment.
REF: S 559

Income Tax Issues in Real Estate Transactions

69. D
There is not a 39 percent federal tax bracket for income tax purposes. The highest tax bracket is 35 percent.
REF: S 593

70. D
According to the IRS, mortgage interest and property taxes are all federal tax deductions for property ownership.
REF: S 594

71. D
Annie and Xavier do not have to pay a capital gains tax on the sale of their property. They have lived in their house for five years and the profit on the sale of $50,000 is less than their $500,000 married couple exemption.
REF: S 595

Mortgage Brokerage

72. A
If an applicant for a mortgage broker's registration also holds a real estate broker's license, he must submit a dual agency affidavit to the NYS Department of Financial Services. An estoppel certificate may be included in a commercial lease.
REF: S 296

73. C
A real estate salesperson needs two years of experience in the mortgage brokerage business to apply for a mortgage broker registration. A licensed real estate broker can use this license as the experience for the mortgage broker registration.
REF: S 295

Property Management

74. D
Advisors to property managers who focus on long-term financing planning rather than day-to-day operations of the property are asset managers.
REF: S 616

75. A
A document submitted to the property owner outlining the commitment of the property manager once he is employed is the management agreement. The management proposal is submitted before the agreement and outlines what the property manager plans to accomplish.
REF: S 617

Salesperson Practice Exam 2

License Law and Regulations

1. C
A person must be at least 20 years old to be licensed as a real estate broker in New York.
REF: S 13

2. A
Attorneys who are admitted to practice in the New York courts are exempt from obtaining a license as long as they do not employ salespeople.
REF: S 16

3.B
According to New York law, brokers must maintain a separate escrow account for client monies including deposits. The office operating account must be separate.
REF: S 32

Law of Agency

4. D
An illegal net listing contract allows the broker to keep as a commission any money obtained from the sale above a sale price specified by the seller.
REF: S 32

5. D
A broker's agent is one who is hired by a broker to assist the broker in selling or finding a property for the principal.
REF: S 70

6. A
Under New York law, dual agency is permissible with disclosure and informed consent of buyer and seller.
REF: S 61

7. D
With an exclusive agency arrangement, the broker is legally entitled to the commission if the exclusive broker or another broker effects sale of the property, but not if the owner sells the property without the assistance of any broker. An exclusive-right-to-sell agreement allows the broker to receive a commission no matter who sells the property. An open listing arrangement allows the property to be listed with a number of brokers who receive a commission only if they sell the property. An illegal net listing contract allows the broker to keep as a commission any money obtained from the sale above a sale price specified by the seller.
REF: S 78

8. C
The first law to address antitrust violations was the Sherman Antitrust Act. The Clayton Antitrust Act is another antitrust law. The Real Estate Settlement Procedures Act addresses regulations having to do with real estate closings.
REF: S 57

9. B
This example illustrates an illegal tie-in arrangement because as a condition of sale, the buyer must obtain financing from a specified company. An illegal group boycott occurs when one group or person is persuaded or coerced to not do business with another group or person. An illegal market allocation agreement occurs when competing companies agree to split a territory among them.
REF: S 57

10. B
An agency relationship created by an oral or written agreement between a principal and agent is an express agency. Implied agency can be created through the acts of the parties. Dual agency occurs when one broker represents the buyer and seller in the same transaction. A power of attorney allows a person to legally manage the affairs of another.
REF: S 54

11. B
Under an exclusive-right-to-sell contract, Martin owes a commission to Broker Gerald even though Martin sells the house himself. This is a possible breach of contract. Reformation permits a court to rewrite a contract perhaps in case of a typographical or other mistake. Injunction is a court order to stop an act. Assignment is the giving over of the contract to another.
REF: S 212

12. D
Under an amendment to Section 443 of the New York Real Property law, buyers or sellers may give advance informed consent to dual agency by indicating consent on the Agency Disclosure Form.
REF: S 61

13. C
In the independent contract relationship, there are no deductions taken for income taxes. Paying income tax is the responsibility of the licensee.
REF: S 94-95

14. A
Real estate licensees are classified as independent contractors under Section 3508 (a) (b) of the IRS Code. Article 12-A applies to the New York salesperson and broker license law. Section 443 of the New York Real Property Law applies to agency disclosure.
REF: S 95

Legal Issues
Estates and Interests

15. C
The unities that make up a joint tenancy are the unities of time, title, interest, and possession. Partition is a court action to divide a property owned by tenants in common.
REF: S 125

16. B
The most complete form of real property ownership is fee simple absolute. Fee simple defeasible estates have conditions for ownership. A fee simple defeasible ownership is recognized by the words "but if" in the transfer. A life estate is ownership for a person's life or another's life.
REF: S 119

17. D
This question is an example of a life estate (with a remainder interest). The property will go to another party after the life tenant. A fee simple absolute estate is complete title to a property. A leasehold estate is not ownership but rental. A joint tenancy is a type of ownership with the right of survivorship.
REF: S 120-121

Legal Issues
Liens and Easements

18. D
A judgment is an involuntary general lien because it is without the permission of the property holder and can apply to all of his property.
REF: S 129-130

19. B
A l*is pendens* is a notice that a lawsuit is pending affecting title or possession of a property. An injunction is a court order to stop an act. A judgment is a lien against all property of the debtor. A mechanic's lien is a lien for unpaid labor or materials.
REF: S 130

20. C
Lionel's property requires an easement by necessity because it is landlocked and Lionel cannot exit the property any other way. An easement by condemnation is created by eminent domain. A negative easement is an easement not to do something such as block a view. An encroachment is the intrusion of an object across a boundary line.
REF: S 136

Legal Issues
Deeds

21. C
A type of deed used in bankruptcy proceedings and foreclosures is a referee's deed. A sheriff's deed, executor's deed, and guardian's deed are other types of judicial deeds.
REF: S 157

22. B
In order to claim title by adverse possession in New York, the use must be open and notorious for ten years.
REF: S 161

Title Closing and Costs

23. C
Discount points, the hiring of an attorney by the purchaser, and a purchase money mortgage are all common closing events. Outstanding liens would generally delay a closing because the title would not be clear.
REF: S 165

24. A
On the closing statement, the earnest money deposit appears a buyer credit. Prepaid real property taxes, a prepaid insurance premium, and the sale of personal property are all seller credits.
REF: S 176

The Contract of Sale and Leases
Leases

25. B
A periodic lease automatically renews itself at the end of the term unless notice is given. A proprietary lease is given to cooperative unit owners along with shares of stock as evidence of their ownership share.
REF: S 194

The Contract of Sale and Leases

Contracts

26. A
An option is a unilateral contract because only one party, the optionor, makes a promise. The option specifies a time limit in which the optionee can choose to purchase. It is not a contract to convey title.
REF: S 225

The Contract of Sale and Leases

Contract Preparation

27. D
Contingency clauses, addenda, and riders are all possible additions to the contract. A codicil is an addition to a will.
REF: S 161

Real Estate Finance

28. C
A HUD agency (Department of Housing and Urban Development) that purchases VA (Department of Veteran's Affairs) and FHA (Federal Housing Administration) mortgages on the secondary market is Ginnie Mae (Government National Mortgage Association). RHS is the Rural Housing Service that makes loans and grants to rural properties. SONYMA is the State of New York Mortgage Agency that loans money for target properties. FDIC (Federal Deposit Insurance Corporation) insures bank deposits.
REF: S 276

29. B
A mortgage clause that allows a lender to declare the balance due if the borrower sells the property is the alienation clause. The prepayment penalty clause is a fine imposed by the lender if the mortgage is paid off before it is due. The granting clause is part of a deed. The defeasance clause gives the borrower the right to pay off the loan.
REF: S 257

30. D
A mortgage that provides for paying the debt by monthly payment of principal and interest and in which the interest portion of the payments decreases as the principal portion increases is an amortized loan. A balloon mortgage does not fully retire the debt. An installment land contract calls for a transfer of title after all payments are made. A swing loan is a type of short-term loan.
REF: S 265

31. B
Regulation Z of the Truth-in-Lending Act addresses the accurate advertising of credit terms. The Real Estate Settlement Procedures Act addresses disclosure of closing costs. The Community Reinvestment Act encourages lenders to meet the credit needs of communities. The Anti-Predatory Lending Law is a New York law that places many restrictions on high-cost (subprime) loans that are first or junior mortgages.
REF: S 277

32. A
An adjustable rate mortgage rate floats based on a standard index as opposed to a fixed rate that stays the same throughout the mortgage term. A straight term mortgage allows interest only payments for a specified time.
REF: S 265

Land Use Regulations

33. B
In New York, variance requests are brought to the zoning board of appeals.
REF: S 347

34. C
The boundaries and physical dimensions of a property are shown in a survey. A feasibility study determines a project's usefulness and projected success in the community. A plat is a subdivision map.
REF: S 347

35.C
Parks and forests are classified as public open space. Institutional properties include hospitals and schools.
REF: S 340

Construction and Environment

36. C
UFFI (urea formaldehyde foam insulation) is a type of spray-inside-the-wall insulation that is not longer allowed. This is because it contained irritating and unhealthful levels of formaldehyde. Loose fill, rigid, and batt are other types of insulation.
REF: S 390

37. B
The amount of electrical current flowing though a wire is the amperage. Voltage is the force or push of the current. Milligauss is a measurement of electromagnetic field strength.
REF: S 397

38. B
The New York Energy Conservation Construction Code mandates minimum R-factors for insulation. The Real Property Law addresses real estate license law and other property issues. The Emergency Tenant Protection Act governs rent control and rent regulations. The Sanitary Code is overseen by the NYS Health Department and addresses health and sanitation issues.
REF: S 380

39. C
Senior citizen housing is generally exempt from disclosure under the Residential Lead-Based Hazard Reduction Act. The Act is aimed at children who might eat lead from paint chips and dirt.
REF: S 408

40. A
One of the most prevalent concerns for underground storage tank is leakage caused over time by erosion, wear, and tear of the tank material.
REF: S 417

Valuation Process and Pricing Properties

41. C
The goal of an accurate CMA is to find properties in as close proximity as possible to the subject property.
REF: S 447

42. B
Surveyors and appraisers fees in relation to property development are indirect costs. Hard or direct costs are costs for labor and materials. Impact fees are made to the municipality by a developer for infrastructure and other requirements.
REF: S 436

43. A
An arm's length transaction means that the parties are not related as relatives or business associates.
REF: S 435

Human Rights and Fair Housing

44. D
In New York, in the sale of a single-family home, there are no exemptions in the New York Human Rights Law whether or not Hattie uses the services of a real estate broker. She also cannot discriminate against a person's race in any real property sale as this violates the federal Civil Rights Act of 1868 where there are no exemptions for racial discrimination.
REF: S 465

45. C
The fine for a first offense in violation of the Federal Fair Housing Act can be up to $10,000.
REF: S 461

46. B
According to the New York Human Rights law, brokerage offices must display the HUD fair housing poster.
REF: S 464

47. C
Federal has fewer protected classes than New York. The New York Human Rights law adds to the federal law the protected classes of marital status, age, sexual orientation, and military status.
REF: S 463

Real Estate Mathematics

48. D
3 × $8,000 = $24,000; $9,000 × 4 = $36,000; $36,000 - $24,000 = $12,000 = 50 percent
REF: S 311

49. C
150 x 500 = 75,000 sq ft; 75,000 ÷ 43,560sq ft/acres =1.72 acres
1.72 acres x $5,000 = $8,600 acreage basis; $20 x 500 = $10,000 front foot basis
REF: S 315

Municipal Agencies

50. B
The building department oversees compliance with the building code, inspects properties during and after construction, and issues building permits. Government agencies in New York cannot require property owners to restore or rehabilitate a historic structure.
REF: S 335

51. A
The conservation advisory council accepts grants made to the municipality for lands under its jurisdiction such as wetlands. The planning board oversees land use issues. The architectural review board oversees building design. The building department oversees the building code.
REF: S 362

Property Insurance

52. B
Perils are events that cause damage and are included on the insurance policy. Some perils are excluded from basic policies but may be added to the policy or obtained in a separate policy (i.e. flood insurance). Lenders require homeowner's insurance to obtain a mortgage, an endorsement is an attachment to the insurance policy, and an insurance policy is a legal contract.
REF: S 485

53. D
Usually, additional property coverage, such as a storage shed, is covered at 10 percent of the residence limit. Therefore, the residence was insured for $200,000.
REF: S 488

Taxes and Assessments

54. B
The level of assessment is the percentage of market value at which properties are assessed. $300,000 × .75 = $225,000.
REF: S 505

55. C
The purpose of a special assessment is to collect payment for a share of improvements made to the area. A judicial review of a tax protest in the New York Supreme Court is called a tax certiorari proceeding. Reassessments can be performed on properties when improvements are made, and on a regular prescribed basis. The tax levy is the amount that a municipality must raise to meet budgetary requirements by taxing real property.
REF: S 511

56. A
An *in rem* legal proceeding is a legal action brought against the real property and not against an individual and his personal property. An injunction is a court order to stop a specific action. A judicial review of a tax protest in the New York Supreme Court is called a tax certiorari proceeding. A reformation is a court order that permits the parties to rewrite a contract when a mistake such as a clerical error is made.
REF: S 521

Condominiums and Cooperatives

57. B
In a cooperative, the board of directors must approve a prospective buyer.
REF: S 534

58. C
In a cooperative, the cooperative corporation owns the common areas.
REF: S 532

59. D
The alteration agreement is a contract between the shareholder and the cooperative to make structural changes to the unit. A letter of intent is an agreement to purchase a condominium that may or may not be binding. House rules govern daily behavior in the cooperative. Subscription agreements are the contracts that the sponsor possesses to purchase shares of stock in the cooperative units.
REF: S 534

Commercial and Investment Properties

60. D
$20,000 x 12 =$240,000; $240,000 ÷ $600,000 = 40 percent
REF: S 568

61. A
The profit from income producing properties, less income taxes is the after cash tax flow. The before cash tax flow is profit before income taxes. Debt service is the payment of principal and interest. Debt is what the investor owes. Equity is the investor's interest in the property. The debt-to-equity ratio describes the percentage of the capital that is invested.
REF: S 569

62. B
$10,000 + $2,000 = $12,000; $12,000 x 0.35 = $4,200
REF: S 569

63. D
A paper income loss on investment property is called a tax shelter. Gross income is income received without deducting operating expenses. Debt service is the payment of principal and interest. Leverage is the use of other people's money.
REF: S 569

64. D
$650,000 ÷ 0.12 = $5,416,667 (rounded)
REF: S 571

65. A
Property owners lease commercial space according to the rentable square footage that is the entire space. The usable square footage does not include elevators and hallways, for example.
REF: S 573

66. B
The loss factor is the area that is part of the rented space that is not specifically usable to the tenant.
REF: S 573

67. A
A loft is a type of commercial space that is not generally divided into rooms.
REF: S 576

68. B
Unlike many residential leases, a commercial lease is generally customized. This is because most spaces are unique and there are different tenant needs for each. A periodic lease automatically renews itself for another period at the end of each period unless one party gives notice to the other at the prescribed time.
REF: S 574

Income Tax Issues in Real Estate Transactions

69. B
The basis is the cost of the property. The adjusted basis includes other costs such as the fire that devalued the property.
REF: S 597

70. B
A limited partner does not materially participate in the managing and operation of the investment. Therefore, under the IRS code, Harry's income from the investment is classified as a passive activity. Active income includes salaries or income from a business in which the taxpayer materially participates. Portfolio income is interest, annuities, dividends, royalties, and profits from the sale of portfolio assets.
REF: S 597

71. C
In a tax-deferred exchange, the individual who accepts the funds from the sale and handles the contract is called the qualified intermediary (QI).
REF: S 600

Mortgage Brokerage

72. D
The pre-application disclosure and fee agreement is used by mortgage brokers to make certain disclosures regarding the mortgage fee and other matters. The agency disclosure form discloses whom the real estate agent represents in the sale of rental of one-to-four unit residential properties and condominiums and cooperatives in any size building. A pre approval letter is a document from a lender stating that a purchaser is pre approved for a loan. A letter of intent is an agreement to purchase a property such as a condominium.
REF: S 298

73. D
A mortgage banker is licensed by the NYS Department of Financial Services.
REF: S 295

Property Management

74. D
There are various fee arrangements between a property manager and owner. One of them is a base fee and a percentage of the rents collected.
REF: S 617

75. D
Because they perform a variety of duties, property managers are general agents. Because of their role as agents, a fiduciary relationship, a position of trust, exists between the manager and the owner. A special agent generally performs one duty such as marketing the real estate.
REF: S 617-618

Broker Practice Exam I

The Broker's Office: Operation, Management, and Supervision

1. B
Once a broker receives a deposit, he or she must immediately deposit it in an escrow account until the money is needed such as at closing. At closing, sometimes the deposit money comprises some or all of the broker's commission. In certain areas, brokers turn over deposit money to the seller's attorney who places it in his or her escrow account.
REF: B 41

2. B
An agent must disclose any material defects he or she knows about to a prospective buyer.
REF: B 44

3. C
Generally, if a real estate broker receives compensation from more than one party in the transaction, the broker must disclose the fact and receive the consent of all parties to the transaction.
REF: B 44

4. C
All ads placed by a broker must indicate that the advertiser is a broker and give the name and telephone number. Ads that do not contain this information are called blind ads.
REF: B 45

5. A
A property condition disclosure form, used in the sale of one-to –four unit residential properties and completed by the seller, assists in disclosing property defects and other issues to prospective buyers.
REF: B 257

6. B
An illegal net listing is one in which a broker sets a sales price for a property and uses any amount that the property sells above that amount for his or her commission
REF: B 43

7. B
The sales agent must obtain permission from the sellers to post a for sale sign on their property. Offering a property for sale or lease without the authorization of the owner is a violation of the license law.
REF: B 43

8. A
Broker Lately must not allow unlicensed salespeople to transact real estate. This is a violation of the license law.
REF: B 61

9. B
Under the IRS code, real estate licensees are independent contractors. As such, work hours for an independent contractor cannot be mandated by a broker. Independent contractors must set their own hours and are paid for work product, not for hours worked.
REF: B 55

10. C
The governmental commission that has the power to declare trade practices unfair is the Federal Trade Commission, also known as the FTC. The FTC oversees antitrust violations.
REF: B 51

11. A
An illegal market allocation agreement is one in which competitors divide or allocate a market area for sales and agree not to compete in those areas. A tie-in arrangement is between a party selling a service to a buyer, that as a condition of sale, the buyer will buy another product from the seller or not do business with another. Price fixing occurs when competitors in a certain group conspire to charge the same or similar price. A group boycott is a conspiracy in which a person or group is coerced into not doing business with another person or group.
REF: B 52

12. D
A tie-in arrangement is between a party selling a service to a buyer, that as a condition of sale, the buyer will buy another product from the seller. A group boycott is a conspiracy in which a person or group is coerced into not doing business with another person or group. Price fixing occurs when competitors in a certain group conspire to charge the same or similar price. A market allocation agreement is an agreement between competitors who are dividing or assigning a certain area or territory for sales.
REF: B 52

13. C
All ads placed by a broker must indicate that the advertiser is a broker and give the name and telephone number. Ads that do not contain this information are called blind ads.
REF: B 45

14. B
All levels of NYS appraisal licensure, payable to the NYS Department of State, require a $325 fee for a two-year term (except for the appraiser assistant license) which is $275).
REF: B 20

15. D
Violations of real estate license law include not providing definitions of exclusive right to sell and exclusive agency listings. This is necessary in the sale of one-to-three unit dwellings but does not apply to condominiums and cooperatives. In all listing agreements, the broker must provide a printed explanation of the difference between the two listings.
REF: B 44

16. A
Associate brokers and salespersons who want additional licenses must obtain permission from each sponsoring broker and submit a statement to DOS from each sponsoring broker indicating acknowledgment of each licensure.
REF: B 39

17. A
When a salesperson or associate broker terminates their association with the broker, the broker must file a termination of association notice online to DOS with a fee in the amount of $10.
REF: B 39

Real Estate Agency Disclosure

18. C
A seller's broker, in his fiduciary role, may not advise a buyer that the seller is anxious to sell because of a job transfer. Because of the fiduciary relationship, the principal is owed loyalty, faith, trust, and confidentiality by the agent hired.
REF: B 73

19. D
A broker must obey reasonable and lawful instructions from the principal. The broker must disclose material defects to the buyer even though the buyer is a third party outside of the fiduciary relationship between the broker and the principal. The broker must obey all human rights laws and present all offers to the sellers.
REF: B 73

20. D
The principal must disclose all information to the agent bearing on the agency relationship. If the agent is found liable to third parties for the principal's misrepresentation, the agent is entitled to repayment from the principal. The repayment is indemnification to the agent and makes the agent financially whole.
REF: B 76

21. C
A franchise is an umbrella organization that lends its name and expertise to member firms that carry the franchise name. In New York, with some franchise firms, the franchise fee portion is deducted from the final commission due the sales associate
REF: B 36

22. D
Giving legal advice to principals or customers may constitute the unauthorized practice of law by real estate agents. Agents should refer legal questions to an attorney. Loyalty, reasonable care, and confidentiality are all common law fiduciary duties of an agent to the principal.
REF: B 42

23. A
A broker's agent is an agent who cooperates or is engaged by a listing agent, buyer's agent, or tenant's agent. In this relationship, the principal is not vicariously liable for acts of the broker's agent. The broker who engaged the broker's agent agents accepts this liability.
REF: B 82

24. B
In New York, dual agency is legal with timely disclosure and informed consent.
REF: B 84

25. B
Subagency can be created when a seller and broker agree, usually by means of an MLS, that other agents will also work for the seller. The principal can agree to accept or reject the option of subagency when signing the listing agreement.
REF: B 80

26. C
Subagents of the seller must also deal honestly and ethically with the buyer or customer and disclose any pertinent information that may affect the value of the specific property.
REF: B 110

27. D
An undisclosed dual agency is a violation of the Real Property Law and is legally classified as a misdemeanor.
REF: B 86

Real Estate Finance II

28. D
Because the balance is being paid off early, the lender may be entitled to or is exercising its right to a prepayment penalty. Not all lenders charge this penalty should the loan be paid off early. The defeasance clause in a mortgage gives the borrower the right to redeem the title and have the mortgage lien released at any time before default by paying the debt in full. The alienation clause entitles the lender to declare the entire principal balance of the debt immediately due and payable if the borrower sells the property during the mortgage term.
REF: B 128

29. A
The loan-to-value ratio establishes how much the borrower will pay from his or her personal funds toward the purchase of the property. This is the down payment.
REF: B 132

30. C
Fannie Mae (short for Federal National Mortgage Association) is part of the secondary mortgage market where mortgage loans are purchased from the primary mortgage market. The VA (Department of Veterans Affairs) and FHA (Federal Housing Authority) are government-backed agencies and are part of the primary mortgage market. SONYMA (State of New York Mortgage Agency) makes mortgage loans to target areas in New York.
REF: B 146

31. B
A swing loan is a type of interim loan in which a borrower uses the equity in one property to obtain the funds necessary to buy another property. A purchase money mortgage is a type of seller financing. A package mortgage is one in which personal property as well as real property is pledged to secure payment of the note. A convertible mortgage gives the lender the option of converting the outstanding balance into an agreed-upon percentage of property ownership.
REF: B 138

32. C
Mortgage liens are generally paid according to priority of the date and time of recording.
REF: B 139-140

33. D
A purchase money mortgage is a type of seller financing in which the seller holds the mortgage on the property. A bridge loan is a legal short-term loan used to obtain interim financing for projects before a long-term loan is in place. With an installment land contract, title is not transferred to the buyer until the mortgage is paid. A wraparound mortgage is a subordinate mortgage that includes the same principal obligation secured by a superior mortgage against the same property
REF: B 138

34. C
Release land subdivision financing is structured so that the borrower has a monetary stake in the land before a mortgage is given. Gap financing is short-term financing until permanent financing is in place. A wraparound mortgage is a subordinate mortgage that includes the same principal obligation secured by a superior mortgage against the same property. A sale-leaseback is a transaction in which a property owner sells a property to an investor who immediately leases back the property to the seller as agreed to in the sales contract.
REF: B 141

35. A
A sale-leaseback is a transaction in which a property owner sells a property to an investor who immediately leases back the property to the seller. A ground lease is a long-term lease of unimproved land, usually for construction purposes. A wraparound mortgage is a subordinate mortgage that includes the same principal obligation secured by a superior mortgage against the same property. A purchase money mortgage is a type of seller financing in which the seller holds the mortgage on the property.
REF: B 141

36. D
A ground lease is a long-term lease of unimproved land, usually for construction purposes. Sale leaseback is a transaction in which a property owner sells a property to an investor who immediately leases back the property to the seller. A periodic lease is renewable at the end of the period and can be for any duration. Gap financing is short-term financing until permanent financing is in place.
REF: B 142

37. C
With an installment land contract, title is not transferred to the buyer until the mortgage is paid.
REF: B 136

38. D
Used by older people who need additional income and want to take advantage of the equity in their homes, a reverse annuity mortgage allows homeowners to draw upon the equity in their homes during their lifetime. A balloon mortgage is an amortized mortgage that calls for a final larger payment at the end of the term. A straight term mortgage calls for an interest-only payment for a specified term. A shared appreciation mortgage allows a lender to share in the profits of the mortgagor.
REF: B 136

39. C
A package mortgage pledges personal property such as furniture in addition to the real property. A mortgage given by a buyer to the seller to cover part of the purchase price is known is a purchase money mortgage. A convertible mortgage gives the lender the option of converting the outstanding balance into an agreed-upon percentage of property ownership. A home equity loan uses the security in one's home for the mortgage debt.
REF: B 137

Real Estate Investments

40. C
By using other people's money (OPM), the investor's buying power is increased. The use of borrowed funds is called leverage.
REF: B 172

41. B
Capital gain is the profit realized from the sale of a real estate investment. Portfolio income includes interest, annuities, dividends, and royalties. Debt service includes mortgage principal and interest payments.
REF: B 181

42. C
A tax shelter is best defined as a paper loss; it is a phrase used to describe some of the advantages of real estate investments. Negative amortization occurs when the monthly payment is less than full interest and does not pay any principal. The interest that is unpaid accrues and the principal balance owed increases. Capital gain is the profit realized from the sale of a real estate investment. Boot is the cash received in a tax-deferred exchange.
REF: B 185

43. D
The cash flow represents the net proceeds after all expenses are met and may be measured before or after taxes are considered. Debt service is the annual amount needed to pay off or reduce a loan.
REF: 184

44. B
Tax depreciation is a provision of the tax law, applicable to certain types of assets, that permits a property owner to take a business deduction for annual depreciation. Depreciation due to physical deterioration is economic depreciation. The adjusted basis consists of the price paid for the property, plus expenses incurred in acquiring the property, and the cost of any capital improvements (less depreciation if applicable). Capital loss occurs when investment is sold at a loss.
REF: B 182

45. A
A type of organization that avoids a double tax on trust income is a REIT or real estate investment trust. This is because the trust is not taxed at the corporate level if income is distributed to the beneficiaries.
REF: B 208

46. B
A participation mortgage is one in which a lender participates in the profits generated to secure payment of the mortgage debt. Gap financing is short-term financing until permanent financing is in place. A blanket mortgage is for two or more parcels of land pledged as security for payment of the mortgage.
REF: B 178

47. C
Projected income is not a classification for income according to the tax law. Active income is earned by salaries or in a business in which the taxpayer materially participates. Portfolio income includes interest, annuities, dividends, and royalties. Passive activity income includes invested funds.
REF: B 180

48. B
Performing an IRS Code 1031 tax-deferred exchange allows an individual to defer capital gains taxes on real estate bought and sold for investment purposes. Investment property would include any industrial property, commercial property, and hotel or motel. According to regulations for a 1031 exchange, a personal residence is not eligible for a tax-deferred exchange.
REF: B 186

49. C
To effectively use the buying power of leverage, investors will NOT want to make a major down payment so as to minimize monthly payments. This is because the purpose of leverage is to use "other people's money."
REF: B 172

50. C

$140,000 ÷$1,166,666 = .12 = 12%

REF: B 176-177

51. A
Property taxes may be deducted on any type of real property including the personal residence, second home, time share, vacant land, income property, or inherited property.
REF: B 180

General Business Law

52. C
Corporations may be set up for profit or nonprofit. A profit-making organization is created to do business and distribute profits to shareholders in the form of dividends. A nonprofit organization includes organizations such as charities.
REF: B 203

53. A
Securities that do not involve a public offering are exempt from the SEC registration requirement.
REF: B 207

54. D
State laws protect investors from buying "blue sky" (or nothing); therefore the term blue sky laws. Securities that do not involve a public offering are exempt from the SEC registration requirement under tithe private placement exemption.
REF: B 207

55. D
Negotiable instruments are a substitute for money so cash is not a negotiable instrument. Negotiable instruments include drafts, checks, promissory notes, and certificates of deposit.
REF: B 197

56. C
Requirements of negotiability must be in writing, be signed, contain a promise or order to pay, be payable at definite time or on demand, and must be a specific or fixed sum of money (any denomination).
REF: B 198

57. C
Sole proprietorship refers to a sole owner of a business. A limited liability company is a business organization that blends elements of partnership and corporate structures.
REF: B 202

58. D
A C corporation is not taxed as a partnership. A C corporation must pay corporate income tax to the Internal Revenue Service (IRS), and the shareholders are also taxed on their dividends that are profits of the corporation. An advantage of a subchapter S corporation is that since it is taxed as a partnership, it does not have to pay corporate income tax, thereby avoiding the double tax a C corporation must pay.
REF: B 203

59. A
The U.S. Bankruptcy Court is a federal district court.
REF: B 209

60. B
Contract law addresses the promises made by different parties to one another. A tort addresses civil lawsuits; namely, wrongful acts that are committed either intentionally or unintentionally. Real property law deals with the acquisition, transfer, and possession of an interest in real estate and the rights attached to it. Due process mandates that anyone involved in a legal matter is entitled to have a legal proceeding according to established rules and regulations.
REF: B 213

61. D
Legitimate causes of action for divorce includes cruel and inhuman treatment, the abandonment of the plaintiff by the defendant for a period of one or more years, an act of adultery , the confinement of the defendant in prison for three or more years, and irretrievable breakdown. Severance is not a divorce action,
REF: B 216

62. B
Chapter 11, a reorganization form of bankruptcy, provides a method for reorganizing the debtor's financial affairs under the supervision of the bankruptcy court. With Chapter 7, a liquidation form bankruptcy. the debtor's nonexempt property is sold for cash. Chapter 13, a consumer debt adjustment, is a rehabilitation form of bankruptcy for individuals.
REF: B 220

63. A
The Statute of Limitations imposes time limits within which litigation may be commenced. The Doctrine of Laches can bar an action even though the specified period has not yet run out if there has been an unreasonable delay. The Statute of Frauds requires that contracts that create an interest in real estate be in writing. A notice of pendency is legal notice that a lawsuit is pending.
REF: B 223

Construction and Development
Construction

64. D
The State Environmental Quality Review (SEQR) is a process that requires all levels of New York and local government to assess the environmental significance of actions for which they have discretion to review, approve, fund, or undertake. Article 9-A of the Real Property Law addresses the sale of vacant subdivided land in New York and outside of New York when sold on the installment plan. The Comprehensive Environmental Response, Compensation, and Liability Act (CERCLA) provides solutions to environmental problems created by uncontrolled disposal of wastes. The Interstate Land Sales Full Disclosure Act regulates sale of unimproved lots across state lines.
REF: B 273

65. D
According to Article 36-B of the NYS General Business Law, implied in all contracts of sale for new housing is a one-year builder's warranty against defects in construction; a two-year warranty for all plumbing, electrical, heating, and air conditioning systems; and a six-year warranty covering material defects.
REF: B 247

66. B
A seller broker must disclose to a prospective buyer, information about any defects in the structure.
REF: B 257

67. B
Most residential service is a minimum of 100 amps but new construction generally has 150- to 200-amp service, which is better.
REF: B 239

68. B
In a due diligence review, Phase I is the investigative phase. Phase II is the testing. Phase III is the clean-up phase, and phase IV is the management phase.
REF: B 251

Development

69. A
New York empowers local government, cities, and counties, through subdivision regulations, or ordinances, to protect purchasers and control property development within the subdivisions.
REF: B 269

70. C
Condemnation occurs when a property is taken by government under its right of eminent domain. Escheat occurs when the government takes property of the deceased if no heirs are found. Estoppel is generally a court order to stop an act. *In rem* is a type of legal proceeding.
REF: B 255

71. C
Building codes require that a property owner obtain a building permit from the appropriate local government authority before constructing or renovating a commercial building or residential property. A certificate of occupancy permits the occupancy of a structure by the tenants or owners.
REF: B 256

72. D
Transfer of development rights (TDR) may occur if development rights are transferred from one building to another such as from a historic property that may possess unused development rights.
REF: B 254

73. A
Covenants and conditions are privately imposed land use controls. A restriction (generally found on deeds) may provide for a reversion of title if violated. The Doctrine of Laches states that if landowners are lax in protecting their rights, they may lose them.
REF: B 280

Conveyance of Real Property and Title Closing
Conveyance of Real Property

74. B
Dedication occurs when land or an easement to land is given for use to the public by an owner. Situations can arise that force a property owner to transfer title against his will. This is known as involuntary alienation.
REF: B 298

75. A
If no valid will exists, a person is said to die intestate.
REF: B 303

76. C
Transfer of title to real property is described in law as alienation. Adverse possession is a method of acquiring a title after compliance with certain statutory regulations over a long period. A tenant at sufferance is a tenant had rightful possession to a property through a lease, but he no longer has the permission of the owner to continue to possess the property. Alluvion is increased soil, gravel, or sand on a stream bank resulting from the current of the water.
REF: B 291

77. A
The sale, gift, or dedications of a property are all voluntary transfers and alienation of property. Bankruptcy, eminent domain, and adverse possession are all involuntary alienations of title.
REF: B 298

Title Closing

78. A
In some real estate transfers, the buyer or buyer's lender requires either a full staked survey or a mortgage survey to assure that no encroachments exist. A survey is the process by which a parcel of land is measured.
REF: B 310

79. D
A constructive notice is a notice in which all affected parties are bound by the knowledge of a fact even though they have not been actually notified of such fact. Actual notice is notice that is expressly and directly given to a person and received by that person. *Caveat emptor* is Latin for "let the buyer beware." A *lis pendens* is a pending lawsuit regarding a property.
REF: B 311

80. B
Cooperatives may have a flip tax imposed upon transfer. This is a revenue producing tax for the cooperative and paid by the seller. The real property transfer tax is a NYS tax imposed on the transfer of real property.
REF: B 327

81. B
A proprietary lease is used in the ownership of cooperative apartments. The deed is the document that conveys the title from seller to purchaser (grantor to grantee). An option is a unilateral contract where one party makes a promise to another. With an installment land contract, title is not transferred to the buyer until the mortgage is paid.
REF: B 310

Real Estate Property Management

82. D
The property manager's fee is negotiated between the property owner and the manager. It commonly consists of a base fee and/or a percentage of the rents actually collected.
REF: B 340

83. A
Duties of a property manager include maintaining the property, collecting rents, and establishing a budget for property operation. Property manager's duties do not generally include investing owner's profits.
REF: B 342

84. C
Legal fees are not included in an annual property management maintenance schedule.
REF: B 342

85. C
The concerns of a property manager when selecting tenants for residential properties include the credit history of the tenants, past landlord references, and employment status. Consideration of marital status for apartment rental is illegal under the NYS Human Rights Law.
REF: B 349

86. B
If a real estate broker enters into a property management agreement with an owner, an agency or fiduciary relationship is created. A trustee and trustor are parties to a trust, another type of legal arrangement. The owner of a property is called the landlord, or lessor.
REF: B 335

87. D
A property management agreement includes the scope of agent's management authority, a manager's fee, and accounting responsibilities. It does not generally include a portfolio of the owner's other investment holdings.
REF: B 340

88. C
If an individual or management office works for more than one owner, a real estate broker or salesperson license is required.
REF: B 338

89. B
Skills needed to manage office property include analyzing demographics, negotiating leases, and scheduling and working with rental schedules. Knowledge of commodity prices is not a skill required to manage office property.
REF: B 346-348

90. A
Developing an appropriate tenant mix is most important with shopping centers. A manager of nonresidential properties must select tenants suitable for each type of center and consider appropriate tenant mix.
REF: B 354

91. C
An illegal actual eviction occurs if a landlord removes the tenant's belongings and locks the doors of the premises so that the tenant does not have access. A tenant can claim constructive eviction when the tenant is prevented from the quiet enjoyment of the premises such as in the absence of heat or electricity. *Lis pendens* is legal notice that a lawsuit is pending affecting title or possession of a specific property.
REF: B 349

92. A
The key feature of the estate, leasehold, or tenancy for years is that it exists for only a fixed period of time that can be as short as one day. In an estate at will, duration of the term is completely unknown at the time the estate is created, because either party may terminate the lease by giving notice to the other party. A freehold estate is ownership for an undetermined length of time until, for example, until the owner sells the property.
REF: B 335

93. D
A key feature of a periodic lease is that it automatically renews itself for another period at the end of each period unless one party gives notice to the other at a prescribed time before the end of the lease.
REF: B 336-337

Taxes and Assessments

94. C
Property is taxed on an *ad valorem* basis—that is, according to value.
REF: B 365

95. B
A special assessment is a specific lien for an improvement to a property or properties that do not affect the entire taxing unit. A general lien is against any or all assets of an individual.
REF: B 384

96. D
An *in rem* legal proceeding occurs when an action is brought against the real property directly and not against an individual and his personal property. A judicial review in state supreme court is called a tax certiorari proceeding. An Article 78 is a type of appeal process according to the New York Civil Practice Law and Rules for administrative decisions. Taxpayers who disagree with their assessment may file a complaint called a grievance.
REF: B 384

97. A
Market value is an accepted type of value for setting assessments. Value in use is based on the property's usefulness to an investor and not necessarily for its market value. Investment value is the amount of return on a certain dollar investment a property will produce.
REF: B 365

98. C
A homestead is a type of residential property.
REF: B 377

99. B
Taxpayers have the right to look at the assessment of their property and compare it with other properties on the assessment roll, and if a property owner believes the assessment is wrong, the owner may file a written complaint, called a grievance, with the local board of assessment review. The zoning board of appeals decides variance requests.
REF: B 379

100. B
$0.75 \times \$80,000 = \$60,000$;
$900 \div \$60,000 = .015 \times 100 = \$1.50$
REF: B 403-404

Broker Practice Exam 2

The Broker's Office-Operation, Management, and Supervision

1. D
Individuals exempt from continuing education are brokers licensed before July 1, 2008, who are engaged in the real estate business full time and licensed with no lapse in licensure for 15 years.
REF: B 40

2. C
A broker who discusses types of deed with a customer is giving legal advice. This act violates New York license law and regulations.
REF: B 42

3. B
A salesperson must be licensed for two years full time in order to apply for a broker license in New York.
REF: B 25

4. B
Violation of the license law is a misdemeanor and is punishable by a $1,000 fine and/or a maximum sentence of one year's imprisonment.
REF: B 47

5. B
Article 12-A of the New York license law states that applicants must demonstrate a fair knowledge of the English language.
REF: B 25

6. B
A broker applicant must be at least 20 years old; a salesperson applicant must be at least 18 years old.
REF: B 25

7. A
George can probably use his equivalent real estate experience as a property manager to become a licensed broker in New York.
REF: B 25

8. C
Trade name brokers conduct business as a sole proprietorship, using a name other than their personal name.
REF: B 29

9. D
If the worker earns more than $600, the employer must only file a Form 1099 misc. with the IRS to report the worker's earnings for the year. W-2, 941, and FICA forms are responsibilities of employers who hire employees, not independent contractors.
REF: B 56

10. C
Admitting pert-time brokers to MLS is an allowable activity under the federal antitrust laws for multiple listing services.
REF: B 54

11. D
Under federal and New York antitrust law, brokerage firms, franchises, real estate boards, and multiple listing services cannot combine to fix commission rates. Commission rates are negotiable between agent and principal.
REF: B 54

12. B
A consent decree (called *nolo contendere* in criminal cases) is used by the government in civil cases. A consent decree is a compromise in which the accused party agrees to stop the alleged illegal activity without admitting guilt or wrongdoing.
REF: B 53

13. D
The NYS Department of State (NYSDOS), Division of Licensing Services, is the regulatory agency that oversees and administers the licensure process.
REF: B 17

14. D
A mortgage loan originator is licensed by the NYS Department of Financial Services to find and negotiate mortgage loans under the employment or supervision of a registered mortgage broker. A real estate salesperson, broker and associate broker are all categories of real estate agent licensure.
REF: B 22

15. B
Property managers who perform tasks such as rent collection for more than one owner must be licensed.
REF: B 24

16. A
A mortgage loan servicer is one who receives scheduled periodic payments from a borrower for a mortgage and is licensed by the NYS Department of Financial Services.
REF: B 20

17. B
Attorneys admitted to practice in the New York courts are exempt from licensure. Attorneys may act as brokers without obtaining a broker license and may collect commissions. However, they must obtain a license if they employ salespersons to work under their supervision.
REF: B 23

Real Estate Agency Disclosure

18. D
The agency disclosure form details consumer choices about representation at the first substantive contact with a prospective seller, and applies to all one- to four-unit residential properties, and residential condominium and cooperative properties in any size building.
REF: B 99

19. C
The overall purpose of the agency disclosure form is to protect the public in making informed choices regarding real estate agent representation.
REF: B 99

20. B
If a buyer or seller refuses to sign the disclosure form, the agent can show the property but must complete a declaration form, have it acknowledged, and provide a copy to the broker to be kept on file for a period of three years.
REF: B 110

21. D
An exclusive single agency is a relationship in which the agent or agents in the transaction represent the interests of either the buyer or the seller.
REF: B 85

22. A
The brokerage firm owns the listing contracts.
REF: B 77

23. A
As of January 1, 2011, new amendments apply to Section 443 of the New York Real Property Law. Buyers and sellers can select and allow a dual agency relationship in advance of it actually occurring. This concept is called advance informed consent to dual agency.
REF: B 84

24. D
The agency form applies to all one- to four-unit residential properties, and residential condominium and cooperative properties in any size building. The form is not required in the rental or sales of commercial property although according to the license law, agents must give full disclosure as to who they represent in all transactions.
REF: B 99

25. D
The listing agent, buyer's agent, or tenant's agent gives direction and instruction to the broker's agent. Therefore, these agents will have liability for the acts of the broker's agent. The seller, buyer, landlord, or tenant does not have vicarious liability for the acts of the broker's agent.
REF: B 82

26. B
The fee or rate of commission paid to a real estate broker is strictly negotiable between the broker and the principal or client. Brokers are typically paid by a percentage commission of the final sales price or less often by a flat fee for services rendered.
REF: B 78

27. C
An illegal net listing occurs when a seller authorizes a broker to obtain a specified amount for the property and then allows the broker to keep as a commission any money above this specified amount obtained from the sale. A net listing may allow a broker to take advantage of a property owner by putting the broker's own interests above the interests of the principal.
REF: B 43

Real Estate Finance II

28. C
The function of the FHA (Federal Housing Authority) is to insure loans to protect lenders against financial loss.
REF: B 143

29. D
The borrower who gives or signs the mortgage note is called the mortgagor.
REF: B 127

30. B
An amortized mortgage is one in which uniform installment payments include payment of principal and interest. A balloon mortgage is an amortized mortgage that calls for a final larger payment at the end of the term. A junior mortgage or subordinate mortgage describes priority rather than a type of mortgage. A convertible mortgage gives the lender the option of converting the outstanding balance into an agreed-upon percentage of property ownership.
REF: B 136

31. C
Disintermediation is the loss of funds available to lending institutions for making mortgage loans. It is caused by the withdrawal of funds by depositors for investment in higher yield securities in times of higher interest rates. Stagflation is an economic condition in which economic growth is at a standstill (stagnant) but inflation still exists.
REF: B 146-147

32. B
A capital-short market occurs when lenders do not have funds for underwriting mortgages.
REF: B 144

33. D
High rates of unemployment have an extremely negative effect on the real estate market. If a local area has a high rate of unemployment, the number of houses for sale will increase while the number of prospective purchasers will decrease.
REF: B 149-150

34. A
An index is a value estimate used by banks to adjust interest rates.
REF: B 150

35. A
Recession is a moderate and temporary decline in economic activity that occurs during a period of otherwise increasing prosperity. Depression is the lowest possible point in the economic cycle. Stagflation is an economic condition in which economic growth is at a standstill (stagnant) but inflation still exists.
REF: B 152

36. D
Stagflation is an economic condition in which economic growth is at a standstill (stagnant) but inflation still exists. Inflation is an increase in money and credit relative to available goods, resulting in higher prices. Depression is the lowest possible point in the economic cycle. Recession is a moderate and temporary decline in economic activity that occurs during a period of otherwise increasing prosperity.
REF: B 152

37. A
Priority of mortgage liens usually is established by the time (date and hour) the lien is recorded. Credit A has filed a judgment before the other creditors so will be paid first.
REF: B 139-140

38. D
In a blanket mortgage, two or more parcels of real estate are pledged as security for payment of the mortgage debt. The shared appreciation mortgage (SAM) allows the lender to benefit from the appreciation of property value in exchange for a lower rate of interest to the borrower. A bridge loan is a legal short-term loan used to obtain interim financing for projects before a long-term loan is in place. An installment land contract is a form of seller financing, can be used on any type of property, and is sometimes called a "contract for deed."
REF: B 137

39. C
In a package mortgage, personal property in addition to real property is pledged to secure payment of the mortgage loan. The shared appreciation mortgage (SAM) allows the lender to benefit from the appreciation of property value in exchange for a lower rate of interest to the borrower. The purchase money mortgage is a mortgage given by a buyer to the seller to cover part of the purchase price. A convertible mortgage gives the lender the option of converting the outstanding balance into an agreed-upon percentage of property ownership.
REF: B 137

Real Estate Investments

40. A
The leasehold mortgage pledges a leasehold estate rather than a freehold estate to secure payment of a note. The leasehold acceptable to the lender is a long-term estate for years.
REF: B 178

41. C
A qualified intermediary (QI) accepts the funds from the sale and handles the contracts for a tax-deferred exchange. Release land subdivision financing is structured so that the borrower has a monetary stake in the land before a mortgage is given. A real estate investment trust (REIT) is a business trust owned by shareholders making mortgage loans.
REF: B 186-187

42. B
Passive activity income consists of invested funds and could include investment in income producing properties. Active income is earned by salaries or in a business in which the taxpayer materially participates. Portfolio income includes interest, annuities, dividends, and royalties.
REF: B 180

43. A
An anchor store is a large retail store that has a well known name that a mall depends on to draw in business.
REF: B 173

44. D
Apartments are generally the most popular form of investment for a beginning investor because it can be carried out on a small scale.
REF: B 173

45. D
Lender participation in financing is not a risk in considering a real estate investment. A downturn in the real estate market, illiquidity of the investment, and environmental problems associated with a proposed development are investment risks.
REF: B 177

46. A
The initial cost to construct the building is not of importance because the building has already been built, and the price will be more relevant to his desired rate of return, the vacancy level of the building, and how long he wishes to hold the property.
REF: B 176

47. B
Because the motel/hotel business is a specialized industry, an investor who has little or no experience in this type of business should hire a professional to help run the operation.
REF: B 174

48. C
The recipient of the cash in the exchange, called the boot, or other nonqualifying property incurs a tax liability on the boot or other unlikekind property in the calendar year of the exchange. The basis of a property is usually its cost.
REF: B 188

49. C
$400,000 – ($16,700 × 12) = $199,600
$199,600 ÷ .135 = $1,478,518
REF: B 405

50. D
If there are construction problems and time constraints, the cost of the property may exceed the market value. One reason is that time is money.
REF: B 169

51. D
A gain or loss realized from a sale or an exchange of property usually is a recognized gain or loss for tax purposes. Recognized gain means that the taxpayer must pay taxes on the gain or profit.
REF: B 181

General Business Law

52. C
The term *lis pendens* comes from Latin, and means pending litigation. A mechanic's lien is a claim by someone who has performed work on a property and has not been paid. Mediation involves the use of a neutral third party to discuss and attempt to resolve a dispute. Torts deals with civil lawsuits; namely, wrongful acts that are committed either intentionally or unintentionally.
REF: B 225

53. A
Corporations that are not subchapter S are known as C corporations. A subchapter S corporation is a type of corporate organization that is permitted to function as a corporation but is taxed as a partnership. A C corporation must pay corporate income tax to the Internal Revenue Service (IRS), and the shareholders are also taxed on their dividends that are profits of the corporation. Therefore, a double tax is paid at the corporate level and the shareholder level.
REF: B 203-204

54. D
Types of local ordinances include zoning laws, traffic laws, and building codes. Agency law pertains to an agreement where one party in the agency relationship (agent) may act on behalf of another (the principal). Torts deals with civil lawsuits.
REF: B 196

55. B
An endorsement is a signature by someone other than a maker, a drawee, or an acceptor that is placed on an instrument to negotiate (or transfer) it to another person. Endorsements may be written on the back of the instrument. An assignment is the transfer of rights under a contract.
REF: B 199

56. D
A limited partnership, which must be created by written agreement, consists of one or more general partners who are jointly and severally liable, and one or more silent, or limited, partners who contribute money or other assets of value to the extent of their ownership interest. Limited partners are not liable for the debts of the partnership beyond the amount of money they have contributed.
REF: B 202

57. A
The Supreme Court Appellate Division is a state level court. Family Court, County Court, and Surrogate's Court are all county level courts..
REF: B 212

58. C
The Court of Appeals is New York's highest court. It hears cases on appeal from lower appellate courts, and in some capital cases, it may rule on questions of both law and fact.
REF: B 212

59. D
Real property law deals with the acquisition, transfer, and possession of an interest in real estate and the rights attached to it. Contract law address agreements between two or more parties. Torts deals with civil lawsuits Agency law pertains to an agreement in which one party in the agency relationship (agent) may act on behalf of another (the principal).
REF: B 213

60. B
A limited liability company (LLC) may be formed by one or more persons. This form of business combines the most favorable attributes of both partnerships and corporations. Owners of an LLC (called members) are not personally liable for the obligations of the LLC; however, an LLC is taxed as a partnership.
REF: B 204

61. C
Statutory laws include all laws that are created by acts of the legislature in contrast to constitutional law (derived from the Constitution) or laws generated by court decisions (case law) and other administrative bodies.
REF: B 213

62. D
If a person receives money or property from another, the donor may be subject to a federal gift tax. If an individual makes a gift to someone else, the gift tax does not apply to the first $13,000 given to that person each year.
REF: B 221

63. C
A mechanic's lien is a specific lien filed by a person who provides labor to a property.
REF: B 224

Construction and Development
Construction

64. C
The Americans with Disabilities Act provides guidelines for construction of public accommodations, commercial space, and new multifamily housing.
REF: B 243

65. D
A selling agent who is working with a buyer must comply with the requirement to place a clause in the contract giving the buyer 10 days to inspect the property (if the selling agent is preparing the contract).
REF: B 259

66. B
New York has specific laws and regulations that govern municipal drinking water, well water, and wastewater treatment, which are regulated by the NYS Department of Health.
REF: B 248

67. D
In New York, local planning boards have the statutory authority to review site plans. The review of the site plan allows the planning board to evaluate the proposal's physical, social, and economic effects on the community.
REF: B 252

68. C
Building specifications are written narratives that explain the building plan. The specifications may include the materials used and any design features not visible in the plan.
REF: B 252

Development

69. A
A study of the demographics of a community, which is its social and economic statistics, helps planners decide if the community can support development. Topography is the physical features and contours of land. The services of a community such as roads, hospitals, police, and fire departments are known as the infrastructure. Sensitivity analysis is a study of how a change in one factor can affect the income to the property.
REF: B 272

70. B
A completion bond, also known as a subdivision bond, ensures the municipality that off-site improvements to the subdivision are made upon completion of the project. In this type of bond, the municipality is the beneficiary.
REF: B 280

71. B
Subdivision planning includes a market study of the area to determine the salability of the proposed project. This includes a feasibility study. Feasibility studies include demographic information ranging from average income to traffic patterns.
REF: B 278

72. D
The State Environmental Quality Review (SEQR) is a process that requires all levels of New York state and local government to assess the environmental significance of actions for which they have discretion to review, approve, fund, or undertake.
REF: B 273

73. A
The purpose of a deed restriction is to limit the use or appearance of a given property. A special-use permit is a permit for a use that is not allowed in the zone without the approval of the planning board or other legislative body.
REF: B 280

Conveyance of Real Property and Title Closing

Conveyance of Real Property

74. B
An individual who makes a will is called a testator if a man and a testatrix if a woman.
REF: B 302

75. B
Avulsion is the loss of land when a sudden or violent change in a watercourse results in its washing away. The gradual building up of land in a watercourse over time by deposits of silt, sand, and gravel is called accretion. Land may also be lost through erosion, which is the wearing away of land by water, wind, or other processes of nature.
REF: B 300-301

76. C
The right of redemption occurs when the borrower redeems his or her property before foreclosure. Eminent domain is the power of the government to take private property for public use with just compensation to the owner. A tenant in common may bring legal action to have a property partitioned so that each tenant may have a specific and divided portion of the property exclusively. Adverse possession is a method of acquiring a title after compliance with certain statutory regulations over a long time period.
REF: B 300

77. C
Acknowledgement is the oath in front of a witness that signing the deed is a voluntary act. Without the acknowledgment, the grantee cannot record the deed and have protection to title against subsequent creditors or purchasers.
REF: B 292

Title Closing

78. B
A cooperative is conveyed through the transfer of shares of stock and is evidenced by a proprietary lease. Condominiums and other types of property are transferred through a deed.
REF: B 309

79. A
Recordation provides protection for the owner's title against all recorded titles. This protection is provided by the theory of constructive notice: all are bound by knowledge of the existence of the conveyance of title if evidence of the conveyance is recorded.
REF: B 311

80. B
According to the Real Estate Settlement Procedures Act, within three working days of receiving a completed loan application, the lender must provide the borrower with a good faith estimate (GFE) of the likely mortgage costs and associated costs at settlement.
REF: B 316

81. C
The Combined Real Estate Transfer Tax Return (Form TP 584) is used to transmit the NYS transfer tax and is furnished by the NYS Department of Taxation and Finance. The form must be completed and signed by all buyers and sellers involved in the transaction, at closing, for the deed to be recorded. The form is submitted with payment to the county clerk.
REF: B 326

Real Estate Property Management

82. A
Public liability insurance is coverage to protect against claims alleging that one's negligence or inappropriate action resulted in bodily injury or property damage. Errors and omissions insurance is a type of professional liability insurance that protects professionals and services providing companies and individuals.
REF: B 341

83. B
The management agreement is a contract in which a property owner employs a property manager to act as the owner's agent. The management agreement creates a general agency, and the manager owes undivided loyalty to the owner–principal.
REF: B 340

84. D
The property manager is required to understand building systems, supervise others, and handle landlord-tenant relations. Property managers may not draw contracts as this constitutes the illegal practice of law in New York
REF: B 42

85. C
If the property manager or owner is careful in selecting tenants, legal actions for eviction and collection of rents are minimal. The owner/manager should attempt to resolve any disputes before they become a lawsuit. If there is a lawsuit, the owner's or property manager's records must show their compliance with all lease agreement terms.
REF: B 349

86. D
A property manager who must be familiar with commodity prices, soil types, and environmental controls would manage agricultural property .Besides understanding accounting methods; the property manager must be familiar with crop production, commodity prices, soil types, environmental controls, and soil conservation.
REF: B 354-355

87. A
To function efficiently, a property management office should effectively service existing clients, and distribute the workload efficiently among the employees of the management company. A property manager cannot engage in the illegal practice of law.
REF: B 355

88. C
If a management office works for more than one owner, a real estate broker license is required. The managers employed by the company would require a minimum of a salesperson license.
REF: B 338

89. C
The owner-manager relationship is formalized by a management agreement. The duties of the manager are outlined in this agreement.
REF: B 340

90. A
If a management office works for more than one owner, a real estate broker license is required. The agent or managers employed by the company would require a minimum of a salesperson license.
REF: B 338

91. A
A lease agreement does not terminate when a landlord sells the premises. The new landlord is bound by the lease terms.
REF: B 338

92. B
A constructive eviction occurs when the tenant is prevented from the quiet enjoyment of the premises. Self-help occurs when the owner violates statutory law by physically removing the tenant and his belongings from the premises. An estate or tenant at sufferance describes a tenant who is originally in lawful possession of another's property but refuses to leave after his right to possession terminates.
REF: B 349

93. A
The property manager's fee is negotiated between the property owner and the manager. It commonly consists of a base fee and/or a percentage of the rents or effective gross income actually collected.
REF: B 346

Taxes and Assessments

94. B
The amount that the municipality must raise by taxes on real property is called the tax levy. The stabilized budget is a forecast of income and expenses as may be reasonably projected over a short-term, typically five years. A special assessment is a specific lien for an improvement to a property or properties that do not affect the entire taxing unit The assessment roll lists all real property in the taxing jurisdiction, including information about each parcel and its assessed value and exempt status.
REF: B 381

95. C
An approved assessing unit is a taxing jurisdiction that has completed a property reevaluation and has been certified by the NYS Office of Real Property Tax Services. Assessing units can include villages, cities and school districts. District court is not an example of an assessing unit.
REF: B 365

96. D
The tax rate must be sufficient to provide the amount of revenue required to accomplish the budgetary requirements of the local governmental unit. It is the amount of the tax levy that is raised through property tax.
REF: B 365

97. A
Property taxes pay for the community's infrastructure and other services.
REF: 366

98. B
At its simplest, an equalization rate is the state's measure of a municipality's level of assessment (LOA). The amount that the municipality must raise by taxes on real property is called the tax levy. The tax levy determines the tax rate. Apportionment occurs if parts of a school district, or special district, exist in more than one city or town. Taxes are apportioned so that the districts in the different municipalities pay their fair share of the district tax levy. The assessed value of a property is is used to determine the taxable base of property that is used to raise tax revenue.
REF: B 382

99. C
If a taxpayer is delinquent in paying property taxes, the taxing jurisdiction initiates a tax lien against the property. A mechanic's lien is a claim by someone who has performed work on a property and has not been paid. Taxpayers who disagree with their assessment may file a complaint called a grievance. A homestead misclassification occurs if the parcel has been designated in the wrong class on the assessment roll, or the allocation of the parcel's total assessed value between the homestead and the nonhomestead part is incorrect.
REF: B 384

100. A
$\$200{,}000 \times .015 = \$3{,}000$
REF: B 403